"The conclusion of a criminal trial is not a closure. *Tough Crimes*, a collection of trial counsels' recollections of cases that leave an indelible mark on them, engages the reader in the haunting and inevitable after-effects of prosecuting or defending notable Canadian trials. This book, carefully edited by C.D. Evans and Lorene Shyba, demonstrates that criminal lawyers do not escape unscathed from serious trials."

The Honourable John C. Major, CC QC
Retired Justice of the Supreme Court of Canada

"*Tough Crimes* provides the reader with a breadth of view into the world of criminal trial work; the characters that occupy it; the impact of this work on the participants and the absolute need for an objective and impartial approach to the investigation, prosecution and defence of a person charged criminally. The essays illustrate the gamut of emotions from exhilaration to fear experienced by those involved whose task it is, in all cases, to 'get it right.'"

The Honourable Felix Cacchione
Justice of the Supreme Court of Nova Scotia

"Well worth the read. There are lots of interesting stories and important lessons contained in them. I would certainly recommend every law student read this book.... Tough Crimes is a mentoring book. Reading stories from talented lawyers, seeing how they struggled with strategic and ethical concerns, is a great way for young and old lawyers to learn."

— Steve Dykstra, *Above the Law*

"Long-time Calgary criminal lawyer Christopher (C.D.) Evans and publisher Lorene Shyba have co-edited an incredible collection of memorable cases ... In Tough Crimes: True Cases by Top Canadian Criminal Lawyers, readers go behind the scenes as lawyers prepare for difficult cases and see how they handle their clients, witnesses, and other evidence during and after trial."

— Daryl Slade, *The Calgary Herald*

"Tough Crimes ... essays that detail the crimes along with the writers' ethical and strategic decisions, their reaction and feelings to finding themselves in the media and legal maelstrom that engulfs high-profile, high-stakes cases. Although written by lawyers, the writing seldom strays into legalese. Instead, they provide a window on their thinking: How do I cross-examine this witness? Do I let my client testify? How do I cope with the horrors? How do I justify defending someone who seems so obviously and abhorrently guilty?"

— Colin Perkel, The Canadian Press

TOUGH CRIMES

True Cases by
Top Canadian Criminal Lawyers

TOUGH CRIMES

True Cases by Top Canadian Criminal Lawyers

C.D. Evans and Lorene Shyba
EDITORS

DURVILE
PUBLICATIONS

Durvile Publications Ltd.
(formerly Durance Vile)

Calgary, Alberta, Canada
www.durvile.com

NATIONAL LIBRARY OF CANADA
CATALOGUING IN PUBLICATIONS DATA
Evans, C.D. and Shyba, Lorene
Tough Crimes: True Cases by Top Canadian Criminal Lawyers

Issued in print and electronic formats.
ISBN 978-0-9689754-6-6 (print pbk), ISBN 978-0-9689754-8-0 (epub),
ISBN 978-0-9689754-9-7 (kindle), ISBN 978-0-9689754-7-3 (audiobook),

1. True Crime —collections
2. Canadian Law
3. Criminal Law
4. Canadian Essays—21st Century

I. Evans C.D. (Christopher Dudley), 1939– editor
II. Shyba, Lorene Mary, editor

Printed by Houghton Boston Printers, Saskatoon

The True Cases Series
Book One: *Tough Crimes True Cases by Top Canadian Criminal Lawyers*
C.D. Evans and Lorene Shyba, Editors (2014)
Book Two: *Shrunk: Crime and Disorders of the Mind*
Lorene Shyba and J. Thomas Dalby, Editors (2016)
Book Three: *More Tough Crimes: True Cases by Judges and Criminal Lawyers*
William Trudell and Lorene Shyba, Editors (2017)

First edition, third printing. 2016.

This printing of Tough Crimes is dedicated
to the memory of Edward L. Greenspan,
a brilliant barrister and a great Canadian.

Other Books by C.D. Evans and Lorene Shyba

By C.D. Evans and L.M. Shyba
5000 Dead Ducks: Lust and Revolution in the Oilsands

By C.D. Evans
• *A Painful Duty: 40 Years at the Criminal Bar*
• *Milt Harradence: The Western Flair*
• *Matthew's Passion*

By Lorene Shyba
Beyond Fun and Games: Interactive Theatre and Serious Videogames with Social Impact

Edited by Lorene Shyba and J. Thomas Dalby
Shrunk: Crime and Disorders of the Mind
Book Two in the True Cases Series

CONTENTS

Reasonable Doubt Continued

Introduction

Justice cannot be for one side alone, but must be for both.
— Eleanor Roosevelt

OUR MUTUAL AIM in editing this collection was to create a publishing first in Canada; a book of true cases written directly by top Canadian criminal lawyers designed not only for the profession, but for informed readers as well. With this in mind, we challenged eminent criminal defence lawyers and prosecutors to think about cases that were perplexing or disquieting, had weird or surprising turns, or presented personal or ethical issues. A good number of them met our challenge and their thoughts eventually emerged as this Tough Crimes anthology; stories about cases that tugged on their emotions as they reflected back on their world of criminal trial work. As William Trudell says in his poignant chapter on the Walkerton water treatment disaster, "Tough crimes demand tough decisions."

As we travelled across the county meeting with prospective authors, we detected an enthusiasm for our concept but neither of us anticipated the intense efforts that were to be made by our authors to meet our guidelines and inject their hearts and souls into their compositions. It took two years to complete this book, but we feel satisfied that readers will appreciate a chance to read more than just the media's take on persons accused of public crime; instead having a chance to hear directly from the lawyers who prosecuted or defended them.

Once we settled with our authors on subject matter, we edited gently, allowing individual voices to come through. We occasionally nudged the writers toward the gritty heart of the story but never curbed the excitement and passion that shone through in their narratives. We didn't mine for answers to unanswered questions as these often provided the energy; seething frustration is sometimes what the story is about. Some of our natural storytellers came up with surprisingly funny twists and turns too. That said, thoughtful and insightful solutions and reprimands have been revealed, worthy of a close read and maybe even ideas for action on policy change.

As a collective voice, our authors discussed the full range of precepts in cases of criminal justice: the presumption of innocence; the right of all accused persons to a defence; the burden of proof; reasonable doubt; and the importance of juries as triers of fact. As the stories dealing with these crucial matters came across our desks, we realized they clustered into themes and it was in this way that we developed our sections on Wrongful Conviction, Homicide, Reasonable Doubt, Collateral Damage, and Community.

In the section on Wrongful Conviction, respected criminal defence lawyer Edward Greenspan QC plunges us into the book with "A Miscarriage of Justice," about the conviction of a client he, and just about everyone else except the jury, considered to be innocent. In "A Perfect Storm," Richard Wolson QC reviews a high-profile Inquiry into a wrongful conviction with details of a criminal investigation and a prosecution that careened off the tracks. Finishing the section is Marilyn Sandford's "Twenty-Seven Lost Years" which gives a compassionate account of the release of a wrongfully convicted man after a long prison sentence.

The Criminal Code of Canada defines "Culpable Homicide" as including crimes of murder, manslaughter, and infanticide. In the Homicide section, Earl Levy QC starts out with "Toronto Loses Its Innocence: the Shoeshine Boy Murder" — a chapter that has social ramifications well beyond its horrendous facts. Next, Justice Peter Martin's "Man's Inhumanity" is a chilling indictment of the profound effect of absolute evil. John Rosen's account of "Defending Paul Bernardo" provides insight into the ethical duty to undertake the defence of all who ask for a lawyer's professional services. Justice Fred Ferguson, in his greatly moving chapter "The Case of John Ryan Turner," informs us of the agonizing decision required of this Crown prosecutor on the just and appropriate charge to prefer. To end the section on homicide, William Smart QC takes us on a surprising ride of twists and turns in "The Rest of the Story," introducing us to "Mr. Big".

In the section on Reasonable Doubt, "Air India" gives us an idea of the magnitude and scope of the four-and-a-half-year commitment through the eyes of Richard Peck QC. In "*Corpora Delicti*," Noel O'Brien QC then illuminates the spectacle of the police and the prosecution scratching their heads over the absence of a body in a homicide trial. In "The Antigonish Beech Hill Murders," a jury in a small community appreciates defence counsel Joel Pink QC's admonition to them on reasonable doubt. Following that, it took the worldly ex-cop Pat Fagan QC to fight for an acquittal in the aftermath of a deadly fist-fight in his story "Boys Will Be Boys." Finishing the section, Brian Beresh QC's "In

Defence of Larry Fisher" emphasizes the isolation of the criminal lawyer who takes on a challenging defence brief for an unpopular client.

Originally a military term, "Collateral Damage," in our context, means disproportional damage visited on sympathetic targets. A prime example is "Democratic Freedoms Undermined," Mark Brayford QC's article that strongly endorses jury nullification in his championship of Robert Latimer. Next, in "Split-Seconds Matter," Marie Henein discloses a courageous defence strategy where harsh damage was caused to the former Attorney General of Ontario, a person who should not have been a target at all. To end this section, in "Weighing Moralities of a Victimless Crime," editor C.D Evans QC fulminates against sanctimonious prosecutions.

In "Community," we encounter observations of defence counsel as they express, in unique ways, feelings of fellowship. Firstly William Trudell's story "The Walkerton Tragedy" describes the generosity and forgiveness of a town stricken with contaminated water. Then Hon. John Vertes' story, "The Case of Henry Innuksuk," depicts the rallying of a remote Inuit community in support of one of theirs who has fallen. Still within the theme of Community, forensic psychologist Dr. Thomas Dalby examines the impacts of "The Taber School Shooting," including factors to be considered when deciding on youth or adult court for young offenders. It remains for Hersh Wolch QC in "The Young Prosecutor's Trial by Fire" to take us into his first homicide case, as the raising of the curtain on an outstanding career.

Just about every Canadian, at one time or another, will come into contact directly or indirectly with the criminal law and our adversarial system; the two-sided system of law under which criminal trial courts operate that pits the defence against the prosecution. On one side of the debate, the Crown prosecutor must do his or her duty to the public, and on the other side, the criminal defence lawyer must do his or her duty to the client.

In Canada, as in other Commonwealth countries, the parties in a criminal case appear as, for example, *R. v. Smith,* with the initial *"R"* being an abbreviation for the Latin *Rex* or *Regina*, representing "the Crown," with the opposing party being the named defendant. In terms of the Crown prosecutor's task, those who prosecute accused persons in the name of Her Majesty Queen Elizabeth II, there are traditional codes of professional conduct — fairness, firmness, transparency, and objectivity. These are the requisites for Counsel for the Crown who are expected to comport themselves and their offices as Ministers of Justice.

In terms of the defence counsel's task, every person in Canada accused of public crime is presumed to be innocent unless a jury of twelve citizens, or a judge sitting without the intervention of a jury, finds guilt, which must be proven beyond a reasonable doubt. Invariably, the only person standing between them and dreary years in prison, not to mention personal ostracism, loss, and exile, is the defence counsel. In response to the usual question put to the criminal defence lawyer of "How can you defend a person you know is guilty?", the answer is straightforward. The criminal defence lawyer does not judge the client, as he or she is neither a judge nor a jury. The defence lawyer, in undertaking the retainer, agrees in the classical essence to act for the accused and not to act against them.

In most instances in this collection, criminal cases were tried in a public courtroom, widely covered by the media, and of gripping interest to the public. Some cases were so sensational and notorious that even decades later they remain prominent in the public consciousness: the echoes of the horrendous facts of a particular case, the name of the accused person, and the issues raised, resonate to this day, and beyond. The findings of the court in any particular case are a matter of public record, and the verdicts reported herein speak for themselves.

We feel strongly that the publication of Tough Crimes is important because of our primary aim to offer readers insights and wisdom from some of Canada's most prominent criminal lawyers, but also to remind them of the immutable precepts of our adversarial system of justice. Producing this book in our unique partnership as best friends is for us an exciting achievement. We have already collaborated to date on five books, fiction and nonfiction. We hope there shall be many more.

— C.D. Evans and Lorene Shyba, 2014

Note: This is the third printing of Tough Crimes and we thank Canadians all across the country for spawning interest in what has now become Durvile Publications' True Cases series: Tough Crimes: True Cases by Top Canadian Criminal Lawyers (2014), Shrunk: Crime and Disorders of the Mind (2016), and More Tough Crimes: True Cases by Canadian Judges and Criminal Lawyers (2017).

PART ONE

Wrongful Conviction

Edward L. Greenspan

A Miscarriage of Justice

PHOTO: AL GILBERT CM

Edward L. Greenspan QC, LSM, LLD, was founding partner of the Toronto law firm Greenspan Partners LLP. Eddie, as he was known, conducted major criminal trials in Canada for forty-one years. The author of Greenspan: The Case for the Defence *with co-author George Jonas, he received the G. Arthur Martin Award in 2001, The Advocates' Society Medal for lifetime achievement in 2009, and the Law Society of Upper Canada Medal in 2013. Upon his death in 2014, both the Prime Minister of Canada and the Minister of Justice extended their condolences.*

The Registrar: Mr. Foreman, have the members agreed upon their verdict?
The Foreman: We have.
The Registrar: And what is your verdict?
The Foreman: Guilty as charged.
His Lordship: So say you all?

The jury nods affirmatively.

THESE LINES are not from a movie, they are from a thirty-year-old trial transcript; the charge was second-degree murder, the plea was not guilty. I was defence counsel. The client was not famous. The case was not front-page news. I don't think it made the news at all. But this two-week trial is burned into my brain as one of the most perplexing verdicts I have ever seen. There were no surprises in the trial, it was not a whodunit. The defence was that the accused fired the gun that killed his best friend while in fear of his life and the life of his family and was acting in self-defence in his own home. The trial went perfectly; every witness furthered reasonable doubt. Following closing arguments, counsel were requested to retire to the judge's chambers to await the jury's deliberations. On the way to chambers, I was congratulated by the senior police witnesses. In chambers, I was congratulated by the Crown and the judge. I was feeling reassured that I had done my best for my client. An acquittal seemed both deserved and inevitable. Yet before long, the jury returned with its verdict and in three briefs words announced, "Guilty as charged." Even after thirty years, the case still haunts me.

As a footnote, I have resorted to pseudonyms for everyone in deference to the compassionate practice of not mentioning the names of bystanders whose involvement in a criminal matter is purely peripheral, and in deference to my client, whose name, I believe, has not appeared in print. It would be ironic for a client whose involvement in a criminal case had never been made public to find his name for the first time in a chapter in a book written by his own lawyer.

My client, Tom James, was thirty-five years old. He was big; five-foot-ten-inches tall and 200 pounds. His lifelong friend, Barry Hawthorne, was bigger; five-foot-eight-inches tall and 255 pounds, with arms the size of tree trunks. They had been in business together, and one night, for reasons that never became sufficiently clear to explain his behaviour, Barry got very angry with Tom. Barry and his wife Lauren came to Tom's townhouse in the east-end of Toronto, where he lived with his common-law wife Ann at around 1:00 *a.m.* Tom was asleep in his bedroom on the third floor, and sleeping in the second-floor bedroom was his younger step-son. His older step-son, Harold, had fallen asleep in front of the television in the basement family room. On the main floor, sitting awake in an unlit living room sipping a cup of coffee, was Ann. She had a headache and had come downstairs to make a cup of coffee in the hope of alleviating it. Suddenly, she heard a bang on the door. She asked who it was, and a voice yelled out, "It's Barry Hawthorn, open up!" She opened the door and Barry barged in, causing her to tumble backwards into the adjacent bathroom, nearly knocking over Barry's wife Lauren. Barry continued to shout, "I want you to get him up. Where is he? Get him up!" Barry was clearly drunk and there was no calming him down, so she went up to the third-floor bedroom and woke up Tom. "It's Barry. He's drunk and he's mad." Tom put on a pair of pants and followed Ann downstairs.

Before Tom reached the bottom of the staircase where his best friend was standing, Barry started swinging. He was punching and shoving Tom, screaming, "I'm tired of your fucking lies." Tom pleaded with his friend, saying "I don't want to fight with you, Barry" but by this point, Barry was too enraged to slow down.

In the basement, Harold was abruptly awakened by the loud noise coming from upstairs. He rushed up to the first floor, tried to intervene, but was frightened off when Barry yelled, "Get out of the way or you'll get some of the same." Harold testified that Lauren, standing off to the side, told Harold "Let them work it out themselves." Barry kept coming at Tom. He was told a number of times by Tom to get out of his house, but Barry wouldn't stop, wouldn't listen and wouldn't get out.

Tom, yelled "I'm going to call the cops" and Barry sardonically replied, "You want the fucking police? You know I'm not scared of them. I'll call them for you." He took off in the direction of the kitchen. Thinking that Barry was going to pull the phone out of the wall, Tom wisely ran upstairs to his bedroom to call the police himself. He ran up to his bedroom, but when he picked up the phone, he heard Barry on the other end asking, "Is this the police?" The other voice on the line said, "Yes, that's right". The last words Tom heard on the receiver was Barry roaring angrily, "...and you'd better bring a few guys." Tom knew at that moment this was very serious. He testified at trial, "I put the phone down and I thought to myself he is just crazy, like he doesn't even care. And I knew that he wanted me. I went to go to the bedroom window."

Tom testified that he ran over to his bedroom window because in his panic he was thinking that maybe he could escape by climbing out onto the roof. (Testimony would later reveal that even if he had made it out the window, he probably would have fallen to his death given the forty-foot drop to a concrete patio below.) Before Tom even had time to slide the window open, let alone remove the window screen cover, Barry had charged up to the third floor and stormed into the bedroom. There was nowhere for Tom to retreat. Barry grabbed Tom and punched him, causing Tom to topple over a chair and tumble backwards onto the floor. Both wives rushed into the room, each one grabbing one of Barry's arms in an attempt to stop him from doing any more harm to his friend. In one swift action, Barry threw both women off. They fell backwards: one into the hall, the other by the bed. In these few crazy moments, gripped by terror, panic and confusion, Tom reached for a small caliber handgun, a Lady Derringer, lying on the television table, grabbed the gun, cocked it and extended his left arm, pointing the gun at his friend. The gun, which was no bigger than a gun-shaped cigarette lighter, was there only because my client had acquired it on a trip to Florida from which he had just returned, and while he had already unpacked his suitcase, he hadn't yet got around to putting his things away and storing the gun for safekeeping. He hadn't even realized he had brought it back in his luggage. No one could have guessed that this gun, purchased, as many law-abiding citizens would do, for his protection while down in Florida, would become his only means of defending himself from his enraged best friend in his own bedroom in Toronto. Barry lunged at Tom, hitting his left arm and triggering the gun to fire. Barry suddenly became even crazier; he let out a laugh, stared at Tom and, before lunging again, declared, "Now, I'm going to fucking kill you!" Tom testified that he thought Barry was going to kill him and his family.

Tom, in complete fear, shot again, but this time it wasn't by accident. Tom meant to shoot the gun and, in fact, he shot Barry through the heart. But as he testified at trial, "I didn't intend to kill anybody. I just wanted to stop him". If he had any intention at all, it was to stop the chaos and insanity that had jolted him and his family awake in the middle of the night. It was later determined by the Crown expert analyst that Barry had about thirteen ounces of alcohol in his system — over twice the legal limit. Lauren testified that he was stone sober. Ann testified she had never been so frightened in her life. She believed Barry was uncontrollable, had a wild look in his eyes and she was panicked, terrified for herself and her husband.

But there was more. The deceased's wife Lauren testified that when Tom fired the gun the second time, Barry was six to seven feet away and wasn't attacking Tom at the time. But the Crown's firearms expert concluded that the firearm residue found on the deceased's sweater meant that the gun would have to have been fired within six to eighteen inches of the deceased for both shots. As important, the deceased's hand would have to have been around the gun, as he had close firearm residue on his hands as well as his sweater. This evidence totally undermined Lauren's testimony.

It was a measure of Barry's strength that he turned around, walked for about sixty to seventy yards to a parking lot carrying a bullet lodged in his heart, and actually got into his car before he slumped over the seat and died.

Tom had lived in Toronto his whole life. He had left school by grade eight and started working early. He worked as a tow truck driver, moved to snack food sales and after working as a district manager for the *Toronto Telegram* newspaper, went into partnership with his dad as a snack food supplier for Northern Ontario. He also found part-time work as the general manager of a motor inn, with a staff of sixty-two employees, among them Barry Hawthorn. This is where their fifteen-year-long friendship began. Later, Tom went full time into auto sales. He would come to be the joint business owner of a few different establishments over the years.

In his personal life, Tom had been married for about a decade before his divorce, and was the father of a son he continued to see on weekends and holidays, as well as support financially. A few years after the divorce, he got together with Ann. She testified that she had known Tom since the age of four; they moved in together, along with Ann's two sons. Though they had never married, they treated each other as husband and wife. Tom's relationship with his step-sons was equally strong; he treated the boys as his own and they called him "Dad." They had lived together as a family for over three years before the events of that evening. Ann had known Barry Hawthorn for over six years.

In Tom's life, there was no pattern of violence or demonstration of any escalating criminal behaviour. By the time this tragic event took place, he was a settled man and a fairly successful businessman.

This was an excellent set of facts supporting self-defence. His best friend of fifteen years stormed into his family home a little after one o'clock in the morning while Tom was sleeping. He was terrified. As he made it repeatedly clear at trial, "Barry was my friend for fifteen years. I never wanted to kill him or anybody else. I thought he was going to kill me and my family. I just wanted him to leave the house. I just wanted him to leave us alone. Leave us alone."

The brief time frame in which the events took place also suggested a sudden volatile attack resulting in this terrible unplanned outcome. Besides Tom, Ann and other witnesses present at the incident there was no witness more compelling than Tom's neighbour, Police Constable Jackson of the Metropolitan Toronto Police Service.

Jackson lived in the townhouse next door. At the time of the incident, he had been sleeping in his bed on the third floor of his townhouse with a partly open east-facing window. He knew his neighbours by name, but as he said at the trial, "other than that, I did not have anything to do with them." He testified he had been awakened at 1:25 *a.m.* by "a loud argument involving male and female voices." He worked the day shift, from 7:00 *a.m.* to 3:00 *p.m.*, and knew the exact time because "the alarm clock radio is right beside my bed on the night table facing towards me. They don't like it if we're late at work so as I was awoken — I usually sleep on my left side — and the first thing I saw was the alarm." He couldn't hear the details of the argument, nor was he certain where the noises were coming from; as he explained, "that townhouse complex, any noises tend to echo and reverberate off the walls." The only thing he knew for sure was that, "it was very loud, people were shouting, there were male and female voices." (In contrast, Lauren testified that there had been no shouting, no arguing, and that she and Tom's wife never said anything.)

Jackson thought the argument had subsided, until he heard, "what sounded like two shots spaced two or three seconds apart. At that time as I was still lying on my left side, I opened my eyes and I then noted the time at 1:30 *a.m.*" It certainly did not seem reasonable to believe that within the short period of time Barry had been raging in his house, my client had developed any intention to harm, let alone kill, his best friend. Furthermore, it was Barry who had shown up on Tom's doorstep, so what was the motive? How could anybody have believed this horrible event was anything more than an act of self-defence, an unfortunate incident?

There was an additional legal concept that came into play in this case that made a conviction even more unlikely. At the time of the trial and still today, evidence of the deceased's violent propensity *known* to the person charged with the crime at the time of the event, was admissible and relevant — not to show that Barry was a bad person but to show instead what was in Tom's mind, so the jury could assess how frightened Tom must have been when Barry attacked him, knowing what Barry was capable of.

Barry had provoked two fights when he was working as a weekend bouncer at the inn where Tom was the general manager. Barry had been criminally charged and convicted of assault on both occasions.

The first incident involved Barry and an off-duty firefighter. The firefighter had come into the bar one night for a few drinks with his buddies and started hitting on a waitress, Carol, who was dating Barry at the time. Barry and the firefighter got into a fight. Barry pummelled him. The firefighter was wheeled off in an ambulance and treated at the hospital for a broken nose, a broken cheekbone, a cracked jawbone, fourteen stitches over one eye, and eight stitches over another.

The second incident was even worse. Three off-duty police officers had come into the bar to celebrate a birthday. The officers, who appeared to be "feeling pretty good," were asked to leave after getting "fresh" with one of the waitresses. Two of the officers left quietly but the third officer didn't leave without a fight. Tom saw Barry pushing the third officer through the bar to the exit when the officer started pushing back. They smashed through the window and ended up outside where Barry pinned the cop to the hood of a car and started beating his head like a punching bag. Throughout the beating, the officer kept screaming, "I'm a police officer." Barry's only response was, "Too bad, too late" and continued beating him. It had taken three guys to peel Barry off the firefighter. It took four to five guys to peel him off the police officer. By the end, the scene was literally a bloody mess and the officer was taken to the hospital.

How was it possible for the jury not to understand, as everyone else in the courtroom seemed to, that this history of violence that Tom had witnessed may reasonably have led him to fear what Barry would do to him and his family in the state he was in that night?

The law in Canada is clear that Tom would be expected to retreat as far as he could were he in a public place. The law is equally clear that in your own home, you are not expected to retreat any further than the front door. Yet Tom retreated as far as he could in his own home, all the way to the window of his third floor bedroom with a forty-foot drop outside. Trapped in his own room, he committed the only act he could to save himself and his family.

What made Barry so angry and violent? What would cause him to do what he did to his best friend of fifteen years? Nothing was proven in the trial to explain this important question. It was all speculation. Some witnesses said Barry was angry and upset at the accused that day but all the accused knew was that he was defending himself and his wife against a murderous and unprovoked attack in his home. Although under no duty to retreat in his own home, Tom did retreat to the third floor of his home and, trapped there, he did the only thing he could do to save himself.

I told the jury that if my client had not fired that gun, they would be here instead to determine the guilt or innocence of Barry for the murder of Tom and the Crown would be telling them about how a drunken, raging bull killed an innocent man in his own home.

At the end of the trial, the jury was charged by the trial judge fairly. I had one serious objection to the charge. I asked the judge to bring the jury back and fully explain defence of home and property. I wanted him to remind the jury that, although when Barry arrived at Tom's house, under the law, he was not considered a trespasser, the first time Tom asked him to leave and he would not, he became a trespasser in the eyes of the law. Despite further requests to leave, he continued to trespass and attacked other residents of the house. It was essential to emphasize to the jury that the accused was not the offender but rather the defender in the situation, that he was defending himself, his family and his home from assault by a trespasser, a trespasser who was, ironically, his best friend. Best friend or not, once Barry was asked to leave and refused, in the eyes of the law, he became a trespasser, giving Tom the justification "in using as much force as is reasonably necessary (a) to prevent the commission of an offence (i) for which, if it were committed, the person who committed it might be arrested without warrant," according to section 27 of the *Criminal Code*. The judge recharged the jury in accordance with my submissions.

Naturally, every person prefers to be tried fairly rather than unfairly. However, if you ever get convicted of a crime you did not commit, pray to God that you get convicted in an *unfair* trial. If your trial has been fair, the higher courts can't help you much. If you had a fair hearing but a jury, or a judge sitting alone, happened to come to the wrong conclusion, you're pretty much out of luck. Courts of Appeal rectify errors of law, but seldom change findings of fact.

I don't know why the jury convicted Tom. It is no longer lawful for a jury in Canada — as it once used to be, and as it still is in the United States — to reveal anything about their deliberations. I think it was an unreasonable verdict, even a perverse verdict. How could the jury actually believe Tom had wanted this to happen? How did they all come to this conclusion and so quickly? I will never understand. In my view, there was more than enough evidence that Tom had acted in self-defence to raise a reasonable doubt about his guilt, and he was entitled to the benefit of that doubt. However, since all of this was set out to the jury with sufficient clarity, when the jurors convicted Tom, they convicted him in a *fair* trial.

The Crown Attorney was fair. The trial judge was also fair, although he made a couple of errors in his charge to the jury which formed the basis of the appeal. The trial as a whole had seemed to be going for the defence. The facts barely supported a murder charge and the way the evidence unfolded during the trial did little to bolster the prosecution's theory. Some key Crown witnesses faltered, while the defence witnesses were unshaken under cross-examination. The attending journalists, some of whom always gamble on the outcome of any interesting trial, were giving four-to-one odds in favour of an acquittal. Before the jury returned with the verdict, the Crown Attorney very graciously came over to the defence table to congratulate my associate and me on what he himself expected to be a defence victory.

I couldn't bring myself to reciprocate *after* the verdict. I was too crushed. How my client must have felt, anyone can imagine.

Generally, higher courts will not interfere with a jury's verdict for anything except major errors in law — such as important evidence wrongly admitted or excluded, or a judge misdirecting a jury on some vital point in his charge — or for some new, relevant, and credible fact that, having emerged only after the trial, would not have been available to the jury. Other than these two reasons, a jury verdict would have to be "perverse," that is, incapable of being supported by the evidence — for an appeal court to interfere with it.

In Tom's case, there was no wrongly admitted or excluded evidence. Despite one or two errors one can always find by going through the judge's charge with a fine-tooth comb, the charge to the jury was fair. This left nothing to submit but that the verdict was unreasonable which, I believed, was the strongest point of the appeal.

It wasn't, however, strong enough. The Ontario Court of Appeal felt there was *some* evidence that Tom committed murder, and the Crown had only to satisfy the jury after a fair trial that it was *enough evidence*: satisfy it beyond a reasonable doubt, to the point of moral certainty. This jury was evidently satisfied, and that was pretty much the end of the matter in law.

Perhaps no other jury would have found murder proven beyond a reasonable doubt. Perhaps no other jury would have found that Tom did not act in self-defence. Perhaps no other jury would have been morally certain that Tom wasn't even provoked sufficiently to reduce his act to manslaughter — but this jury was. On the evidence, it was just barely, if at all, open to these twelve good men and women to reject Tom's defence — but they rejected it. They sent a man to jail for life who, I firmly believe, virtually any other group of twelve good men and women would have found to be totally innocent.

Like all lawyers, I have alas received some guilty verdicts. Like all lawyers, I've been dismayed over losing. But I've seldom been totally perplexed by the outcome. Tom's jury genuinely shocked me by their verdict.

Despite what I believe to have been the wrongful conviction of an innocent man, my faith in the jury system remains, although it was severely shaken by this case. I continue to be persuaded that, on the whole, twelve ordinary men and women are far more likely to arrive at a just result than any one individual would, no matter how learned and sincere. Nor can I envisage any panel of experts or scholars bringing a greater sense of responsibility and fair play to their task, or making a more inspired guess at whether witnesses are telling the truth, than twelve honest people picked almost at random from the community.

Unfortunately, no legal system is perfect or mistake-proof. Mistakes are made and innocent people are convicted. DNA evidence has been effective in establishing innocence in some cases, but serious miscarriages of justice can and do occur that cannot be righted by DNA evidence. As this case sadly demonstrates, even a seemingly perfect trial can lead to the conviction of a perfectly innocent man.

Mr. Greenspan is deeply indebted to Samantha Greenspan (B.A., New York University; M.A. Centre of Criminology, University of Toronto) for the quality of her research and her analysis of the case that assisted him greatly in the writing of this article.

Richard Wolson

A PERFECT STORM FOR A WRONGFUL CONVICTION

Richard J. Wolson QC, as well as representing clients in all courts, has participated as counsel in high profile inquiries that have had a profound impact on the practice of law in Canada. He is a Fellow of the American College of Trial Lawyers and the International Society of Barristers. A past Faculty member of the National Criminal Law Program, he writes and lectures on criminal law.

At the heart of the Thomas Sophonow case is a tragedy beyond comprehension; one that created a great depth of harm. A family lost their beloved teen-aged daughter, an innocent man went to jail for a crime he did not commit, and the perpetrator was free with an opportunity to kill again. Days before Christmas 1981, beautiful sixteen-year-old Barbara Stoppel was brutally attacked while working alone at a donut shop. She died a few days later, leaving behind a family who suffered immensely at the loss of their daughter whose life was taken so viciously and unfairly.

The people of Winnipeg, Manitoba were outraged and rightfully so. They wanted answers. The killer had to be arrested. The police did everything in their power to solve this crime. The media coverage of the crime was rampant. Ultimately, three months later, police arrested Thomas Sophonow in Vancouver and charged him with the murder. Sophonow endured a preliminary Inquiry and three trials. He languished in jail for forty-five months. In 1985, he was acquitted by the Court of Appeal of Manitoba after his third trial. He spent the better part of the next fourteen years attempting to clear his name and prove his innocence. His dogged determination succeeded when a re-investigation of the case by the Winnipeg Police commenced in 1998.

From 1998 to 2000, the Winnipeg Police Service reinvestigated the circumstances surrounding the death of Barbara Stoppel. The investigation revealed that Thomas Sophonow was factually innocent and it was recommended that he be exonerated. Fifteen years after his acquittal, on June 8, 2000, the Manitoba Government announced that it had apologized to Tom Sophonow and that there would be a Commission of Inquiry to review the police investigations and court proceedings, and deal with the issue of compensation.

An Opportunity Not to be Ignored

I remember it like it was yesterday. I was just finishing a murder case in Vancouver in June 2000 and the verdict had been delivered that morning. When one does murder cases, one is energized and all the adrenaline is flowing, but when the verdict arrives, it all vanishes. Though it was a verdict I welcomed, I went back to my hotel room exhausted. I fell into a chair; I was going to fly home that night, and I turned on the television looking for the news. As I flipped channels, I caught a glimpse of Winnipeg's Chief of Police, Jack Ewatski and, of course, it piqued my curiosity. I was surprised when I heard him exonerate Tom Sophonow. I had no idea this announcement was going to be made.

While I did not know Tom Sophonow, I was very happy for him because I knew it had been a long journey. As I was getting ready for my flight that day, I called my office, as I routinely do, for messages. I received a message from Bruce McFarlane, then Deputy Attorney General for Manitoba, but did not necessarily connect the message to the Sophonow matter. When Bruce and I spoke, he asked me if I would consider being Commission Counsel to the Honourable Peter Cory in the Public Inquiry into the wrongful conviction of Thomas Sophonow. It took me about two seconds to answer in the affirmative. This was an opportunity I could not turn down. Of course I had to meet Commissioner Cory and be accepted by him as his counsel.

My adrenaline began to flow. I flew back to Winnipeg that night. I have to say that while I did not consume any intoxicants, I was higher than the airplane. For a criminal lawyer (and I have practiced criminal law since 1973) to do a post mortem on a murder case — to find out what went wrong and even in a small way to be a part of recommendations for change — is an awesome task. I could not have been happier and more excited to be a part of the Inquiry. A few weeks later I met with Commissioner Cory, over dinner. I knew Peter as he and I were part of a teaching faculty, but I did not know him well. I was awestruck. He is simply an unbelievable person. I knew him to be a great judge of the Supreme Court of Canada but I did not know the kind of person that he was: a gentle man, kind, decent, caring, compassionate and so humble. He regaled me with his many stories of flying bombing missions in World War Two. That night he asked me formally to become his Commission Counsel, and of course, I readily accepted. It was the start of a beautiful mentorship and friendship that I cherish to this day.

When I began my term as Commission Counsel, I wanted to meet Tom Sophonow so I flew to Vancouver to meet with him and his counsel. At the end of the meeting I asked his counsel if I could have a few minutes alone to talk to Tom. It was blatantly obvious to me that he was a fractured man; he was tormented. I recall saying to him "Tom, what is this about for you? Is it about vindication or compensation?" His response was one I will never forget — it was music to my ears. He told me that it was not about compensation nor was it about vindication. It was about, he said, "working to ensure that there is not another Tom Sophonow." I knew his intentions were honourable.

To say that the wrongful conviction of Tom Sophonow scarred him for life is an understatement. He was the victim of a grave miscarriage of justice: a victim of tunnel vision, police and prosecutorial misconduct, faulty eyewitness identification and false admissions by jailhouse informants. He was incarcerated in a facility referred to as a "hell hole" by one of its custodial officers. At another facility he spent twenty-three hours in segregation in a cell that measured five-and-a-half by ten feet. Unimaginable that someone could endure such hardship for a crime he did not commit. After he was released from jail, having been acquitted, he lived with this crime hanging over his head. His house was firebombed. Everywhere he turned he was presumed guilty.

Facts Giving Rise to the Inquiry

The year was 1981. Days before Christmas, Tom Sophonow drove from Vancouver to Winnipeg to visit his young daughter. Tom, because of his own difficult childhood, had a practice at Christmas time of taking candy to sick kids in hospitals and did so on the evening of December 23rd. Tom had purchased the candy earlier that day while he was waiting for his car to be repaired at the Canadian Tire in Winnipeg on Pembina Highway, some distance from the Ideal Donut Shop. There was a Safeway store adjacent to Canadian Tire, making it convenient to do so. After placing a call to his mother from Canadian Tire, he attended local hospitals to distribute the candy.

That same evening in a different neighbourhood, sixteen-year-old Barbara

Stoppel was working the evening shift at the Ideal Donut Shop. She was working alone.

At approximately 8:30 *p.m.*, Barbara Stoppel was attacked. She was strangled with a piece of nylon twine. The attacker was seen both inside and leaving the donut shop by no less than four eye-witnesses. One of the witnesses, Lorraine Janower, who worked close by, went for coffee, only to find the donut shop locked. She peered inside and saw the attacker heading toward the washroom. Her husband arrived to pick her up. He watched as a man in a cowboy hat moved around the store. Later, this man approached the door and turned the "open" sign to "closed" and left the store. He was observed carrying a brown cardboard box.

Another witness saw a tall man in a cowboy hat pass her in the parking lot shortly after the attack. John Doerkson, a Christmas tree salesman who worked in the parking lot, followed the man. Doerkson watched the attacker exit the store, followed him, and grappled with him on an adjacent bridge before he got away. He saw the attacker throw something over the bridge. Police later recovered the twine used in the attack, gloves, as well as the cardboard box from under the bridge. The police sealed the parking lot and inspected vehicles. There was no vehicle with a British Columbia licence plate located.

Tragically Barbara Stoppel died a few days later in the hospital. On the day of her death, a man had attended to the hospital inquiring about her condition. This man was interviewed by the police. The murder of Barbara Stoppel rocked the city of Winnipeg and accordingly there was a great deal of public sentiment over the killing. The four eyewitnesses aided the police and multiple composite sketches were produced and released across the city.

The eyewitnesses described the attacker as a large man, certainly fitting Tom's description, wearing cowboy boots and a cowboy hat, with a pitted face, and dark glasses. Winnipeg Police received a tip that Tom Sophonow resembled the police sketch and they sought the assistance of Vancouver Police to interview him. On March 3, 1982, in Vancouver, a non-verbatim notebook statement was obtained from Sophonow by a member of the Vancouver Police Department. The most salient comment recorded was "I could have been in Ideal Donut Shop, 49 Goulet." (At the Inquiry, Sophonow testified that the statement should have read "I could not have been in Ideal Donut." He further testified that while he indeed signed the notebook, he did not read the statement.)

Interrogations and Three Trials

On March 12, 1982, two Winnipeg Police officers travelled to Vancouver to interview Sophonow. He was interrogated five times over four hours. While the officers claimed to have taken verbatim notes, it was clear that this was not the case. On critical points, their notes were significantly different. During the interrogation, between the second and third session, police strip-searched Sophonow and searched his anal cavity to determine whether he was carrying drugs. There was no possible reason for this — the officer who met with him on March 3rd did not consider him to be a physical threat at any point. He was never challenging or threatening to the officers during the March 12 interview. Moreover, he was patted down prior to the commencement of the interview. Sophonow ultimately testified at the Inquiry that this strip search had the effect of taking his dignity from him, of shaking him to the core. Sophonow testified that the interview haunted him to the very day of his testimony at the Inquiry. He testified that the police broke his will. He reported to his psychiatrist that at the end of this interview, he thought for a while that he might have committed the crime, even though he knew that he had not. In the interview, police purported that Sophonow made statements that were indicative of guilt. Tom Sophonow testified at the Inquiry that at no time did he make such statements. Tom Sophonow was arrested, brought back to Winnipeg and was charged with murder.

The interview, the Commissioner noted, was hardly fair and crossed the line in several instances. The Commissioner found that the officers were not taking verbatim notes of the interview and it was not audio or video recorded. The police did not charge or caution Sophonow nor did they give him the right to a lawyer even though he asked for one. They lied to him, and they told him he was lying. They strip-searched him. Overall, Commissioner Cory had serious concerns about the conduct of the Winnipeg police.

Before arresting Sophonow, police considered a man named Terry Arnold as a suspect. He was the man who attended to the hospital just days after the attack to ask about Barbara Stoppel's condition. He told Barbara Stoppel's mother that he regularly went to the donut shop and knew her daughter. He lived a short distance from the Ideal Donut Shop. Arnold, as noted by police, matched the description of the killer. Furthermore police were told by one of Arnold's friends that he wore a cowboy hat and cowboy boots. While Arnold initially put forward an alibi, it could not be substantiated. Arnold's prints were on file with the Winnipeg Police, however they were never compared to those found at the donut shop. Despite all of these facts, he was dismissed as a suspect. An insidious case of tunnel vision was at work.

Police were convinced that Sophonow was the man responsible for the murder. Between his arrest in March 1982 and April 1986, and while in custody, Sophonow underwent a preliminary Inquiry and three trials. A mistrial was declared at the first trial on the basis that the jury could not reach a unanimous verdict. The second trial resulted in a conviction. On appeal to the Manitoba Court of Appeal, the Court ordered a new trial. The Crown sought leave to appeal in the Supreme Court of Canada however it was not granted. The third trial resulted in a conviction. Sophonow appealed. While the Manitoba Court of Appeal found that there were grounds for a new trial, it considered that Sophonow had already spent forty-five months in custody and that if a new trial were ordered, it would be the fourth. The Court set aside the guilty verdict and directed an acquittal. While the Crown sought leave to appeal the acquittal, the Supreme Court of Canada denied the Application.

The Inquiry and Breach of Duty

Historically the official stakeholders in the criminal justice system, politicians, judiciary, bench, bar and law enforcement agencies, have taken great pride in the near-certain infallibility of the adversarial system of criminal justice. Today the rising tide of post-conviction DNA exonerations has shed a harsh and unflattering light on the staples of classic investigative tools and trial evidence: investigative and prosecutorial tunnel vision, eye-witness fallibility, hair and fibre junk science, opportunistic jailhouse informants, self-induced and other induced false confessions and disclosure failures. These classic tools, alone and in combination, have been the cause of numerous wrongful convictions.

In Canada, with the veneer of systemic infallibility now breached in numerous cases, the key structural response for the investigation and analysis of errors and misconduct is the Public Inquiry. While the Public Inquiry process has multiple goals, the primary goal is to determine the particular errors that contributed to the wrongful conviction in the instant case. The backward-looking process of a Public Inquiry is essential to determine the specific causes that resulted in wrongful conviction and it may inform the compensatory aspect of any Inquiry. It is the forward-looking application, however, that has broader social policy impacts, because of the publication of findings, and more importantly, recommendations that provide stakeholders with a weighty reminder of pitfalls that must be avoided.

By Order-In-Council dated June 7, 2000, the Attorney General accepted the conclusion of the Chief of Police that Thomas Sophonow had no involvement in Barbara Stoppel's death. Terry Arnold was, at that point, considered the number one suspect by police. By the time of the Inquiry he had been convicted of sexually assaulting four girls in Newfoundland and the murder of a fifteen-year-old girl in British Columbia. Further, he was the prime suspect in the murder of another girl. He took his own life in 2005 and was never brought to justice.

The mandate of the Inquiry was two-fold. Firstly, we were to inquire into the conduct of the investigation into the death of Barbara Stoppel and the circumstances surrounding the criminal proceedings against Tom Sophonow. The second task was to determine whether Sophonow was entitled to financial compensation. My role as Commission Counsel was to gather the evidence, to review it, disclose it, and to put witnesses before Commissioner Cory. I took the position that I would cross-examine these witnesses in search of the truth. My task as Counsel was to put all the evidence before Commissioner Cory in a fair and impartial way. I was mindful that we were dealing with peoples' reputations, specifically, the reputations of the prosecutors, the investigating police officers, and the witnesses who would appear before Commissioner Cory.

Approximately sixty-five witnesses testified at the Inquiry. Commissioner Cory identified a number of problem areas such as statement recording by police, eyewitness identification, tunnel vision, police notebooks and exhibits, testing of material evidence, prosecutorial discretion on potentially prejudicial matters, and alibi and jailhouse informants. Systematically, when one looks at wrongful convictions there are a number of factors, and most, if not all of them were present in Sophonow's case. I learned quickly that, from start to finish, the Sophonow case was the perfect storm for wrongful conviction. It had all the ingredients, the recipe was there, and the outcome could have been predicted. In the subsequent paragraphs I will touch briefly on some of the areas of concern as identified by Commissioner Cory. In particular, the ethical obligation of prosecutorial disclosure comes into sharp focus.

Eyewitness Identification

Eyewitness identification, I can tell you, as a criminal defence lawyer, is devastating evidence against the accused. Picture a witness coming forward who says, about your client, "I saw the fellow leave the scene of the crime, and that's the man sitting in the prisoners dock," well, that is pretty powerful. In this case there were four such accounts provided. Four eyewitnesses — that is the kind of evidence that would give you grey hair prematurely as a defence lawyer.

In a study called "Eyewitness Identification, a Policy Review," conducted by The Justice Project which works toward public awareness of needed reforms, it is shown that in about seventy-five percent of wrongful convictions, misidentification plays a significant role. In the Sophonow matter, John Doerkson had the most interaction with the attacker. Recall that it was Doerkson who went to the donut shop for coffee sometime after 8:15 pm only to find that the door was locked. He observed a large man inside the shop and when he left, Doerkson followed him to the nearby Norwood Bridge where an altercation ensued.

A few weeks after the attack, Doerkson called the police from the Norwood Hotel claiming that the killer was at the hotel. The police quickly determined this to be an erroneous identification and cleared the man. Doerkson also erroneously, identified a newspaper reporter as the killer. Moreover, he later reported that he was seeing the killer everywhere and that all tall men looked like the killer. None of these misidentifications were disclosed to defence counsel. At the Inquiry a number of Crown Counsel testified that the misidentifications ought to have been disclosed to defence as it affected the credibility of a key witness. According to ethical obligations, evidence should be disclosed as soon as a person is charged, or certainly when brought to the attention of the Crown.

Of significance is that when Doerkson attended a line-up parade in which Sophonow participated, he did not identify Sophonow. It gets worse. A few days after the line-up parade, Doerkson was picked up on a warrant for unpaid fines. While in police custody he caught a glimpse of Tom Sophonow. Coincidentally he had with him a copy of a newspaper containing Sophonow's photo. He asked to see Sophonow face to face again. Approximately nine days later, Doerkson attended Court and saw Sophonow in the courtroom. At that point he advised police that he was ninety percent sure that Sophonow was the man on the bridge. That fact was not disclosed to the defence. The fact that he had glimpsed Sophonow's face while in custody, and possibly even in the newspaper was never disclosed to defence either. Crown counsel testified at the Inquiry that this too ought to have been disclosed.

Somehow, when it came to the preliminary hearing and over the course of the three trials, Doerkson claimed to be a hundred percent certain that Sophonow was the man. A skeptic might argue that Doerkson had seen the pictures of Sophonow in the newspapers and had been influenced by them.

Evidence at the Inquiry revealed that in 1982, John Doerkson required glasses and that he had trouble with his eyes at night and in poor lighting conditions. This too was not disclosed to defence counsel at trial. Further evidence at the Inquiry disclosed that John Doerkson had developed a friendship with Barbara Stoppel's family and in particular, with her father. This leaves a reasonable inference to be drawn that the friendship may have influenced Doerkson's identification of Sophonow as the killer.

Over the years, Courts have recognized the frailties of eyewitness identification. A good example that illustrates this is the following one: when I was preparing for the Inquiry, I interviewed one of the eyewitnesses who had made a positive identification of Sophonow at trial. I had pictures of both Tom Sophonow and the new police suspect, Terry Arnold. The witness, pointing to the picture of Terry Arnold, said "there is Tom Sophonow." At the Inquiry one of the four eyewitnesses testified that when they saw the picture of Terry Arnold in the newspaper, they not only thought it was the killer, but they thought it looked more like the killer than Sophonow did.

The evidence of the four eyewitnesses was devastating to Tom Sophonow. None of these witnesses made positive identifications at the beginning, but all of them, by the time of the preliminary hearing, were positive that the person they saw leaving the donut shop was Tom Sophonow. It is therefore not difficult to see why eyewitness identification has been described as frail at the best of times, in the best of cases. There is no doubt that eyewitness evidence played a significant role in the wrongful conviction of Tom Sophonow. If four eyewitnesses weren't enough, there were three jailhouse informants who testified at Sophonow's trials.

Jailhouse Informants

Jailhouse informants played a prominent role in the conviction of Tom Sophonow. By the time of his third trial, there were three informants who testified that Sophonow had confessed to each of them at different times. While only three were called to testify at trial, police had offers from several other jailhouse informants, including Terry Arnold, the man who ultimately became the prime suspect in the killing. In his Report, Commissioner Cory noted that jailhouse informants, "[a]s a group, they have an unsurpassed record for deception and lying…they do merit very special attention and caution must be exercised in the use of their evidence."

The first informant, who I will refer to as Informant #1, testified that Sophonow confessed to him. His evidence was that Sophonow told him that he went to the donut shop to rob it and when the young employee would not cooperate, he got mad and took her into the washroom and used a rope to kill her. From the defence perspective, if the jury believes the informant, it is just as problematic as a confession from the accused to the police. When defence cross-examined Informant #1, it was suggested that he made a bargain with police in exchange for his testimony. Informant #1 denied this. When the prosecutor re-examined Informant #1, he told the Court that he did not ask for any consideration for his evidence and while he hoped for favourable treatment, the chief reason he came forward was that it bothered him to see a murderer on the street.

Informant #1's testimony was false. He directly contradicted what he told a police polygrapher prior to trial; that the most important reason for his coming forward was to get his twenty-six charges of fraud dropped. The charges were withdrawn by the Crown. Remarkably, this was never disclosed to defence counsel. Informant #1 was released and was never seen again.

The second jailhouse informant, Informant #2 was a regular informant for the Winnipeg Police Service. He had often bargained information for some kind of compensation. He was arrested on break and enter charges. He told police that he would give them information on some drug matters but they were not interested. So he offered to be placed in a cell with Sophonow. He was asked to obtain any information about the murder. Informant #2 reported to the officer with whom he made the arrangement that Sophonow did not say anything to him about the murder. The officer recorded this in a police report. This police report was never disclosed to the defence.

Fast forward. Informant #2 changed his story and told police that Sophonow did, in fact, confess to the murder. At the third trial, when Informant #2 was about to be called as a witness, he told police that if they put him on the stand, he was going to sabotage their case. He told them that he did not want to testify. The police told Informant #2 that they would publicly expose his identity as a police informant, which Informant #2 feared would jeopardize his life. He cooperated and testified that Sophonow confessed to him. At the Inquiry, defence counsel testified that he was not told of Informant #2's initial position that indicated that the two men did not talk about the murder. Furthermore, defence counsel testified that he was never informed that Informant #2 changed his mind about testifying and did so after having been threatened.

The danger of jailhouse informant reliability is illustrated best by Informant #3's testimony; Informant #3 being the informant who testified at Sophonow's third trial. Prior to the Sophonow trial, Informant #3 had testified at least nine times in Canadian courts as an informant. He had previously been convicted of perjury. He too testified that Sophonow confessed to him. To say that Commissioner Cory was not impressed with jailhouse informants is an understatement. In his Report, with regard to Informant #3, Commissioner Cory asserted that he seemed to have heard more confessions in his life than the most dedicated priest.

In Commissioner Cory's view, jailhouse informants "rush to testify like vultures to rotting flesh or sharks to blood." Ultimately Commissioner Cory recommended that the use of jailhouse informants should not be permitted except in the rarest occasions, and only then with certain guarantees of trustworthiness.

Crown Misconduct

The origin of the twine ligature found around Barbara Stoppel's neck became a significant issue at the three Sophonow trials. The prosecution argued that the twine was manufactured on the west coast, and it was used by BC Hydro on a number of sites in Vancouver. Tom Sophonow was living in Vancouver. The "Vancouver connection" was an indicator that Sophonow was the killer. The twine was therefore considered by the Crown to be a compelling piece of evidence linking Sophonow to the crime.

The cost of testing the twine to determine its origin would have been a hundred dollars. The testing would have yielded a conclusive result as to the source of the twine. This was not done. To compound matters, in the first trial, the day before he was to testify, a witness from BC Hydro disclosed an important piece of information during a meeting with the junior prosecutor. He advised that the twine recovered from the crime scene was also produced in Portage-la-Prairie, Manitoba. This was a devastating revelation which significantly weakened the Crown's case. The information provided by the BC Hydro witness was never disclosed to the defence. The Commissioner concluded that the failure of the Crown to disclose pertinent evidence amounted to a serious breach of the duties of Crown counsel.

The Alibi

Tom Sophonow, through his counsel, put forward alibi evidence. He maintained that he was having his car repaired at the Canadian Tire on Pembina Highway around eight o'clock on the night Barbara Stoppel was attacked. While waiting for the car to be repaired he went to the adjacent Safeway store and bought red mesh Christmas stockings to distribute to sick kids in hospital. Furthermore, while at Canadian Tire he placed a phone call to his mother in B.C., minutes before 8:00 *p.m.*, which is reflected by telephone records. When he left Canadian Tire he proceeded to visit two hospitals for the purpose of providing the kids with the Christmas stockings. He talked to a nurse at one of the hospitals.

The prosecution took the position that the alibi was unreliable, that it was put forward at a late stage and that there was no mention of it to officers who interviewed Sophonow in Vancouver. They argued that the alibi was not true.

The prosecution argued that Sophonow, accepting that he was at the Canadian Tire around eight *p.m.*, had sufficient time to drive to the murder scene and commit the crime. Police testified that it took them fourteen minutes to drive that distance. I have driven that distance on a number of occasions, one of those being on the 23rd of December, after I had been appointed as Commission Counsel. It took me longer than fourteen minutes. Consider too that this was just days before Christmas, when traffic would have been heavier and road conditions may not have been ideal. Of importance as well is that Sophonow's vehicle, which had a British Columbia licence plate, was not located at or near the crime scene.

For the prosecution's argument to succeed, Sophonow would have had to have parked his vehicle and walked to the donut shop. There was not time to do so.

At the Inquiry it was revealed that a man had attended at the St. Boniface Hospital on the night of December 23rd and delivered the Christmas stockings. In fact, the police had seized a stocking from the hospital. This was not disclosed to defence. Had disclosure been made, surely the alibi would have been given great consideration by the jury.

Aftermath

Commissioner Cory made several recommendations, a number of which were accepted and adopted across Canada. He was a perfect fit for this Inquiry, firm, but very fair. Sophonow, who had justifiable trust issues, trusted Commissioner Cory. He could see in the Commissioner a man who would treat him justly and with compassion.

A term of the request by government in calling an Inquiry was to determine compensation for Thomas Sophonow. A number of witnesses were called to assist the Commissioner in determining the appropriate compensation. Commissioner Cory assessed compensation in an amount of slightly more than $2 million.

As I reflect on the Inquiry, I will always remember the fractured man who was a victim of wrongful conviction. A man who suffered so greatly and relived his nightmare publicly as a result of the Inquiry. There were days when Tom could not attend at the Inquiry because he was too depressed.

The last time I saw Tom was at another Manitoba Inquiry in 2006. When I walked up to Tom he was smiling — I had never seen him smile before. I asked him how he was, he gave me his hand, and told me that he was doing great. I could see on his face that he had some sense of peace. To say it made my day is an understatement. At the first break in proceedings I phoned Peter Cory and told him about Tom. I could hear the relief in his voice. Commissioner Cory had felt so much for this man.

I am extremely proud to have been a part of this process. Every time an individual is exonerated it reinforces the fallibility of our application of the laws of the criminal justice system. Efficiency should not displace the notion that it is better that a guilty man goes free rather than an innocent man be convicted by the State. That is the greatest tragedy a civilized society can inflict upon its citizenry.

This Inquiry stands for the proposition that if members of the criminal justice system fail to carry out their job fairly, honestly and honourably, the tragedy of Thomas Sophonow will be repeated. We, as Canadians, must never forget the calamity of wrongful conviction and must be diligent to ensure its prevention.

Richard Wolson acknowledges the assistance of his daughter Sarah Wolson in the writing of his chapter. Ms. Wolson, of the Manitoba and Ontario Bars, is Associate Investigation Counsel at the Law Society of Upper Canada. Mr. Wolson notes that comments by him on the Sophonow Inquiry have been previously published in The Drake Law Review *and* The Manitoba Law Journal.

Marilyn Sandford

TWENTY-SEVEN LOST YEARS

Marilyn Sandford was Called to the Bar of British Columbia in 1990, and since that time has been in private practice. Her practice involves criminal defence work as well as civil and constitutional litigation. She teaches a course in wrongful conviction at UBC's Faculty of Law and has guest lectured at other universities. She practices in downtown Vancouver with the law firm Ritchie Sandford.

IN MAY 2008, I returned to my office after taking a break from practice for some months following the conclusion of the Robert Pickton serial murder trial. The Pickton case, on which I had been a member of the defence team, had been very challenging, involving multiple murder counts and highly complex forensic evidence arising from an investigation of unparalleled magnitude. Having lived and breathed that case for six years, it was difficult to imagine returning to more routine files. While I was happy to be getting back to my practice, I wondered whether my cases would now seem rather dull.

Waiting for me on my first day back was a phone message from a colleague, Cameron Ward, with whom I had worked on cases in the past. Little did I know when I returned Cameron's call that this would be the commencement of another lengthy legal saga.

Cameron told me that he had recently been retained to represent a man named Ivan Henry. One of Ivan Henry's daughters, Tanya, had for some years provided childcare services to Cameron's children. Unbeknownst to Cameron until recently, Tanya's father had been in prison since his arrest in 1982, having been declared a dangerous offender following 1983 convictions in Vancouver for a series of sexual assaults. Ivan and his family had learned that a Special Prosecutor had now been appointed, however, to investigate whether he may have been wrongly convicted.

Cameron asked me if I was interested in joining him in his representation of Mr. Henry. I immediately agreed. During the time I had attended law school in Halifax in the 1980s the Donald Marshall Inquiry had held public hearings at a hotel near the Dalhousie campus, and I had sat in on the hearings when I could find the time. Part of my childhood had been spent in Cape Breton, Nova Scotia, living close to the Membertou Mi'qmaq Reserve where Donald Marshall grew up. I later read the scathing Marshall Inquiry Report. Its indictment of a justice system that had "failed Donald Marshall Jr. at virtually every turn from his arrest and wrongful conviction for murder in 1971 up to and even beyond his acquittal by the Court of Appeal in 1983" had a powerful effect on me as a young lawyer. The opportunity to participate in some small way in efforts to attempt to overturn a wrongful conviction was thus not something I could pass up. I considered a case such as this to be a defence lawyer's dream.

I suggested to Cameron that a lawyer in my office, David Layton, work with us on the case. David, who had been counsel with me on the Pickton case, has particular expertise in wrongful convictions as he taught a University of British Columbia law school course on the subject. Cameron readily agreed, and thus the Ivan Henry defence team was formed. We were soon joined by a law student, Tony Paisana, who worked with us for the next couple of years.

A Curious Twist

I learned early on that, through a curious twist, the Robert Pickton investigation played a role in Ivan Henry's wrongful convictions coming to light. As part of the police investigation into the disappearances of women from the streets of Vancouver, police had investigated unsolved "cold case" sexual assaults dating back to the 1980s in an effort to determine whether those unsolved crimes might shed light on the Missing Women/Pickton investigation. DNA testing of exhibits containing perpetrator semen from three sexual assaults that had occurred in Vancouver in the 1980s had resulted in matches to the DNA profile of a man named Donald McRae. The three offences where the perpetrator DNA matched McRae's had formed part of a larger group of unsolved sexual assaults that police had named the "Smallman" offences, based upon victims' descriptions of the short stature of the perpetrator.

Police in the 1980s had believed, based upon a common *modus operandi* (M.O.) as well as geographic links among the assaults, that these numerous sexual assaults had been committed by a sole perpetrator, dubbed "Smallman," including the three offences where Donald McRae's DNA had now been identified. In 2005 Donald McRae pleaded guilty to the three sexual assaults.

As the McRae charges were being processed by the Crown office in Vancouver, a prosecutor, Jean Conner, noticed a similarity between the perpetrator M.O. in the McRae cases and the M.O. employed in the sexual offences for which Ivan Henry had been convicted in the early 1980s. As a result of Ms. Conner's concerns, the Crown office took steps that ultimately led to the appointment of a Special Prosecutor, Leonard Doust QC, to investigate whether Ivan Henry's convictions may have been a miscarriage of justice. In 2008 Mr. Doust issued a report that included recommendations that the Crown make full disclosure to Ivan Henry of the Project Smallman investigation and of previously undisclosed evidence relating to the offences Henry had been convicted of, as well as other sexual offences he had been a suspect in that had not proceeded to trial. He also recommended that a second Special Prosecutor be appointed for further matters related to the case. Subsequently, David Crossin QC was appointed as the second Special Prosecutor.

Soon after I first spoke to Cameron Ward about the case I met our client Ivan Henry for the first time when Cameron, David Layton and I travelled to meet with him at Mountain Institution federal penitentiary. A congenial and talkative man in his sixties, Ivan was and is eccentric and engaging, always ready with a quip and quick to laugh. He is also a man of tremendous fortitude and energy, having fought for a quarter of a century as his own jailhouse lawyer to prove his innocence. At that first meeting, one of many to come, our client began to share with us details of his incredible story, other aspects of which we were to learn about through our research.

That story commenced in 1980 when a series of more than twenty sexual assaults began to occur in Vancouver. They shared a distinctive M.O. that involved a perpetrator breaking into ground-floor suites at night where a lone female occupant was sleeping. He awakened his victim, usually with a knife to her neck, and told her that he was looking for a woman who had stolen or "ripped off" money from his bosses. The frightened victim typically attempted to persuade him that she was not the woman he was looking for. Eventually the intruder appeared to be convinced that he had made a mistake, and would tell the victim that he would have to sexually assault her as his "insurance" that she would not go to police. A sexual assault would then follow. The intruder often covered the victim's head, or his own face. He asked the victim to count to fifty when he was about to leave, and suggested that she get better locks on her doors or windows. These assaults occurred in clusters in certain Vancouver neighbourhoods. The police believed them to be the work of a common perpetrator, due to this distinctive M.O. and the locational nexus.

The circumstances of these sexual assaults were not conducive to the victims being able to provide detailed, accurate descriptions of the perpetrator. The initial descriptions of their assailants that they provided to police were, not surprisingly, vague and general.

For a number of the assaults perpetrator semen samples were recovered. While these assaults pre-dated forensic DNA testing, it had been forensic practice in jurisdictions around the world since the 1960s to test semen in order to determine perpetrator blood type. While such testing could not identify a particular suspect as the perpetrator, it could be used to eliminate suspects.

As the offences continued through 1981 and 1982 they attracted considerable media attention. In a city rattled at the time by the notorious child murders perpetrated by the infamous Clifford Olson, the news that another serial offender was on the loose no doubt led to considerable pressure on the Vancouver Police Department to solve these crimes.

One police suspect at the time was Donald McRae. A short man then in his twenties, with brown curly hair, he had for years lived in a house in the heart of a Vancouver east-side neighbourhood that was one of the locations where the assaults had occurred. Police reports documented that he had a history of late-night predatory sexual behaviour.

In 1982 police attention focussed on another suspect, Ivan Henry. Ivan was quite a bit taller than McRae, a red-head, and then in his thirties. After a number of the assaults had occurred Ivan Henry moved into a house that was, coincidentally, located across the street from where Donald McRae had lived for years. Having recently been released from prison, Ivan Henry was attempting to make a fresh start in Vancouver, where his former wife and two young daughters, Tanya and Kari, resided.

The police arrested Ivan Henry and on May 12, 1982 forced him to participate in a live line-up that was viewed by eleven of the women who had been sexually assaulted. As he did not cooperate with the line-up procedure, the police physically compelled his participation. He struggled in the line-up as he was forcibly held by uniformed police officers.

Of the eleven women who witnessed the line-up, six were later complainants at Ivan Henry's trial. Of those six, three did not identify Henry on their ballots, one wrote the number of Mr. Henry as well as that of a foil, while two provided tentative identifications of Henry, one based solely on his voice, and the second based in part on her having detected that Henry's voice in the line-up evidenced what she thought was a French accent. Henry did not have a French accent.

Following the fiasco of a line-up, the police released Ivan Henry from custody. Subsequently another woman was sexually assaulted by a perpetrator who utilized the same M.O. That complainant was presented by police with a photo line-up that included Henry, who was depicted standing in front of a jail cell: a portion of a uniformed police officer's arm was visible in the photo. The foils in the photo array did not resemble Henry. The victim selected the photo of Ivan Henry as her attacker. Henry was then re-arrested and charged with offences relating to a number of the women who had been assaulted.

After Ivan Henry's arrest, many of the complainants were re-interviewed. They were shown a photograph of the line-up in which Henry had struggled and was restrained by police officers. They then provided new witness statements. Their descriptions of their assailant in these new witness statements contained many material inconsistencies with the statements that they had provided prior to the time they saw Ivan Henry in the line-up.

After his preliminary hearing, Henry discharged his lawyer and proceeded to trial without counsel on counts relating to eight women. Ivan increasingly felt that the system was framing him for something he did not do, and that made him suspicious of all participants in the system, including defence lawyers.

The only issue at Henry's jury trial was the identity of each complainant's assailant. They identified Ivan Henry in court as their attacker based solely on his voice and/or his appearance. No other evidence was led that connected him to the assaults. Ivan Henry testified, and denied having committed the assaults. In March 1983, the jury convicted Ivan Henry of all counts. He was declared a dangerous offender and sentenced to an indefinite period of incarceration.

Fifty Attempts to Establish Innocence

Ivan Henry's conviction appeal was dismissed by the British Columbia Court of Appeal for want of prosecution, on application by the Crown, a mere three months after the date he was sentenced: Henry had failed to obtain the trial transcripts as he could not afford them. Unbeknownst to Ivan at the time, the *Criminal Code* required that the trial proceedings be transcribed in all cases where a convicted person had been declared to be a dangerous offender, and thus the transcript would in due course have become available.

Subsequently, over the course of the next quarter century, Ivan Henry filed more than fifty applications to various Courts and to the Minister of Justice attempting to overturn his convictions. All of his efforts proved fruitless. But for the Missing Women/Pickton investigation, that might still be the case.

At my first meeting with Ivan in the penitentiary he told us about a

The line-up picture showing Ivan Henry being restrained by police officers.

photograph in his possession that depicted the line-up in which he had been forced to participate. He explained the extraordinary measures he had taken throughout his many years in custody to keep that photograph intact and prevent it from being seized, discarded or lost. For many years he had kept his copy wrapped in plastic: this allowed him to take it into the shower with him so that it could not be taken from his cell or effects while he was showering.

I was astonished when I initially saw the line-up photograph. As criminal lawyers, we learn early in our careers about the frailties of eyewitness identification, and the importance of there being no steps taken that might lead to a tainting of an eyewitness's identification of a suspect. The Henry line-up photograph depicted a line-up that was likely to taint any subsequent witness identification. It would have been clear to any victim who viewed the line-up that Henry was the police suspect. His appearance also differed significantly from that of the foils.

We began our work on Ivan's defence case by reviewing the thousands of pages of documents that our client had carefully preserved in his cell for years, including the trial transcript. We also reviewed new disclosure materials that had been obtained by the Special Prosecutor.

One might have expected that in a situation where such an obviously flawed line-up was employed, the Crown at trial would, in fairness, have ensured that evidence about the line-up was before the jury from the witnesses who viewed it, so that the jury would appreciate the problematic background relevant to the victims' in-court identifications of Henry. One might also have expected that the Trial Judge would have strongly cautioned the jury about the line-up circumstances that so acutely brought into question the integrity of the identification process and the reliability of any subsequent identifications. Reading the trial transcript, I discovered that this had not occurred.

At trial, the Crown led evidence in chief from a victim that on May 12, 1982 she had heard Mr. Henry speak and had tentatively recognized his voice as that of her assailant. To this point in the trial no evidence about the tainted May 12 line-up had emerged. The Crown did not elicit from this witness in chief that this occasion when she had an opportunity to hear Henry's voice was when she had witnessed the perverse line-up. It was only when Mr. Henry, in cross-examination, put to the witness that when she heard him speak on May 12, 1982 she had been witnessing a line-up, one in which he had been restrained by police officers and shouting, that the tainted circumstances of the line-up emerged at trial, through the defence. The photograph of the line-up was then introduced in evidence.

The trial judge's charge exacerbated the difficulty with the line-up. Rather than strongly warning the jury that the reliability of any ensuing identification by complainants who had viewed the line-up was highly suspect, if not wholly destroyed, the trial judge instructed the jury that had the Crown attempted to lead the evidence of the line-up photograph he would probably have ruled it inadmissible. He also reminded the jury that the Crown's position was that Henry's obvious reluctance to participate in the line-up led to an inference of consciousness of guilt.

Rather than cautioning the jury, then, concerning the potential tainting effect of the line-up on subsequent identifications, and instructing them that Mr. Henry had a legal right to refuse to participate, the trial judge belittled Henry for introducing in evidence the circumstances of the line-up, and suggested that it was open to them to find that those circumstances could be used to infer consciousness of guilt.

Upon reading the trial transcript I discovered that the line-up was just the beginning of the many disturbing circumstances in this case. While there were additional errors in the charge and in evidentiary rulings, what struck me most was the fact that there was no reliable evidence implicating Henry. The complainants identified him in the dock based on his voice and/or aspects of his appearance, after having seen him and heard his voice at the tainted line-up and at the preliminary inquiry, and without being able to point to any truly distinctive characteristics of voice or appearance. That was essentially the case against Henry. It amounted to no case at all.

Heightened Concerns

My concerns about the case were heightened once I moved from the trial transcript to a review of the disclosure materials that had been withheld at trial. Mr. Henry's lawyers had made written disclosure requests for all of the complainants' statements. Once he became self-represented, Henry renewed that request. Notwithstanding these requests, the Crown failed to disclose at trial approximately thirty of the statements made by the eight trial complainants. Those statements contained material and significant inconsistencies with their testimony at trial. The undisclosed statements also showed that their initial descriptions of their attackers changed, by the time of trial, to become more consistent with those of the other complainants and to more closely resemble Mr. Henry, whom they had viewed in the farcical line-up.

The difficulties with disclosure went beyond the complainants' statements. Prior to trial, the defence had made requests for disclosure of forensic reports, including serology reports, serology being the forensic science of body fluids. At his trial, Mr. Henry requested disclosure of medical evidence and offered to provide a blood sample for comparison purposes. Notwithstanding these requests, the prosecutors failed to disclose the existence of medical and lab reports, and of the fact that testing had identified spermatozoa with respect to four of the offences that police believed were committed by the common perpetrator, including one assault for which Henry was later convicted. By the time I became involved in the case all of the exhibits that had contained semen had been lost or destroyed, and were no longer available for testing.

Another very significant matter that had not been disclosed to Mr. Henry at trial was that Donald McRae, a. k.a. "Smallman," had been a police suspect in the offences Ivan Henry was convicted of committing. In addition, it had not been disclosed at trial or afterwards that unsolved sexual assaults involving the same M.O. and occurring in the same neighbourhoods as the alleged "Henry" assaults had continued to occur after his arrest. For example, a month or so after Ivan Henry was convicted, and while his case was still before the courts, a woman who lived across the hall from one of the women he was convicted of assaulting was sexually assaulted by an intruder who utilized elements of the same M.O. This assault was never disclosed to Mr. Henry.

In addition to review of materials collected by our client and by the Special Prosecutors, our team worked on assembling additional evidence that we would require for the appeal. Tony Paisana, our law student, obtained documentation from court registries concerning the criminal history of Donald McRae and discovered, to our surprise, that some old McRae Court files contained disclosure documents such as Reports to Crown Counsel. We reviewed old criminal files at the Vancouver Archives and were able to identify additional unsolved sexual assaults from the 1980s that involved the distinctive M.O. of the assaults for which our client had been convicted.

We furthermore located a forensic expert in California who provided us with an affidavit regarding the state of the science of serology in the 1980s and his own involvement in that decade with the Vancouver forensic lab concerning serological issues. We also collected documents relating to efforts made over the years by Ivan Henry's younger daughter, Kari, to bring issues concerning her father's convictions to the attention of authorities.

We also needed affidavits from the women who had been sexually assaulted after our client was detained in custody, for the purpose of a fresh evidence application. An experienced senior lawyer, John Banks, agreed to make approaches to the victims once we had located them. We were gratified that a number of the victims agreed to meet with Mr. Banks and were willing to prepare and swear affidavits setting out the difficult circumstances of the assaults on them that had occurred so many years earlier.

In January 2009 the British Columbia Court of Appeal granted Mr. Henry's application to re-open his appeal, which had been dismissed for want of prosecution twenty-five years earlier. Thereafter, I spoke with Ivan about applying for bail. He was initially quite reluctant to seek his release from custody, as he had a concern that if he were released from custody he might be wrongly accused of some new offence. Our client eventually agreed to have us seek his release from custody. Thomas Sophonow, himself a victim of a miscarriage of justice and wrongful conviction, kindly and quietly agreed to step forward to provide a surety if necessary. (The Sophonow case is written up in this collection by my colleague Richard Wolson.)

As it turned out, the Court of Appeal did not require a surety, and in June, 2009 Ivan Henry was ordered released from custody. When I told Ivan that one of the terms of his release was that he wear an electronic bracelet he was delighted. It was his view that if someone wrongly accused him of committing a crime during his liberty, he would be able to provide an alibi as the bracelet would establish his whereabouts at all times.

Ivan's release from custody and his taking up residence with his daughter Tanya and her family was a momentous step for him. Having been excluded from society for twenty-seven years, everything was new for him. Ivan had never used a lap-and-shoulder seat belt. He had never used a cell phone. He was unfamiliar with one and two-dollar coins. As the days went by, he expressed astonishment over things such as the quantity of clothing that people typically owned, the amount of traffic on the streets, the size of television screens, and the fact that the world population had grown from four billion to more than seven billion people within the duration of his incarceration.

After Ivan's release from custody, we continued to prepare his appeal. The materials relevant to the appeal issues included not just the usual trial record, but also a significant volume of documents relating to matters such as the history of disclosure and non-disclosure, and the Smallman investigative file. Fortunately, with the co-operation of the Special Prosecutor, and following careful research on both sides, we were able to reach agreement on the factual record of out-of-court events. At the hearing of Ivan Henry's conviction appeal before the British Columbia Court of Appeal, the Special Prosecutor, Mr. Crossin, conceded a number of grounds of appeal, including that the evidence was such that no reasonable jury could have convicted and, furthermore, that the non-disclosure of the complainant statements could possibly have affected the overall fairness of the trial.

On October 27, 2010, the Court of Appeal delivered its judgment allowing the appeal, overturning the convictions, and entering acquittals. That day was a highlight for the members of our defence team, and was rewarding in a way that perhaps only those who have represented the wrongly convicted can truly appreciate.

Although it has been a tremendous privilege to work on Ivan's case, it has also opened my eyes to the reality that there exists a surprising resistance to acceptance of the fact that a perfect storm of tunnel vision, breach of Crown disclosure duties, and a badly flawed police investigation, resulted in a case of wrongful conviction. While the Special Prosecutors conducted careful and thorough investigations and their efforts assisted in the convictions ultimately being overturned, and while the Court of Appeal overturned the convictions and entered acquittals, as of the date of this writing no public apology or acknowledgement of wrongdoing has been offered by those with institutional responsibility for the wrongful conviction of Ivan Henry, and no financial compensation has been offered to him.

The sad reality is that while the British Columbia public has embraced Ivan Henry as an innocent, wrongly convicted man, the institutional players have not accepted their responsibility for wrongly convicting him. Just as with Donald Marshall, the justice system's failure of Ivan Henry has persisted long after his acquittal.

PART TWO

Homicide

Earl Levy

TORONTO LOSES ITS INNOCENCE

Earl J. Levy QC is a past President of the Ontario Criminal Lawyers' Association and authored Examination of Witnesses in Criminal Cases (6th ed.). He received the Arthur Martin Criminal Justice Medal in 1996 and the Osgoode Hall Alumni Gold Key Award for Achievement in 2011. He is a Fellow of the American College of Trial Lawyers and a Life Member of the National Criminal Law Program Faculty.

IN 1977, I was retained to represent Mr. Werner Gruener in the Emanuel Jaques Trial, also known as the Shoeshine Boy Murder. The summertime slaying of Emanuel Jaques on what was known as Toronto's sin strip — a seedy stretch of Yonge Street that was a site of prostitution, drug dealing, and body rub parlours — elicited an uncommon display of public outrage and media coverage. Wire services spread the story throughout Canada, in Europe and throughout the United States, where cities such as Los Angeles and New York picked up the story because of its sensational elements of homosexual pedophilia and homicide.

Public anger in Toronto reached the point that after the first day of jury selection, one of the jurors received a phone message, "Find guilty or else." As a result, the trial judge, Justice William Maloney, agreed that the jury should be sequestered and so the jurors were kept away from their family and friends for two months. Sequestration is rarely granted, particularly when a trial is expected to be a long one. My family and I also received threatening calls; one so threatening to my wife that police protection was provided around my home.

Scenario

At 7:40 on the morning of Friday, July 29, 1977, twelve-year-old Emanuel Jaques was reported missing to the Metropolitan Toronto Police Service by his sister, Valdemira Jaques. An intensive search of the city followed, and particularly of the downtown core, with police receiving assistance from concerned members of the community. Valdemira told police that on the afternoon of Thursday, July 28, 1977, Emanuel had been at his homemade shoeshine box on Yonge Street, shining shoes with his fourteen-year-old brother Luciano, and a twelve-year-old friend, Shane McLean. At about 5:30 *p.m.*, the boys were approached by Saul Betesh who, with his co-accused Robert Kribs, had planned with one of his buddies to pick up a young boy and take him to 245 Yonge Street. Under the pretext of paying Emanuel $35 to help him move camera equipment, Betesh talked Emanuel into coming with him.

245 Yonge Street is located on the east side of Yonge Street, midway between Shuter Street and Dundas Square. The building housed "Charlie's Angels Body Rub Parlour," owned and operated by Joseph Martin. The body rub was located on the second floor. Werner Gruener, my client, and Robert Kribs shared a bedroom in the small, third-floor apartment and Josef Woods occupied another. Although Saul Betesh did not apparently live with them, he was a frequent visitor.

Saul Betesh left Emanuel on the street and went up to the apartment where Gruener, who was the only one in at the time, answered the door. Betesh told Gruener that he had a boy with him and that he would bring him in by the back door, which faced the laneway at the rear of the building. Gruener unlocked the back door and Emanuel was led up the fire escape stairway. Meanwhile, Kribs and Woods arrived at the apartment in time to greet Betesh and Emanuel. They had coffee and watched television. After a short time Emanuel was coaxed into Woods' bedroom where he was photographed, clothed and unclothed, by Betesh and Kribs.

It appeared that Emanuel had first agreed to certain acts of sex but withdrew when matters went too far. Emanuel was forced to commit acts of oral copulation. He was tied hand and foot with wire and handcuffed. He was anally penetrated, gagged and threatened with death, then choked by Kribs and Betesh in their efforts to force him to co-operate.

At one point during the evening, while Betesh and Kribs were taking turns with Emanuel in the bedroom, Joseph Martin Jr., together with his brother

Charlie and a friend came upstairs from the body rub parlour with the intention of smoking marijuana in the apartment. While there, Joe Martin Jr. attempted to go into Woods' bedroom but was stopped by Kribs outside the door. Later that night, Joe Martin Jr. returned to the third floor for some marijuana and was met by Gruener on the landing outside the apartment door. Martin Jr. asked Gruener what was going on and Gruener replied that nothing was going on.

Betesh and Kribs then decided to drug Emanuel by giving him sleeping pills, which Gruener supplied. Firstly, Gruener mixed an orange drink. One sleeping pill was put into the drink and given to the boy. This had no apparent effect on him and, as a result, it was decided to give him a second pill, intravenously. Gruener and Betesh prepared the drug and Betesh, allegedly with Gruener's assistance, tried to inject it into the boy's arm vein. They failed.

Shortly thereafter, Betesh and Kribs realized they could not let Emanuel go, so they decided to kill him. Kribs however, having previously held boys captive, at first wanted to take the boy away with him to Vancouver. After deciding to kill Emanuel, Betesh first tried strangling him to death, using an elastic cord he had taken previously from the back of a bicycle in the apartment. Kribs and Woods were present when the attempt was made. Gruener was allegedly guarding the door from the hallway. Woods locked the downstairs door. Betesh could not complete the strangling. He and Kribs then carried Emanuel, who was now in a semi-conscious state, from the bedroom to the kitchen where they held his head in the water until he asphyxiated. Betesh then took three dollars from the dead boy's pocket, giving Kribs a dollar.

Woods and Kribs wrapped Emanuel's body in garbage bags and they decided to conceal the body in the building until darkness fell that night so they wouldn't be seen digging a grave. With Betesh's help, they put the body in the rear stairwell leading to the back laneway.

Later that morning Kribs made reservations at the CNR for the train to Vancouver leaving Saturday, July 30. The Friday evening train, for July 29th, was full. Next afternoon, July 29, Betesh, Woods and Gruener went to the hardware store where Betesh purchased a shovel, later used to dig a grave. During that night Betesh and Kribs abandoned the idea of digging a grave because the ground was too hard. The accused finally selected a spot on the fourth-level rooftop at the rear of 245 Yonge Street. There, they concealed the corpse in the air duct.

Woods, Gruener and Kribs left Toronto by train at 11:30 pm on Saturday July 30, 1977. There was some talk that Betesh would meet them in Vancouver at a later date.

While the search for Emanuel intensified, Betesh realized he could be identified as the last person seen with Emanuel. An inveterate liar, he decided to go to the police with a false story. Betesh first contacted Mr. George Hislop, the head of the Canadian Homophile Association. Hislop in turn enlisted the aid of Mr. P., a solicitor. Mr. P. then contacted the police and accompanied Betesh to No. 51 station on Sunday, July 31, 1977. Betesh spun a false tale extricating himself, but he agreed to help the police with their investigation. His assistance continued through the night. Mr. P. left Betesh with them in locating persons responsible for Emanuel's disappearance. But the police were becoming more and more suspicious of Betesh as a result of certain things he told them. Betesh finally confessed and much of this scenario derives from his statements to the police. As a result of Betesh's confession, the Ontario Provincial Police at Sioux Lookout Detachment were advised to detain Woods, Gruener, and Kribs when the train stopped there.

Betesh told the police where the body could be found and later, with police photographers snapping, he voluntarily re-enacted the murder of Emanuel Jaques. Examination of the body revealed a bruising to the neck, which was indicative of ligature strangulation; there were needle puncture marks on the inside of both arms; there was a tearing in the wall of the boy's rectum, and there were traces of a drug in the boy's system.

At Sioux Lookout, Woods, Kribs, and Gruener were taken from the train and incarcerated until homicide officers arrived. There they gave signed statements. Kribs and Woods completely implicated themselves in the murder; Kribs as a principal, Woods as a party. They stated that Gruener was present during the discussion to kill Emanuel. Gruener admitted that he opened the back door of the 245 Yonge Street to let Betesh in with Emanuel. He stated they watched television for a while and then the others took Emanuel into Joe's room. Gruener said he did some packing and then went to Howard Johnson's to buy some ice cream. He said that while he was watching television, Saul Betesh had come out and asked for a sleeping pill. Gruener said he thought the boy was tired and was going to stay overnight. The others then debated what they should do with him. Woods talked about hypnotizing Emanuel. Betesh wanted to leave him in the park. Kribs wanted to take Emanuel to Vancouver. Gruener told them to take Emanuel back to his parents. Hoping they would let him go, Gruener went to sleep. Gruener admitted that the following day he had gone to the hardware store where Betesh had bought a shovel but said he was only interested in looking at the ten-speed bicycles. All four of the accused were avid bicycle riders and in fact originally met due to this mutual interest.

Both Kribs' and Betesh's statements concurred, in that Gruener helped them hide the body of Emanuel Jaques. On this evidence, if believed, Werner would have been convicted of accessory after the fact to murder but he was never charged on a separate indictment with this offence. Offences other than murder could not be included on the same indictment charging murder at the time of this trial, although that is not the law now.

On the way back to Toronto, Staff Sergeant Gerald Stevenson, Robert Kribs, and Werner Gruener sat three abreast. Stevenson testified that during the flight Kribs talked freely about his being homosexual and indicated Betesh and Woods were also homosexual. However, he said that Gruener liked little girls and that he also liked to watch when they had little boys in sexual activity. This evidence, if unchallenged, could have had an important bearing on the jury's deliberations. If Gruener was not homosexual, why would he have any interest in what was going on at 245 Yonge Street with Emanuel Jaques?

The Trial and the Verdict

THE DEFENCE decided not to move for a change of venue from Toronto — the publicity would follow the trial anywhere in Ontario. We agreed that Toronto being the most cosmopolitan location, provided the best chance for a fair trial. Each of the four accused had the right to challenge prospective jurors without cause. On behalf of my client, Werner Gruener, I decided not to challenge any prospective jurors and so advised the court in the presence of the jury panel, with the hope of conveying to them that my client stood in a different position from his co-accused.

Talking to Gruener was like swimming through a pool of peanut butter. Twenty-eight years old, he looked somewhat like Rasputin and acted like Mortimer Snerd. Although quite friendly, he never volunteered an answer. When he did answer it was brief as possible, after which he would lapse into a dreamy silence until asked another question. He belonged to the Children of God sect, was never without his Bible, and saw nothing wrong in working in a body rub parlour or co-habiting with pedophiles.

The great concern I had for Werner Gruener's defence was that, when heard by the jury, he would be tainted by the same prejudicial evidence that directly affected his three co-accused. I urged the court twice unsuccessfully for a separate trial for Gruener but instead, it proceeded as a joint jury trial.

Since there was no evidence that Gruener took part in the actual killing of Emanuel Jaques, it was the Crown's theory that he was guilty of first-degree murder by virtue of the sections of the *Criminal Code* which relate to aiding and abetting a crime. In the circumstances of this case, therefore, it was incumbent upon the prosecution to prove beyond a reasonable doubt that Werner Gruener formed an intention in common with any of his co-accused to commit the offence of indecent assault on Emanuel Jaques, or forcibly confine him and assist such co-accused therein, and knew or ought to have known that bodily harm leading to Emanuel Jaques' death would be a probable consequence.

Numerous photographs of young boys in various nude positions had been found in Josef Kribs' luggage that had been seized by police in Sioux Lookout, including photographs of Emanuel Jaques in sexual poses with Betesh. Also found were rolls of film, which were subsequently developed. A number of boys in these photos were traced and called to give similar fact evidence notwithstanding objections by the defence.

The Crown led evidence from some of these witnesses that Werner Gruener had taken the incriminating photographs but Gruener, in his testimony, denied taking such photographs. I pointed out to the jury the frailties in the evidence of these witnesses, raising a doubt on that issue. To demonstrate that Gruener would have to be set apart in evidence from his unsavoury friends, I cross-examined Joe Martin Sr. and Joe Martin Jr., who knew him well as their employee for four years at Charlie's Angels Body Rub Parlour.

The Martins were helpful in detailing his childish, simple, and soft nature. They stated how Gruener was always reading his Bible and would even talk about it to some of the customers at the body rub parlour. He was a good employee, honest and well-liked by those who worked around him. He had a collection of toy tanks that he liked to play with and at times was seen to drive his bicycle in the early hours of the morning down Yonge Street, pretending he was a soldier. There were times that he would hand out his Children of God pamphlets to passing pedestrians on Yonge Street. He liked to wear his Davey Crockett coonskin cap even in the heat of the summer. His bicycle had to be seen to be believed — it had streamers and a coonskin tail and all sorts of gadgets including a CB radio on the handlebars. The Martins felt that they and the girls who worked in the body rub parlour were Gruener's only family and that he enjoyed being told what to do by the girls because it was an indication that they had taken an interest in him. Their evidence was that Gruener had lived at 245 Yonge Street for four years and that Woods and Kribs were new-found friends who had moved in about two months before Emanuel was killed.

The psychiatric evidence we led was important. Insanity was not a defence but I felt it necessary to explain how Gruener could be so detached from events on the night in question that he could go to sleep. This is not a normal reaction of a normal person under the circumstances. Gruener tested at low-average intelligence. The conclusions of psychiatrist Dr. Donald Atcheson were that Gruener suffered from a personality disorder and that he periodically demonstrated psychotic symptoms at which time his contact with reality was inappropriate and inadequate. There was no evidence of deviant sexual behaviour. After trying to ascertain a chronological account of the events of the night in question, it was Dr. Atcheson's clinical impression that although Gruener was present much of the time, he was in the type of dissociated state that the doctor observed periodically during his examination. That is, he was in a world of his own and almost completely withdrawn from the reality of the situation. He did not feel, however, that Gruener was certifiable in that he did not present a risk to himself or others. Dr. Atcheson felt that Werner Gruener was a lonely person who sought out the Children of God sect for that reason. It was of course an explanation why he became friendly with his co-accused after they found each other through their mutual interest in CB radios and bicycle riding.

When one of the police officers from Sioux Lookout was called by the Crown to testify, I requested in cross-examination that Gruener's suitcase that she had seized, be opened. Prior to trial, I had arranged with the Crown, Frank Armstrong, to see its contents and I had felt that they strongly set Gruener apart from his co-accused. In it were: a picture from the *Toronto Sun* of Gruener sitting on that strange bike of his with earphones on his head and caption underneath reading that "Werner Gruener, an international cyclist was on his way from Vancouver to Florida and had stopped off in Toronto," an indication of the fantasy world in which he lived and a certain childlike quality; two Bibles (one Bible was also found on him when he was arrested and which he read continuously whilst in custody in Sioux Lookout and during the course of the police interrogation by the homicide squad); a group of religious drawings that he'd made; a pile of religious literature; a collection of wallet-sized photographs of movie stars; and a card indicating he was a member in good standing in a Rocket Club. There was also a receipt from American Express showing he had bought two hundred dollars worth of travellers cheques about a week before he took the train to Vancouver. This was important evidence insofar as the question of flight was concerned as it negated the allegation that he left Toronto as an acknowledgement of his guilt.

Gruener's Testimony

It was Gruener's testimony, consistent with part of the statement he gave to the police, that he had left Toronto not as some indication of consciousness of guilt, but that it had been a pre-planned trip. This evidence was corroborated by the Martins who testified that Gruener had told them about a month prior to Emanuel's death that he was going out West.

Before Frank Armstrong and Peter Rickaby QC had finished the Crown's case, Robert Kribs had changed his plea to guilty as charged, but not before his counsel, Gordon Goldman, first tested the admissibility of Kribs' incriminating statements and the similar fact evidence.

Woods had attempted to enter a plea of guilty to second-degree murder before the jury but this was not accepted by the Crown. He elected to call no defence and George Marron, his counsel, went to the jury on the basis that Woods was guilty of second-degree murder. In my view this was an excellent tactical move that paid off in the result as that was the jury's verdict instead of a verdict of guilty of first-degree murder.

Betesh's defence was insanity. Notwithstanding the impossible task that faced him, Betesh's lawyer Paul Tomlinson never once wavered in pursuit of this defence. I say his task was impossible for a number of reasons. His client's instructions to him were constantly changing, even during the course of the trial. Throughout the trial Betesh would constantly send him annoying messages. At one point, Betesh fired Paul, then rehired him the next day. Although several psychiatrists had seen Betesh prior to trial and there was a history of psychiatric illness diagnosed as far back as childhood, the most that could be said was that he had a mental illness. According to the psychiatrists, he could appreciate the nature and quality of the act and could distinguish right from wrong. This finding meant that Betesh was not insane within the meaning of the word used in *The Criminal Code of Canada.*

During the course of the trial, and after lengthy argument, Mr. Justice Maloney agreed to have Betesh further examined by a panel of several psychiatrists at Penetang jail over a period of approximately four days, including a weekend. Their finding was that Betesh was not insane. Dr. Andrew Malcolm, the Crown psychiatrist, concluded that Betesh was not insane within the meaning of the *Criminal Code* section at the time dealing with insanity. However, Betesh continued with the defence of insanity, without the support of a psychiatrist.

Betesh wanted to take the stand. Prior to doing so, his counsel called numerous members of his family including his mother, father, sister, and brother-in-law as well as acquaintances. They testified to his unpredictability, violent escapades and his lack of conscience. For example, he had thrown knives at his sister, he had thrown his mother down a flight of stairs and his parents were so afraid of him that they had kept a lock on their bedroom door. There was evidence of previous psychiatric treatment, special schools, and a fact that a male teacher had raped him when he was at one of these schools.

Most of all, these witnesses testified that Betesh was a pathological liar from the time he was a child. He could convince anybody of the truth when telling a lie because he couldn't recognize the difference himself. This evidence went to Betesh's disease of the mind but Betesh's history of lying was very helpful insofar as Gruener was concerned because of what Betesh had told the police about Gruener's alleged part on the night in question. However, it was still a very anxious moment for Gruener's defence when Betesh decided to take the stand. In his testimony he denied the truth of most of the things he had said in his statements that had implicated Gruener. He said that he had lied because he was angry with his co-accused when they had gone to Vancouver without him. So, he decided to implicate them all. He admitted that he relished the publicity. This was consistent with the evidence of others who had known him, who testified that he could be vindictive with little provocation. However, he maintained that Gruener helped to inject the boy with drugs, tied off his arm and held the candle to light the spoon containing the drug. There was now evidence from which the jury could have made Gruener a party to a forcible confinement that could have lead to a conviction of first-degree murder against Gruener, if believed.

At this juncture, I had an important decision to make about whether or not to cross-examine Betesh. If he was to be challenged on the evidence of forcible confinement regarding Gruener and he stuck to his story, that evidence would stand out like a sore thumb. He was an extremely unpredictable person, but the odds were that he would not change that evidence one iota, even though he had chosen to change his position with respect to all other incriminating matters involving Gruener. Notwithstanding he was mentally ill, Betesh was extremely bright and would be difficult to challenge. On the other hand, what was there to gain if, as a result of cross-examination, he did change his testimony regarding the forcible confinement? He had been painted as a pathological liar by close members of his family. If he was to change his testimony as a result of cross-examination, by his co-accused's counsel, would the jury give it any weight? Would it not be better to leave the cross-examination up to the Crown and if anything favourable for Gruener was elicited, would it not carry more weight with the jury as a result of the Crown's questions? In any event, would we not be going to the jury saying that Betesh was such a stranger to the truth that the jury should disregard his evidence entirely insofar as it related to his co-accused? These were the things that George Marron, Robert Kribs' counsel, and I discussed when we asked Mr. Justice Maloney for a time-out, designed to decide whether to cross-examine or not. Our discussion was brief. With a look of disdain on our faces to signify Betesh was a worthless witness, we advised the court we did not wish to cross-examine him.

Whether or not to call Gruener to testify gave me many anxious moments. In fact, it is the accused's choice as to whether he/she testifies or not, but it is my experience, and the experience of many other long-practicing counsel, that the accused wants our advice, which occurred in this case. No doubt most counsel have felt this anxiety more than once with their own trials. The case against Gruener was mainly circumstantial and he did have a number of previous criminal convictions involving property offences, vagrancy, and living off the avails of prostitution. However he had no conviction over the past four years since he took up with the Children of God. One could not fail but to consider whether a jury would convict Werner Gruener of first-degree murder on the case the Crown had presented. If the jury was satisfied that Gruener was a party to either an indecent assault, by opening the door to let in Emanuel Jaques, or to forcible confinement, then the key issue remaining was whether he knew or ought to have known that bodily harm would probably result. Even though I had hoped that a picture had been painted to show Gruener as immature and child-like, incapable of fully understanding what was going on around him (to be supported by the evidence of a psychologist and a psychiatrist), I was still not very sure about what the jury thought about him in these very prejudicial circumstances. It has always been my policy to call an accused in a criminal case to give him or her an opportunity to deny guilt, hopefully in a credible manner, and particularly in a homicide case when the penalty is so high; unless, of course, the choice not to do so is a clear and obvious one. In my view, a jury will be very suspicious if you do not call your client, in spite of what you say about his rights in your jury address; a jury wants to hear a credible denial of guilt by the accused. In this case I concluded that the choice not to call Gruener was not clear, not obvious. I felt that his quiet and unassuming manner and his different personality from his co-accused would help his cause before the jury. Knowing the way that he responded to questions from his friendly counsel, psychiatrist and psychologist, I did not feel that an unfriendly Crown would make important headway with him in cross-examination.

So Gruener took the stand. He admitted opening the back door but merely thought they were bringing Emanuel up to take photographs of him during the relevant time frame. He described how he had watched television, was in and out of his own room packing for his trip to Vancouver, and on one occasion went to Howard Johnson's down the street for some ice cream. He denied hearing any screams coming from Emanuel. At Betesh's request he provided a sleeping pill but did not think it was for any nefarious purpose. There had been discussions about what to do with Emanuel. Woods wanted to hypnotize him, which was "his thing." Kribs wanted to take the boy to Vancouver with them. Betesh wanted to drug Emanuel and put him in a park. At this time, Gruener was made aware Emanuel was tied up, although he was not concerned because he had been shown photographs where Kribs had tied up boys for the purposes of picture-taking. Some of these photographs had been made exhibits by the Crown. Very importantly, Gruener testified he told them to let Emanuel go home and then went to sleep. He never thought that they would do harm to the boy. He denied that he helped hide the body the next day. Woods had told him he was buying a shovel to hide some dope he was going to be selling. Gruener testified he never knew Emanuel had been harmed until they were arrested in Sioux Lookout, when Kribs told him what happened whilst they were locked up in the cells there. Kribs had told him the following morning that they took Emanuel home.

A very interesting thing occurred during his cross-examination. Gruener's attention was drawn to Betesh's three-page police statement and he was asked questions by the Crown regarding that statement. His attention was then drawn to his own one-page police statement and he was asked questions pertaining to it. It then dawned on me that Gruener was turning the pages of the Betesh statement instead of referring to his own. This didn't make sense, because, as I said, his statement was only one page long and Betesh's statement was three pages long. I stood up and asked His Lordship whether my client was looking at his own statement or Betesh's statement when answering the questions. I believe that when the jury realized Gruener was looking at Betesh's statement whilst answering questions about his own statement, it gave them a spontaneous insight into his impaired thinking processes.

After a two-month trial, the jury returned with their verdict within two hours. Betesh and Kribs were found guilty of first-degree murder, Woods guilty of second-degree murder, and Werner Gruener was acquitted. Valdemira Jaques, the 19-year-old sister of Emanuel, who was present throughout the trial to hear all the gruesome evidence, flanked by a priest and her aunt, demonstrated her first emotions by bursting into tears and running from the courtroom.

Insights

Now that I have had the chance to think back at the Shoeshine Boy case that occurred over forty years ago, a few things come to mind as being particularly significant. Firstly, only in gangster movies does one normally hear about threats to jury members but this was a reality with the phone call to the juror saying, "Find guilty or else." Coupled with the fact that the jury was sequestered because of that threat when sequestration is rarely ordered and certainly not for such a length of time as this, it is clear to see how this murder pushed up the public blood pressure.

Tied in with the ramping up of citizen outrage and activism, it may be correct to say that the day Emanuel Jaques lost his life was the day that the City of Toronto lost its innocence. No criminal case in the history of Toronto, no matter how notorious, has had a more intense social impact than the murder of Emanuel Jaques. I believe the public's perception was that the body rub parlours and adult stores were emblematic of the sleaze that existed on Yonge Street at that time. The case precipitated numerous protest marches, demanding that the city clean up the area. Adult stores and body rub parlours were shut down and as a consequence, Yonge Street was revitalized.

As a final reflection, when I first became involved in this murder trial, I was doubtful about a successful defence for Werner Gruener, given the fact that Gruener was lumped in with individuals against whom very inflammatory evidence would be presented. Such adages come to mind as, "You are judged by the company you keep," "Birds of a feather flock together," and "When you lie down with dogs you get up with fleas." I felt that the pre-trial publicity would overwhelm potential jurors nothwithstanding they would take an oath to come to their verdicts based only on the evidence and the law as given to them by the trial judge. I was not confident at all that the safeguards against a wrongful conviction that had been built into our justice system over many decades would be sufficient to help Werner be viewed apart from his co-accused by the jurors. But in fact what happened was that the jurors were true to their oaths. By virtue of returning with three different verdicts, including the acquittal of Werner Gruener, as opposed to summarily convicting all four accused with first-degree murder, the jurors had analysed the evidence against each of them separately, as instructed by the trial judge.

While there are those who may disagree with me, the jury's verdicts showed that our justice system worked after being so severely tested; that the presumption of innocence is not a meaningless phrase and that the media and public opinion will not supercede what twelve impartial jurors have considered in the courtroom. Such has not always been the case.

Peter Martin

MAN'S INHUMANITY

PHOTO: NOEL ZINGER

A Senior Crown Prosecutor in Calgary from 1980 to 1995 and then practicing criminal defence, Peter Martin QC was appointed to the Alberta Court of Queen's Bench in 1998 and to the Alberta Court of Appeal in 2005. He has lectured extensively and is a Life Member of the National Criminal Law Program Faculty. He also served as President of the Law Society of Alberta.

I'VE BEEN asked by the editors of *Tough Crimes* to write about a case that was "disquieting" to the community and to me. While I have been involved in a number of such cases, I have chosen to discuss one of such savagery that it shocked the community and as a young prosecutor, marked me. It was this case that led me to the sad realization that man's inhumanity is limited only by the imagination. This is the tragic account of two men, who, in 1981, embarked on a plan to kidnap, rape, and murder women.

At the time they met, both men were married. Robert Brown lived with his wife and children near the hamlet of Blackie, Alberta, about thirty kilometres southeast of Calgary. Brown was a short, pudgy man in his early thirties and bore a remarkable resemblance to the serial killer, Clifford Olson. Both men had that same cunning, evil look. Brown was raised in foster homes and reform schools. He was an outcast and a loner, with a lengthy criminal record. He did odd jobs when he could find them. His family led a subsistence living in a run-down rental property surrounded by worthless junk that Brown had collected over time.

By contrast, Jim Peters was a tall, physically strong man of limited intelligence. He was twenty-nine years old and had no prior criminal record. He worked at minimum wage jobs. He and his wife were from Nova Scotia and were at that time drifting across Canada. In December of 1981, they found a house to rent near Blackie, Alberta and settled there temporarily while Peters worked as a labourer nearby.

The two men met by chance late one night in December 1981 on a dark, deserted country road. Brown was driving an old, very large clunker of a car. He was on his way home. Peters was standing on the shoulder of the gravel road, hitchhiking. He too was going home. Brown later told the police that as his car approached the hitchhiking Peters, he decided to run him over. He sped up and at the last instant swerved his vehicle to hit Peters. As his car left the road and bounced along in the darkness between the shoulder and the ditch, Brown was unable to tell whether he had actually hit Peters, and if so, whether he was dead. Once he was able to stop the car he backed up slowly to check.

As Peters later explained, he reacted to the unexpected swerve of the vehicle by diving into the ditch just as he was about to be hit. Then, as he saw the car stop and back up, he thought the driver was returning to give him a lift. So he got out of the ditch and stood in the darkness by the road and as the car slowly approached, he opened the passenger door and jumped in.

Stunned, Brown drove his unexpected passenger home. En route the two men began chatting. They took an instant liking to one another. By the time they parted company that night, they had become friends. In the days that followed, they met often. Eventually their wives also socialized. Although the two women were friendly, the two men had bonded and often spent their time driving idly around the countryside.

Exactly how it happened was never told, but it appears that on one of those nights, with nothing else to do, Brown proposed that they find a woman to rape and kill. Remarkably, Peters agreed. I later asked a forensic psychiatrist, at another murder trial of two men who had both been diagnosed with anti-social personality disorders, how it is that one could feel comfortable suggesting such an outrageous plan to another. The psychiatrist replied; "God makes them and they find each other." I cannot believe that God had anything to do with it, but I accept there is something about the make-up of such people that attracts, or at least is recognized by, a kindred spirit.

Now Brown and Peters roamed the countryside with a purpose and after several "missed opportunities" as they called them, perverse chance brought them together with a beautiful, twenty-three-year-old woman named Debbie Stevens. Ms. Stevens lived in High River and worked for an oil servicing company. On the evening of December 12, 1981, the company had its annual Christmas party, in Calgary. Ms. Stevens stayed late and it was not until after 2:00 the following morning that she began her drive home, alone.

Brown and Peters were also in Calgary that night. They had been "hunting," as they called it, unsuccessfully for hours, looking for a woman "to take." They left the city at about 2:30 that morning, intending to return home, but at the last minute they decided to go to High River to look for one last "opportunity."

It was just after 3:00 *a.m.* when Debbie Stevens' car ran out of gas by a railway crossing only one kilometre north of High River. She had begun to walk the remaining distance when Brown and Peters drove up and offered her a ride. She accepted and got into the back of their car. She told them where she lived but almost immediately had misgivings and asked to be let out at a nearby hotel instead. But by that time, Brown had signalled to Peters that they'd found their victim.

Peters moved to the backseat of the car to restrain Ms. Stevens while Brown drove to a deserted location several kilometres from town where both men raped her. Then Brown instructed Peters to drive to an even more remote location. There they told her to dress and that she would be allowed to walk home. Brown instructed her to stand by the car and close her eyes. As she did so, Peters approached her with a tire iron and struck her head repeatedly as she fell to the ground, gravely injured but still alive. Brown took the weapon and continued to hit her, while Peters repeatedly kicked her until she was dead. They then dragged her body from the roadway to a farmer's field, stole what money and valuables she had, and drove home. They told their wives they were late returning home because their car had run out of gas.

A few nights later, fearing that they had left evidence on the body that might lead the police to them, they returned with gasoline and set it afire. Ms. Steven's remains were found the following day, after a massive search.

Six weeks later, on January 30, 1982, the two men drove to Calgary again to find another victim. Once again, they were thwarted. As they later explained, they were about to "grab" a woman at a bus stop but, after circling back to get her, had to abort that plan because a bus was coming and they feared the bus driver was close enough to identify them.

So they drove to Okotoks because Brown remembered a pretty young girl who often worked alone at night at a convenience store there. That pretty young girl was sixteen-year-old Laurie Boyd, a grade ten student who worked part time at the Red Rooster store.

The two men arrived at the store around ten-thirty that Saturday evening. Peters went in. He saw that Ms. Boyd was working alone and reported back to Brown. They moved their car to the lane behind the store. Brown went in and literally dragged Ms. Boyd through the back of the store to the car, while holding a screwdriver to her neck. They drove her out of town, to a deserted location where they sexually assaulted her. Then Brown killed her with a knife. Thereafter, as Brown sat on the hood of his car to have a cigarette, Peters poured gasoline on the body and set it afire. They left Ms. Boyd burning on that deserted country road.

On the way home, Brown realized that in the frenzy of the killing he had stabbed himself in the arm. Concerned his wound may become infected, he decided they should drive to a hospital in Calgary to have it treated.

The next customer in the convenience store called the police to report the store was open, but abandoned. Fearing that Ms.Boyd may have met the same fate as Debbie Stevens, the RCMP immediately set up roadblocks checking all traffic travelling on Highway 2 north and south of Okotoks. It was now almost midnight and hellishly cold out.

Twenty-five-year-old Jackie O'Neill and her common-law husband were on that highway driving back to Calgary when their car broke down. They decided that she would have better luck hitchhiking to Calgary to get help than would he.

The two men couldn't believe their luck as they stopped to pick up Ms. O'Neill. She got into the back seat. As he drove, Brown tried desperately to signal Peters that they had another victim, but before he could do so, they found themselves in the RCMP roadblock, from which there was no escape. All three occupants had to identify themselves before being allowed to pass. The police recorded their names. There would be no more killing that night.

At the roadblock the police instructed Peters, who was driving, to go back and get Ms. O'Neill's husband, which he then did before continuing on to the hospital. What followed was by any measure, bizarre. Brown, who was said to be in a jovial mood, advised his passengers that he enjoyed killing people. He then turned on O'Neill's husband for allowing her to hitchhike alone, because it was so unsafe. Brown threatened to hunt him down and kill him if that ever happened again.

In the early 1980s, Okotoks was a small, quiet and safe country town approximately thirty kilometres south of Calgary; and High River, about the same distance south of Okotoks, was only slightly larger. The area had been homesteaded a century before and most residents had lived there all of their lives, many still using the land for farming and ranching. It seemed that everyone knew each other and generally trusted one another. What crime there was, was not of the serious kind — impaired drivings, joy ridings, and minor thefts. Homicides were uncommon. Random, brutal murders such as these were completely unheard of. So it was understandable that these killings left the entire area terrified. Fear and outrage replaced tranquility. Women and children were not left alone. Firearms were left standing loaded by the front door.

In Alberta, smaller cities and towns are policed by the RCMP. Immediately upon discovering the body of Debbie Stevens in December 1981, the investigation into her death was turned over to an RCMP Major Crime Investigation Unit. Those officers then relocated their headquarters to the RCMP detachment in High River. After the murder of Laurie Boyd in February 1982, a larger contingent of major crime investigators were brought in to assist, and for a time there were thirty officers dedicated solely to this investigation.

While the police were doing all they could to apprehend those responsible, Brown revelled in a game of cat and mouse. The day after Debbie Stevens' charred body was found, Brown personally went to the High River RCMP detachment and falsely reported that his jacket had been stolen. That was a ruse to allow him to gain access to the detachment where he hoped to overhear how the police were progressing with the investigation. Later, after the killing of Laurie Boyd, Brown telephoned a television news reporter, identified himself as a close friend and confidant of the killer, then taunted the police who he referred to as "pigs" and "retards", for being unable to find his friend, the killer.

As with most random killings, these proved hard to solve. Initially there were very few leads and no good suspects. The police feared another attack before the perpetrators could be apprehended. They believed they were in a race against time. They held meetings to formulate contingency plans in the event of another kidnapping. Those plans were elaborate. For example, it was decided that in response to the next reported kidnapping, every peace officer in the area, including Fish and Wildlife and By-Law officers, were to become part of an emergency response, to immediately form roadblocks to stop all vehicle traffic on all roadways in the area of the next crime.

Then the hard work of tracking down hundreds of leads, provided by anxious citizens, began. Dozens of potential but tenuous suspects were identified and put on a list to be interviewed.

One such report came from Jackie O'Neill. She thought that Brown and Peters behaved strangely and talked bizarrely on the ride back to Calgary after clearing the roadblock. The following day, on hearing of the abduction and murder of Laurie Boyd, she phoned the police to share her concerns. The police were able to establish the full names and addresses of Brown and Peters from the information they gave when stopped at the roadblock with Ms. O'Neill. Their names were added to the growing list of persons-of-interest that the police intended to interview.

A few days later, on February 5, 1982, two RCMP officers visited Brown at his home and questioned him about his activities on the night of Laurie Boyd's abduction and specifically how he came by his wound. He offered that he had been driving around all that night with Peters and had been cut accidentally when the two men were play-fighting with a knife. The officers accepted that explanation and left. Later that evening, Brown's wife called 911 to request an ambulance for her husband who had attempted to commit suicide by taking a cocktail of stupefying drugs. The ambulance attended but Brown refused to get in and threatened to fight the emergency response people. They called the local RCMP for assistance. When the uniformed officers arrived, Brown began screaming at them words to the effect that they didn't have enough evidence to charge him with the Stevens/Boyd murders and that the police would never be able to prove that he and Peters had killed the two women.

He was placed in an ambulance and en route to the hospital, the attending police officers reported Brown's rants to the investigative team. Those officers instructed their colleagues to maintain a constant bedside vigil and to record every word Brown said while he was in hospital recuperating from his overdose.

This development caused Brown to skyrocket to the top of the list of suspects literally overnight. The following morning, two officers investigating the homicides met Brown as he was about to be released from the hospital. They took him to the High River detachment to question him in earnest. Two other officers went to the car dealership where Peters was then working as a lot boy and took him to another detachment to question him.

Very quickly, both men offered what were to be lengthy and detailed confessions, every word of which was tape-recorded. They also agreed to re-enactments and took the police to the scenes of the crimes, during which property stolen from each victim, and subsequently discarded, was recovered. With that, the nightmare that had gripped the area ended.

I'd joined Alberta Justice in 1976, as an articling student fresh from law school, and was called to the bar in 1977. I had been a lawyer for four years when I was assigned to prosecute this case. I had prosecuted a few murder cases by that time, but always alone. This was the first case for which I was assigned a junior, or second counsel. That lawyer was Balfour Der, who had joined the prosecution service just the year before and is now a prominent criminal defence lawyer in Calgary.

Following the arrests, we met with the investigative teams and their supervisor. I knew two of those men; one a relatively young officer, Corporal Al MacIntyre, who I had met two years earlier when I prosecuted a case he had investigated. MacIntyre had just been promoted to the Major Crimes Unit and this was the first of many homicides that we would work on together. He was a serious, hardworking, by-the-book investigator. I liked him immediately and trusted him completely. The head of the investigative teams was a more senior man, Sergeant Ray Forsythe. He also had a tremendous capacity for work and was a natural leader. I always thought that he too went by the book, so long as the book was adequate for the demands of the case. I did not know the other three men; Sergeant Dennis Schaefer, Constable Robert Kewley, or Constable Terry Mehmel, prior to this case but all impressed me with their diligence and ingenuity. As the trial judge later commented; "They [these investigators] have lived up to the highest traditions of that well-known and respected police force."

At the time, the law provided that all murder cases begin with a preliminary inquiry where the prosecutor would call witnesses to satisfy a Provincial Court judge that there was sufficient evidence to warrant a trial; in very simple terms, enough evidence that if it was heard by a jury, they could convict.

As the killings had occurred near High River, so too would the preliminary inquiry be held there. There was only one courtroom in that plain, small-town courthouse and I remember the first morning of the preliminary inquiry well. A large contingent of media people met us in the parking lot and asked questions about the case as we walked into the courtroom. Questions like, how long we expected the preliminary inquiry to take, how many witnesses we would be calling and so on. I had expected the media and I was also not surprised when I walked into the courtroom to find it packed with spectators. But what amazed me was that virtually all of them were men. I cannot now recall seeing a single woman sitting in that courtroom, and almost all of the men were ranchers and farmers; men used to heavy labour and it showed. I live among these people now, they are my neighbours, and I have yet to meet one rancher who is not hardworking and honest, with a very clear sense of what is right and what is wrong. These are by any measure salt of the earth, conservative people.

My immediate concern was that if one man in the audience moved forward or shouted, "Let's get them," the accused would not be leaving there alive.

In those days, security in country courthouses was provided by uniformed members of the RCMP, particularly members from the local detachment. While the case was being heard, officers would escort the prisoner in and out of the courtroom and sit beside the prisoner's box, facing the judge, with their backs to the spectators.

We had a large complement of officers to provide security for this preliminary inquiry, and as additional insurance, a large bullet-proof glass shield was placed behind the prisoners box. To pre-empt the possibility of any disturbance, I asked two of the officers to stand, one on each side of the prisoner's box, but facing the audience. It was a time when the RCMP uniform and the officers who wore them were universally respected by the communities they served and I was convinced that no one would attack those officers to get at the two accused men.

Once the judge was in the room, Brown and Peters were brought out from cells and the preliminary inquiry began. Throughout that hearing and the trial that followed, they sat impassively, almost bored, as the evidence of their outrageous crimes was introduced for all to hear.

These offences happened long before the discovery of DNA testing, which can now often conclusively match a criminal to the offence. Although there was considerable physical evidence to establish that these two were the assailants, the mainstay of the prosecution's case were the lengthy confessions both accused had provided to the police. In Canadian law, all statements made by an accused to any person in authority such as a police officer must be proven to have been freely and voluntarily made before that statement can be admitted at trial as evidence against the accused person. Confessions that were obtained as the result of threats or inducements held out by a police officer are ruled inadmissible and cannot be relied upon as evidence by the prosecution.

The voluntariness of a statement is usually established by the prosecutor examining all of the police officers who participated in the interview, as well as those who may have influenced the accused to talk. Typically these witnesses would be asked whether they at any time had physical contact with the accused, whether they produced their weapons during the interview, whether they threatened or made any promise to the accused and so on. On the basis of such evidence, the judge would decide whether the statement was voluntarily made and therefore admissible. If the prosecutor could not establish this high standard, then the statement would be ruled inadmissible and could not be introduced at trial to prove the accused's guilt.

In this case, we adjourned for lunch just as I was asking these questions of Constable Kewley, the officer who, along with Corporal MacIntyre, interviewed

Brown. It is uncommon to have police witnesses also provide security for trials at which they are testifying, but because of the unique situation facing us, all of the officers, including those who were there to testify, agreed to remain in the courthouse over the lunch hour.

The accused were kept in cells immediately behind the courtroom, where they were also fed. Constable Kewley walked by the cell area as Brown was having his lunch. He called out; "Hey Kewley, come here." As Constable Kewley walked over, Brown continued; "What's with that prosecutor asking all those stupid questions: '... did you hit me ... did you point your gun at me?' Is he nuts, nothing like that happened. We were close man, we were like brothers."

Constable Kewley immediately took out his notebook to record Brown's comments. When court resumed after lunch, I recalled Kewley to the witness stand to have him tell the judge what Brown had just told him. That was the end of that exercise; it had never been easier to establish the admissibility of such a critical confession.

Predictably, both accused were ordered to stand trial on two counts of first-degree murder, the most serious charge in our *Criminal Code*. The trial took place in the Court of Queen's Bench in Calgary in the winter of 1983. It was presided over by Mr. Justice William Brennan, a decorated war hero and an imposing judge. As then required by law, murder trials were to be decided by a jury. The accused were represented by two very experienced criminal lawyers, Larry Ross for Peters, and John Davison for Brown. They had approached me prior to trial to ask whether I would accept guilty pleas to lesser charges; I told them that was out of the question.

The trial began, again before a packed courtroom. During the second week of the trial, both accused capitulated and offered to change their pleas from "not guilty" to "guilty." That request was quickly accommodated. The law is somewhat different now, but at that time, as the accused had been placed "in charge of the jury" and as the trial had begun, only the jury could return a verdict. After advising the judge that the accused wished to change their pleas to guilty, the jury was brought in to hear them do that. I then told the jury of the remaining evidence which we had intended to call in proof of the Crown's case. Both accused agreed that information was correct. Thereafter, Justice Brennan instructed the jury to accept the additional information I had presented and the accused's guilty pleas as proof of their guilt and return verdicts of guilty on each charge for each accused. The jury went out and returned a few minutes later with those verdicts. Then, all that was left was to sentence the accused.

In Canada, a person convicted of first-degree murder must be sentenced to imprisonment for life without eligibility of parole until they have served twenty-five years of that sentence. At the time, that was the mandatory minimum sentence for that offence and also the maximum sentence available in Canadian law. Before passing that automatic sentence, each accused was asked whether they had anything they wished to say. Neither did. It was then Justice Brennan's turn. Before a packed courtroom of several hundred people, he ordered Brown and Peters to stand. Some of his remarks follow.

> Peters and Brown, I find it impossible to put into words the absolute and utter contempt with which I and all members of society feel toward you because of the crimes you have each committed against these two victims, Debbie Stevens and Laurie Boyd. With respect to each of them, you have committed the most nefarious crimes that a man can commit against a woman. What you did to each of these young woman was so cowardly, violent and vicious and revolting, that it is virtually impossible for any decent member of this society to either imagine or comprehend what you did.

Justice Brennan then imposed a sentence of life imprisonment, and that was it. The prisoners were removed from the courtroom and taken away to spend the rest of their lives in jail. Saddened spectators shuffled quietly out of the courtroom until only the Boyd and Stevens family members were left with their grief and their anguish.

I have often been asked how having to deal with such outrageous crimes has affected me. I usually answer that by the time we as lawyers are exposed to such crimes, we have dealt with less serious offences of violence so when we become involved in murder cases, we have become somewhat desensitized. I think that is true for most cases — even most murders. But there are some, like these, which are so barbaric and so cruel, that they mark everyone involved. The poet John Dunne wrote that, "Every man's death diminishes me." That may be so, but killings like these have an even more profound effect. I think that to varying degrees, after being exposed to such inhumanity, most people are never the same again. Of all the judges, lawyers and police officers I know who have dealt with such cases, I know of only one man who in my opinion has remained untouched by them.

Brown found his time in prison unbearable. He killed himself in the Kingston Penitentiary a few years into his sentence. I am told that he used an electrical cord from the radio in his cell to hang himself. He left a suicide note ironically lamenting that Canada no longer had the death penalty because, as he put it, suicide took a lot of courage. So far as I know Peters is still in jail.

The Town of Okotoks erected a plaque on a lamppost in memory of Laurie Boyd. Sadly, it is gone now. Thirty years on, very few people recall the case and those who do rarely speak of it. Almost every week, I pass by the lamppost that carried that plaque and the railroad tracks where Debbie Stevens' car ran out of gas. And every time I do, it is with sadness that I think of both young women, the horror that befell them, and the evil some men are capable of.

John Rosen

DEFENDING PAUL BERNARDO: AM I THE DEVIL'S ADVOCATE?

John M. Rosen has defended serious criminal cases at all levels of court in Ontario, the Supreme Court of Canada, and other jurisdictions. He received the Law Society Medal and is a Fellow of the American College of Trial Lawyers. He was Treasurer and Vice-President of the Ontario Criminal Lawyers' Association, and is affiliated with advocacy associations. He is actively involved in continuing legal education initiatives.

PAUL KENNETH BERNARDO will forever be known for the murders and other crimes he committed with his wife, Karla Homolka in Southern Ontario the late 1980s and early 1990s. In addition to his being the long-sought-after "Scarborough Rapist," what makes Bernardo and Homolka so infamous is that, outwardly, they appeared entirely normal. As a young, attractive, seemingly normal, white and upwardly mobile couple, they appeared to represent everything middle class Canadian society strives to be. But when his crimes came to light, to the general public Bernardo became the Devil incarnate. Does that make me, his trial lawyer, the Devil's advocate?

Before Bernardo came to me as a client in August 1994, I took my role in Canadian criminal justice for granted. I was called to the Bar of Ontario in 1970 and by the summer of 1994 had practiced as a criminal defence counsel for almost twenty-five years. I had represented numerous people charged with the full range of criminal offences, but was best known at the bar for having represented some two hundred people charged with murder. I was a lawyer, not a judge, and did not judge my clients. I represented their interests, gave them my best advice, tried to protect their rights and, if possible, get them off their charge. My job was to ensure that they got a fair trial and a just result. I always tried to win, and very often succeeded. This is the stuff that criminal lawyers do.

My decision, however, to take Bernardo on as a client fundamentally shook my belief in my role, particularly with the surfacing of the Bernardo tapes early in that process. The case was difficult at best and the subject of intense media coverage. The heinous nature of the allegations and the public's revulsion threatened to impair my ability to do my job properly. Once the videotapes emerged, the case appeared to be un-defendable. Absent a plea bargain involving a lesser charge, which I knew would never happen, the case would proceed to trial. I would be expected to produce a defence. Under the glare of the media, my ability as a criminal lawyer would be scrutinized and perhaps called into question. In other words, taking on the case forced me to ask myself, would this case be my undoing?

Although the case and the four-month trial that ended September 1, 1994 proved difficult in the extreme, my concerns were groundless. From a defence lawyer's perspective, it turned out to be a typical murder case, although one that was especially grueling and unusually media-frenzied. Nevertheless, I survived by doing what I always understood to be my job: I analyzed the problem facing the client, developed a credible strategy, advocated my position in Court and ignored the media hype. Even though I eventually lost the trial, my client paid me the ultimate compliment. As the jury's foreperson announced that he was guilty as charged, Paul Bernardo turned to me and said, "Well, at least I got a fair trial." What follows is perhaps some insight into why he — and others — paid me that compliment. [1]

Background

Paul Bernardo and Karla Homolka met in Toronto on October 17, 1987. He was an accounting student at the Toronto office of a national accounting firm. She worked in St. Catharines, Ontario a city in Niagara Region east of Niagara Falls, as an assistant in a pet store and part-time as an assistant in a veterinary clinic. She and a friend had come to Toronto for a pet food convention. By chance, they met Paul and his friend, Van Smirnis, at the restaurant in the Howard Johnson Motel located in the east-end Toronto suburb of Scarborough, where the women were staying. It was lust at first sight.

Unbeknownst to anyone at the time, Paul Bernardo was a serial sexual predator. Between May 4, 1987 and May 26, 1990, he physically and sexually assaulted and viciously raped fourteen young women in Scarborough, where he lived, and one in Mississauga. The victims were in their teens or early twenties.

On each occasion, his victim was returning home at night, in many cases walking between a bus stop and home.

Bernardo's *modus operandi* included stalking his victim, then attacking from behind, dragging her into a driveway or bushes, punching and beating her before raping her anally and vaginally. Afterwards, he would take a trophy such as jewellery or an article from the victim's purse. In some cases, he took personal identification including addresses and other personal identifiers.

The rapes were accompanied by some or all of: death threats, demand for oral intercourse, tightening a ligature or electrical cord around his victim's neck, digital penetration, cutting or biting the victim, threatening further violence, gagging, cutting clothes and underwear with a knife, smashing the victim's head on the ground, forcing the victim to say she loved him, and forcing the victim to utter words of self-deprecation. In some cases, Bernardo threatened to return later to the victim's house to rape and kill her. In other cases, he made it clear that he had been stalking the victim for some time before the attack, and described her bedtime routine as seen by him through her bedroom window.

Police dubbed the perpetrator the Scarborough Rapist and were actively searching for him.

Paul Bernardo's name first emerged as a potential suspect in January 1988 after the fifth Scarborough rape. A young woman called police about Bernardo refusing to repay money to her. Her description of his bizarre behaviour caused the officer who took the report to target Bernardo for investigation in connection with the Scarborough rapes. The tip received no priority and was not investigated. The rapes continued.

On September 26, 1990, Alex Smirnis, the brother of Bernardo's friend Van Smirnis, was interviewed by police. He named Bernardo as a potential suspect. By this time, the rapes had stopped.

As a result of this tip, on November 20, 1990, police interviewed Bernardo. He was still living in Scarborough. He assumed a totally innocent demeanour and cooperated with their investigation. He told the police he was engaged to Karla Homolka and was planning to move to St. Catharines where she lived. He voluntarily provided to police, at their request, hair, blood, and saliva samples.

Although Bernardo's biological samples were submitted to Ontario's Centre of Forensic Sciences (CFS) the next day, as matters transpired they received no priority for testing and sat on a shelf untested until early 1993.

Indeed, Bernardo and Homolka were engaged to be married. Following their meeting at the Howard Johnson Motel, Bernardo pursued Homolka and drove regularly to St. Catharines to be with her. Their wedding was planned for June 29, 1991.

Sex dominated their relationship. Paul was obsessed with the idea of virginity and of being the first to have sex with a girl. He was disappointed that Karla was not a virgin when they met. They fantasized about engaging in three-way sex with Karla's youngest sister, Tammy, who they believed was a virgin. Tammy looked very much like Karla. She was infatuated with Paul.

At his trial, Bernardo testified that on July 24, 1990, Karla gave her sister's virginity to him. To do this, Karla laced spaghetti sauce with crushed Halcion, a mild sleeping pill sometimes used on animals, and served it to Tammy. When Tammy became unconscious, Paul raped Tammy while Karla watched. This event portended a similar but tragic event several months later.

On December 23, 1990, at a family party in the Homolka home, Tammy got very drunk. When the parents and Karla's other sister retired for the night, Paul, Karla, and Tammy adjourned to the basement area to watch pornographic videos. As Tammy nodded off, Karla applied a cloth soaked with Halothane, an anesthetic used on animals that she stole from work. She then held the cloth to her sister's nose and mouth. When Tammy was fully unconscious, Karla and Paul sexually assaulted her.

Like many of their sexual exploits, the assault was videotaped. At Paul's trial, Karla testified that Paul forced her to participate in the assault. She relied on the video in which she was depicted resisting Paul's efforts to have her perform oral sex on Tammy. She was cross-examined with the use of the videotape, which showed that she was initially a willing participant but balked when she realized Tammy was menstruating.

As Tammy became conscious, she vomited, aspirated her stomach contents and died. Paul and Karla called 911 and cleaned up the scene. At the time, responding police and EMS treated Tammy's death as an accident.

Paul eventually dropped out of accounting and turned to smuggling cigarettes and alcohol across the Canada-United States border, which can be reached by car within minutes from St. Catharines. On February 1, 1991, he moved into the grieving Homolka residence with Karla and her family.

Neither Paul nor Karla demonstrated any apparent remorse for the death of Tammy. When the parents went to Toronto for a weekend away, Paul and Karla continued their sexual escapades, which they videotaped. I will never forget the moment when the clips of Karla and Paul having sex were first played for the jury. The opening scene showed Karla on her back with her legs spread. One juror initially smiled and turned bright red before catching himself, remembering the tragic context in which the videotape was made and was then being played. Sexual activity followed for some minutes, with Karla using her dead sister's underwear to stimulate Paul. Karla then suggested they adjourn to Tammy's bedroom where Karla performed oral sex on Paul for several more minutes while he lay across Tammy's waterbed. The public gallery was shocked. One lady could be heard throughout repeatedly saying, "Oh my goodness," until Karla was done, while others appeared to hold their breath for the several minutes it took for Paul to orgasm before they left the courtroom.

At the same time, Karla's parents were pressing her to postpone or even cancel the wedding. Karla refused. In a candid and revealing letter to a friend, Debbie Purdie, which was filed as an exhibit at trial, Karla complained about her parents' grief for Tammy, especially her father, and how it was getting in the way of her wedding plans:

> Fuck my parents. They are being so stupid. Only thinking of themselves. My father doesn't even want us to have a wedding any more. If he wants to sit at home and be miserable, he's welcome to. He hasn't worked except for one day since Tammy died. He's wallowing in his own misery and fucking me! It sounds awful on paper (but I know you'll really see what I'm saying). Tammy always said last year that she wanted a forest green Porsche for her 16th birthday. Now my dad keeps saying 'I would have bought it for her if I'd only known.' That's bull. If he really felt like that he'd be paying for my wedding because I could die tomorrow, or next year, or whenever. He's such a liar.

Karla and Paul rented and moved into a newly renovated house at 57 Bayview Avenue in Port Dalhousie, now a suburb of St. Catharines. Over the following two years, their sexual exploits escalated. On April 6, 1991, shortly after 5:30 *a.m.*, Paul raped a fourteen-year-old girl as she walked from her home in St. Catharines to nearby Henley Island for rowing practice. As was captured on video, they also drugged, raped and sexually assaulted, on at least one occasion, another fourteen-year-old; this time a co-worker from the pet store where Karla worked and who Karla brought home as a "gift" for Paul. This young woman was later identified only as "Jane Doe," to protect her identity. They also drove around St. Catharines, stalking young girls and women, following them home and videotaping them through their bedroom windows while they undressed. They also raped and murdered Leslie Mahaffy and Kristen French.

Paul and Karla married, as scheduled, on June 29, 1991. The lavish wedding was celebrated at a hotel in nearby Niagara-on-the-Lake. Videotapes of the celebration, together with other videotaped events in their lives, were repeatedly played on television news during the murder trial and are now widely available for viewing on the Internet.

In December 1992, Bernardo allegedly beat Homolka with a flashlight during a domestic argument. The couple separated. Bernardo stayed in the house, while Homolka went to live with relatives. Their career as the "Ken and Barbie" killers finally ended.

The Murder of Leslie Mahaffy

In the early morning hours of Saturday, June 15, 1991, Bernardo drove to Burlington, Ontario, a city west of Toronto and east of St. Catharines, where he began prowling through a residential neighbourhood looking for licence plates to steal for his cross-border smuggling business. Unexpectedly, he came across Leslie Mahaffy in the backyard of her family's home. Leslie missed her curfew and was locked out of the house and relegated to sitting on the family picnic table until morning. Bernardo decided to steal her rather than licence plates.

Bernardo kidnapped Leslie at knife-point, blindfolded her with her own coat and forced her into his car. He drove her back to the house in Port Dalhousie where she was physically and sexually abused and repeatedly raped while being videotaped.

Leslie remained blindfolded throughout her ordeal. Bernardo later testified that he wanted to drive her back to Burlington and release her but Homolka refused. Homolka was afraid they would be caught, even though Bernardo was confident that Leslie saw nothing and could not direct police to their house.

Leslie was later killed and her body was dismembered. The killing was not videotaped. The dismemberment masked the cause of death. Karla later claimed Bernardo strangled Leslie with a wire. Bernardo claimed that Karla got on Leslie's back on her knees and pushed her head into a pillow to smother her while he was out of the room. The autopsy demonstrated deep bruising to tissue under Leslie's shoulder blades, which tended to support Bernardo's version.

Although who killed Leslie was an issue at trial, both Bernardo and Homolka admittedly participated in her dismemberment and the cleanup of the house. Leslie's body was not immediately dismembered. Her body was first wrapped in a carpet and hidden under the basement stairs in the Port Dalhousie house while Homolka and Bernardo entertained Homolka's family for Fathers' Day, June 16, 1991. The dismemberment occurred afterwards. The body parts were encased in cement after which Bernardo drove them to Lake Gibson, a reservoir that services St. Catharines, and threw them into what he thought was deep water.

The police investigation into the disappearance of Leslie Mahaffy began as a missing person investigation conducted by the Halton Regional police commencing June 15, 1991. On June 29, 1991, when the water level in Lake Gibson fell, her body parts encased in concrete were discovered. As a result, Niagara Region Police Service commenced a homicide investigation.

Because of the condition of the body and the manner of its disposal, it took over a week before the body was identified as Leslie Mahaffy. On July 10, 1991, Niagara Regional Police Service and Halton Regional Police Service agreed to cooperate in the investigation into Leslie's murder.

The Murder of Kristen French

As the Easter weekend of 1992 approached, Bernardo and Homolka discussed bringing another young girl to the house in Port Dalhousie for their sexual gratification. On April 16, 1992, the Thursday before the Easter weekend, Bernardo and Homolka drove through the streets of St. Catharines looking for a victim. Shortly after 3:00 *p.m.*, they spotted Kristen French as she walked home along Linwell Road from Holy Cross Secondary School. They stopped their car near her. Homolka got out and asked for directions. While Kristen was speaking to Homolka, Bernardo came around the car and pushed Kristen onto the floor of the back seat, where she was threatened and assaulted into submission. She was not blindfolded.

Bernardo and Homolka drove Kristen to their home in Port Dalhousie. Once there, she too was physically and sexually abused and repeatedly raped throughout the weekend. All of these activities were videotaped.

The killing of Kristen French was also not videotaped. Who killed Kristen was also an issue at Bernardo's trial. Again, Homolka claimed that Bernardo strangled her to death. Bernardo claimed that he wanted to release her too but that Homolka refused. He testified that, while he was out of the house getting food, Homolka hit Kristen on the head with a rubber mallet used to subdue the girl and then strangled her. This time, though, with Kristen not being blindfolded and having suffered significant physical and sexual abuse, as recorded on the videotapes, Bernardo's evidence probably had less credence with the jury.

Although who killed Kristen French was an issue at the trial, Bernardo and Homolka admittedly cleaned and scoured Kristen's body of all trace evidence before Bernardo drove it to Burlington, where he dumped Kristen's naked body by the side of a road not too far from the Mahaffy home and the cemetery where Leslie Mahaffy was buried.

Green Ribbon Taskforce (GRT)

Police experience has shown that serial predators are very aware of police boundaries. Often, they deliberately make use of police boundaries in order to confuse the authorities in an effort to escape detection. They are also known to leave the bodies of their victims, as a symbolic act, in an area of some significance.

It is not clear which motivation drove Bernardo to dump the body of Kristen French near Leslie Mahaffy's home and burial site. It may have been a symbolic act, or it may have been an effort to confuse the authorities. In any event, the police in both jurisdictions recognized the possibility that the homicides were committed by the same person and agreed to merge the two investigations. They also agreed to continue their cooperative efforts pending provincial approval and funding of a joint forces task force.

On May 15, 1992, the Province of Ontario granted funding under the auspices of the Criminal Intelligence Service Ontario (CISO) for a creation of a dedicated joint force to investigate the Mahaffy and French murders. A joint forces operation was named the Green Ribbon Taskforce (GRT) after the Green Ribbon of Hope Campaign started by Kristen French's high school classmates when she was abducted. Originally comprised of twenty-eight officers from Halton and Niagara Regional Police Services, other Ontario police forces contributed investigators and the task force grew to forty officers from eleven different police forces.

Bernardo as a Suspect

During the GRT investigation, Bernardo first came up as a suspect in a tip from an Ontario Provincial Police (OPP) officer who was an acquaintance of the Smirnis family. The tip was based on information he received from Van Smirnis, who wished to remain anonymous at that time. The officer reported the information on May 2, 1992, first to Halton Police and then to the task force.

As a result of this tip, GRT officers interviewed Bernardo at his house at 57 Bayview Drive in Port Dalhousie. Before the interview, the police conducted background checks on Bernardo, including a check of the Canadian Police Information Centre (CPIC) database, which showed no prior criminal record history or reported criminal activity by Bernardo. The officers did not check directly with Toronto Police Service for more information about Bernardo before conducting the interview.

Nothing came of the interview and the officers went on that day to conduct interviews of other possible suspects who had been named by anonymous callers to the GRT. When they returned to the station, they then ran Bernardo again on CPIC and checked him on the Niagara Regional Police System computer information system. The Niagara database search showed that Bernardo had made an assault complaint to police as a result of an altercation in a bar in

Niagara Falls, that he had reported a break-in at his home, and that he had been a witness at the sudden death of Tammy Homolka.

On May 13, 1992, the day after the interview, the GRT officers called the Toronto Police Service Sexual Assault Squad. Their call was returned on May 20, 1992 by one of the lead investigators. He told the GRT officers that Bernardo was just one of many suspects in the Scarborough rapes investigation from whom Toronto Police had collected blood, hair, and saliva samples. There is some suggestion, but no evidence, that this call from the GRT caused the Toronto officer who took the call to inquire into whether CFS had tested Bernardo's samples.

Apparently as a sheer coincidence, CFS finally got around to testing Bernardo's samples in late 1992 or early 1993. On the morning of February 1, 1993, CFS reported their first DNA test result on the samples, namely, a one-probe DNA match that pointed to Bernardo as the Scarborough rapist. Over the next two weeks, further DNA tests were conducted with a view either to strengthen the case against Bernardo or exclude him.

Notwithstanding the uncertainties inherent in the first test results, Toronto Police immediately began reviewing all information in their possession about Bernardo. Within a day, teams of Toronto officers were assigned to keep him under twenty-four hour mobile surveillance. Officers observed Bernardo cruising nocturnally in St. Catharines and Toronto, allegedly stalking young women who were waiting for buses or walking alone at night.

Because of the initial inconclusive CFS results, Toronto police decided *not* to notify either the GRT or Niagara Regional Police Service that they had evidence pointing to Bernardo as the Scarborough rapist and that he was under mobile surveillance by Toronto Police in Niagara Region. Four days later, however, on Friday, February 5, 1993, Toronto Police did notify the GRT of their investigation because of the surveillance results. All eyes focused on Bernardo.

On February 8, 1993, the CFS reported a second, more conclusive DNA result that matched Bernardo to the Scarborough rapes. Bernardo was now the prime suspect in the murder and rape investigations.

The Deal with Homolka

Targeting Bernardo as their prime suspect, police first approached Homolka as a potential source of information about Bernardo, particularly because she was separated from him and was a complainant against him in a domestic assault case. They found her to be surprisingly hostile and uncooperative.

Clearly the police visit to Homolka spooked her into action. She immediately sought legal advice from Niagara Falls criminal lawyer, George Walker.

While their communications remain privileged and secret, subsequent events suggest that Homolka told Mr. Walker about the Mahaffy and French murders. I say this because Mr. Walker soon after approached the local Crown Attorney at the time, Ray Hoolihan, to commence negotiations for Homolka's cooperation in return for immunity, or at least leniency.

Immunity and leniency discussions for accomplices are commonplace in virtually all systems of criminal justice. Human nature drives the desire for self-preservation, and people involved in criminal activities routinely try to better their position by selling out others, especially those the police believe are more legally blameworthy. With Bernardo being suspected as a serial rapist and murderer, Homolka's approach and the response of the authorities exactly fit this paradigm.

The process that followed for Homolka's deal was the same as that generally followed in all such cases. Her lawyer proffered a set of facts that immediately interested the authorities. This was followed by police questioning Homolka as a "queen for a day," meaning that her statements could not be used against her in any subsequent prosecution. Police and prosecutors generally do not buy a pig in a poke and usually want to hear what the proffered accomplice has to say before agreeing to any deal. They obviously liked what they heard, because prosecutors offered a deal. Given her involvement in the crimes, immunity was out of the question. All she could expect was leniency. She took what she could get.

The deal brokered for Homolka by her lawyer required her to provide a full and complete statement, under oath, of all of her crimes and those of Bernardo and to testify against Bernardo at any subsequent trial or trials. In return, she would be allowed to plead guilty to two counts of manslaughter in respect of the deaths of Leslie Mahaffy and Kristen French, and would receive a total sentence of ten years — five years for each homicide, consecutive one to the other.

Homolka's "queen for a day" statements, together with the DNA evidence relating to the Scarborough rapes, provided the police with grounds to arrest Bernardo in late February 1993 for the murders of Leslie Mahaffy and Kristen French as well as the rapes. But the police could not and did not charge Bernardo with the homicides until the deal with Homolka was completed two months later.

Pursuant to her plea bargain, Homolka provided her formal statements under oath in early May 1993. On May 18, 1993, police charged Bernardo, who was already in custody on the Scarborough rapes, with the first-degree murders of Leslie Mahaffy and Kristen French. At around the same time, Mr. Walker and prosecutors set June 28, 1993 as the date for Homolka's "trial," meaning that day she would plead guilty and be sentenced, as agreed in their deal.

While in custody awaiting her appearance to plead guilty, Homolka became concerned that she had failed to tell the police about the circumstances leading to the death of her sister Tammy. Through her lawyer, she re-negotiated her deal to include that event. It was agreed that her total sentence would now be twelve years, meaning two additional years consecutive for her role in her sister's death. Bernardo was charged with manslaughter as well.

Prosecutors representing the Attorney General of Ontario did everything in their power to shield Homolka and her deal from public scrutiny. At the June 28, 1993 appearance, the prosecution sought a publication ban on the guilty plea proceedings, which was granted by the presiding judge. That decision was later overturned by the Court of Appeal, who ruled that the trial judge ought to have issued only a temporary ban on naming Bernardo until his trial was completed, thereby protecting his fair-trial rights. There was no basis to protect Homolka or her deal from public scrutiny.

The publication ban exacerbated the public's perceived unfairness in the leniency granted to Homolka. The deal drew severe public criticism and condemnation and forever vilified Karla Homolka in the public's mind.

To make matters worse, it also turned out that Homolka not only delayed telling the authorities about the circumstances leading to Tammy Homolka's death, but also failed to mention her participation in the drugging and rape of Jane Doe. Many have since argued that her breach of the original deal ought to have resulted in the rescinding of the entire plea agreement, which would have required her to stand trial for the murders of Leslie Mahaffey and Kristen French either with Bernardo or alone.

What is important to remember is that, as the police later admitted, at the time the deal was made with Homolka, there was no basis to charge Bernardo with any homicide.[2] What is of greater importance is that Homolka told the police that she and Bernardo videotaped their crimes, although not the actual killings, and that he hid the videotapes somewhere on the Port Dalhousie property or in the house. The later failure of police to find the tapes during their search of 57 Bayview Drive cannot be laid at her doorstep and does not in any way diminish the importance of her cooperation in the investigation, prosecution, and eventual conviction of Bernardo.

While discussions continued between Mr. Walker and prosecutors from Niagara Region, and later with special prosecutors from the Office of the Attorney General in Toronto, police prepared search warrants for 57 Bayview Drive. Initially they were searching generally for any evidence linking Bernardo to both the Scarborough rapes and the murders of Leslie Mahaffy and Kristen

French. The search process was long and extensive and required judicial extensions of the original warrant.

Prior to the expiry of the first warrant, Homolka provided information about the use of videotapes and their possible location. The searching officers failed to discover the tapes before the search warrants expired. Their failure would later have an enormous impact on the lawyers defending Bernardo.

Defending Paul Bernardo

I was not Paul Bernardo's first choice of lawyer. When he was charged with domestic assault against Homolka in December 1991, Bernardo retained another lawyer on that charge. Shortly after his arrest in February 1993, Bernardo discharged his original counsel on the assault charge and retained Kenneth Murray, a former prosecutor who was then practicing as a criminal defence counsel in Newmarket, Ontario area, to defend all charges.

On May 6, 1993, twelve days before Bernardo was charged with the murders of Leslie Mahaffy and Kristen French, and a few days following the expiry of the search warrants for 57 Bayview Drive, Murray, his junior associate and his law clerk entered the house with the landlord's permission, ostensibly to retrieve Bernardo's personal belongings. Acting on Bernardo's specific instructions[3], Murray went alone to the second floor bathroom where he removed the ceiling light fixture and reached into the crawl space to retrieve six mini-cassettes.

Each mini-cassette was contained in a clear plastic case. Each case was labelled in Homolka's handwriting. Two of the cases specifically referenced Leslie Mahaffy and Kristen French. All cases displayed stickers of hearts and flowers placed there by Homolka. These two mini-cassette tapes depicted, among other things, the physical and sexual abuse and rapes of Tammy Homolka, Leslie Mahaffy, Kristen French, and Jane Doe.

Although Bernardo appeared to be the prime actor, he was clearly aided and abetted by Homolka, who both videotaped some of the scenes and participated in many of the acts. As noted before, the murders were not depicted.

Murray kept the mini-cassettes for sixteen months without telling anyone he had them. He also rented a special machine that allowed him to copy them to VHS format. He did not claim the rental cost as a disbursement expense when he billed Legal Aid Ontario.

In due course, the prosecution and defence targeted February 1994 for a preliminary inquiry into the all charges pending against Bernardo.

The preliminary inquiry presented a number of problems for the prosecution. First, the prosecution was split. One team from Toronto was assigned carriage of the Scarborough rape prosecution. Another team from St. Catharines was assigned prosecution of the homicides. Was there to be one or two proceedings? Second, without the tapes, the prosecution was obliged to present the substance of its case on all charges to get a committal for trial. This meant calling Homolka as a witness and exposing her and her deal to public scrutiny and defence cross-examination. Although there would have been a standard publication ban on the evidence until the end of Bernardo's trial, by that time the case had attracted so much international attention and the prosecution feared that Homolka's evidence, particularly regarding her deal, would be disseminated by foreign media and on the Internet before Bernardo reached trial.

To get around these problems, the Attorney General for Ontario authorized a rarely used power and directed his prosecutors to prefer two indictments in the Superior Court of Ontario. The first charged Bernardo with two counts of first-degree murder relating to Leslie Mahaffy and Kristen French and one count of manslaughter relating to Tammy Homolka. The other charged him with the rapes and related charges. This meant that all charges would proceed directly to trial without a preliminary inquiry.

In compensation for the loss of the preliminary inquiries, and to stave off a defence motion attacking the direct indictments, the prosecution offered to give the defence an opportunity to cross-examine Homolka at the Kingston Penitentiary for Women, where she was serving her sentence. Murray agreed. He later testified at his own trial for attempting to obstruct justice that the arrangements for the cross-examinations were unsatisfactory. There was no judge to make rulings. The exercise was conducted in a small windowless room with the participants sitting around a table. Homolka appeared to be medicated or tired for the first half-day session. Nonetheless, the cross-examination went on for seven days in May through July of 1994. Questions were put and answered that went beyond the norm for those that might be asked at a preliminary inquiry.

Although he was present, Murray decided that his junior associate would conduct the cross-examination. Little if any attempt was made to pin down Homolka using information Murray gleaned from the videotapes. Murray kept them a secret even from his associate.

On May 2, 1994, prosecutors met with Murray and offered his client "a room with a view," meaning less onerous confinement while serving imprisonment for life in return for a guilty plea to the charges in the indictments. Murray recommended the deal to Bernardo, who turned it down.

On May 4, 1994, Murray found himself appearing before then-Associate Chief Justice Patrick LeSage in the Superior Court of Justice in St. Catharines, the assigned trial judge. Bernardo was arraigned and entered not guilty pleas.

When Murray complained that he needed more time to prepare, Justice Lesage essentially told Murray that if the defence was ready earlier to proceed with a preliminary inquiry in February it ought to be ready to proceed with a trial in September. The indictment charging the murder and manslaughter counts would proceed first. Justice LeSage set September 12, 1994 for the commencement of pre-trial motions, with jury selection and the actual trial to commence in January 1995.

As it turned out, Murray did not want to conduct the trial. I do not know all of his reasons, but clearly he was in a bad position. He had Bernardo's tapes and had told no one about them. In Canada, under the common law, lawyers cannot withhold physical evidence of the crime or the instrumentality of the crime and are obliged to deliver such evidence in their possession to the authorities. Rather than seek outside assistance or advice about what to do with the tapes, Murray elected to try to pass the murder/manslaughter case off to another lawyer. He approached me.

At Murray's request, he and I met at my office on August 15, 1994.[4] Murray asked me to take over Bernardo's defence in the homicides. When I asked him why he wanted off the case, Murray told me: "Because I can't handle it. I'm being inundated with motions from the Crown, factums have to be drafted, case books put together. The Crown is preparing motions that I should be bringing and the file is just enormous and I don't have the resources or the wherewithal to do this. You are more experienced than me and I want you to take over the file." After probing further as to the nature of the case, I asked Murray, "Well, you know, why do you need me?" to which Murray responded, "Look, it's just a difficult case and I just can't handle it." Murray also mentioned that he had a "minor conflict" that would probably never arise but that might require him to be a witness.

I spoke to my family and my law partner, who were opposed to the retainer. On August 16, 1994, I left a telephone message at Murray's office saying that I would not take the case. When Murray returned the call, he appeared to be agitated and continued to press me to agree. He urged me to speak to his junior associate. Murray did not say anything about the videotapes.

When I spoke to the associate, she did not tell me about any videotapes. After speaking to her, I became concerned about the state of preparation of the defence. As it happens, at that precise moment, the prosecution of O.J. Simpson was in full swing. Media coverage was gavel to gavel. American criminal justice was being scrutinized as if under a microscope. None of the participants appeared to be acquitting themselves in their respective roles. Given the media attention to Bernardo's case, I feared that Canadian justice might take a black eye if Bernardo's trial was not properly defended. I also felt ethically obliged to act absent some very valid reason for refusing.

On August 25, 1994, I agreed to take over the murder case only. My agreement to act, however, was subject to three specific conditions. First, the client, who knew nothing of Murray's decision to resign from the file, had to agree. Second, Legal Aid Ontario had to agree to allow a change of counsel, which meant a further expenditure of public funds to prepare a case that another lawyer had been working on for almost a year. Third, Justice LeSage had to agree to adjourn the trial sufficiently long enough to allow me to properly prepare the defence.

With regard to the first condition, Murray and I met the client on August 27, 1994 at the Thorold Detention Centre, which services Niagara Region and where Bernardo was being held pending his trial. Murray spoke privately to Bernardo for about fifteen minutes before I was introduced. I was not privy to their discussion, so it came as no surprise later that Bernardo did not mention the videotapes at that meeting. When I joined the meeting, Bernardo said he was happy to have me as his lawyer, since he knew me by reputation and understood I was more experienced than Murray. It was agreed, however, that Murray would remain as counsel on the Scarborough rapes file.

With regard to the second condition, I was well known to Legal Aid Ontario as an efficient counsel, and the change was readily approved.

The third condition proved more problematic. On September 1, 1994, Justice LeSage met with defence counsel and the prosecutors on both indictments in his chambers by way of an unrecorded judicial pre-trial conference. When Murray announced his intention to resign from the case, and I voiced my requirement for an adjournment before going on record as Bernardo's lawyer, Justice Lesage refused to indicate whether he would allow Murray to withdraw or whether an adjournment would be granted. Justice LeSage and the prosecutors insisted that Murray file an application to be removed as counsel of record together with a supporting affidavit explaining why he was resigning from the case on the eve of trial. That application would be heard by the Court on September 12, 1994, the day scheduled for pre-trial motions to start. Any motion for an adjournment would also be heard at that time.

In light of the positions taken by Justice LeSage and the prosecutors, I made it clear that I would not appear on the record unless and until an adjournment was granted.

There can be little doubt that the prospect of having his resignation from the case subjected to public scrutiny and potential scrutiny by the Law Society of Upper Canada drove Murray to retain his own lawyer, Austin Cooper QC.

In so doing, Murray must have revealed the existence of the videotapes because Mr. Cooper applied for and received advice from an *ad hoc* committee of the Law Society.

By letter dated September 8, 1994, the *ad hoc* committee speaking for the Law Society directed Mr. Cooper to have Murray put the videotapes in a sealed envelope and file the sealed envelope with the Court at the next appearance. I believe the members of the *ad hoc* committee were influenced by the manner in which the knife used in the O.J. Simpson case came to be filed with Judge Ito. No consideration appeared to have been given by anyone to the rights and interests of the client, Paul Bernardo.

On receipt of the letter from the Law Society, Murray and one of Mr. Cooper's associates travelled to the Thorold Detention Centre to serve Bernardo with it. Although I was determined not to become involved in the absence of the adjournment, I was nonetheless interested in knowing what was going on with Murray's application. I called the detention center to speak to Bernardo to find out what was happening with his case. It happened that when I called, Bernardo was being served with the letter from the Law Society, and he called me back afterwards. When I heard what was in the works I realized the potential prejudice to Bernardo if the sealed package was presented to the Court without objection from him. I felt obliged to become involved.

That evening I drove to the Thorold Detention Centre and received Bernardo's written direction addressed to Murray terminating Murray's retainer on all matters and requiring Murray to deliver all of Bernardo's files to me. I faxed the direction to Murray and Mr. Cooper that evening and prepared to appear in Court.

Unbeknownst to me, Murray had gone to the detention center to see Bernardo on August 30, 1994. He arrived with four typed directions he prepared for Bernardo to sign. In essence, these directions authorized Murray to remove the videotapes from the homicide file and place them into the rape file without telling me or anyone else. I did not know about the directions until Murray later produced them as part of his defence at his own trial.

In preparation for the Court appearance on September 12, 1994, I arranged for Clayton Ruby, a well-known criminal lawyer and a Bencher of the Law Society to accompany me as co-counsel for Bernardo for that day only. I felt that I needed Mr. Ruby to offset the prestige Mr. Cooper commanded at the time as the *de facto* Dean of the Ontario Criminal Bar.

When we appeared, I attempted to stop Mr. Cooper from speaking by speaking first and presenting the Court with Bernardo's direction to Murray terminating his retainer. Justice LeSage, however, insisted on hearing from Mr.

Cooper, who presented the Court with the letter from the Law Society. Justice LeSage read the letter but refused to accept the proffered sealed package from Mr. Cooper, observing that we were not in Southern California and that he was not Judge Ito. The parties asked for a short recess to attempt to resolve their differences.

The prosecutors suspected that the proffered package contained the missing videotapes. Mr. Ruby and I met with them, and they agreed that I could take possession of the sealed package on my personal undertaking to deal with the contents legally, professionally, and ethically. They also agreed that, in return, Murray would be allowed to withdraw as counsel of record for Bernardo without comment.

The two defence teams then met privately. Going into the meeting, I knew only about tapes in general, and that Murray's associate and clerk had advised me previously that a machine to convert mini-cassettes to VHS had been rented. Murray's law clerk and associate were also in attendance at my request. Mr. Ruby received the sealed package to minimize the risk of me becoming a witness to the chain of custody. He opened the package and emptied the contents on a table. The six original mini-cassettes slipped out. Based on the information I previously received from Murray's former staff about the VHS converter, I asked for the VHS copies. Mr. Cooper asserted there were no such copies. When one of Murray's former staff said that there were copies, Murray confessed that the VHS copies were at his home. Mr. Cooper, who was so angry he appeared to implode, ordered Murray to deliver them forthwith to Mr. Ruby, which he did later that day.

When we returned to Court, Murray was removed as counsel of record. Murray was later charged with attempt to obstruct justice in connection with his handling of the videotapes. On June 13, 2000, Murray was acquitted. At his trial, he admitted that after he and I first met with Bernardo, he returned to the detention centre and got Bernardo to sign the typed instructions to remove anything in his discretion from the murder file and place it into the rape file.

After some hesitation on his part, Justice LeSage eventually granted me a long adjournment of the trial. He set April 1995 for pre-trial motions and May 1, 1995 for jury selection with the trial to immediately follow. I then went on record as Bernardo's trial lawyer.

The Tapes and the Trial

Much has been written about the videotapes, the failure of the police to find them and the horrific nature of their contents. But nothing has ever been said about the impact of the tapes on the lawyers.

After taking possession of the tapes, Mr. Ruby and I met at his home to view them for the first time. We played the VHS tapes so as not to damage the originals. We also fast-forwarded through most parts. Our intention was to get an understanding of what was depicted so we could assess my legal, professional, and ethical obligations.

In truth though, the images depicted shook me to the core. At one point, I needed to stop and excuse myself for a few moments. The images were deeply disturbing and the implications were obvious. How was I going to defend this case in the face of these tapes? What would prevent the jury from coming over the boards at me for having the gall to advance any defence for this accused? Moreover, I am a father myself — what would my own family think of me? How was I going to survive a trial with my health and reputation intact?

I could have avoided my responsibilities by claiming I was a witness to the chain of custody of the tapes. But what would that have said about the twenty-five years of my life that, at that point in time, I had dedicated to the criminal law? After a moment's hesitation, I decided to set aside my personal feelings and interests and get on with the job at hand.

The first issue was what to do with the videotapes. Having briefly viewed them, I determined that they were evidence of both the crime and the instrumentality of the crime, and that I was legally, ethically, and professionally obliged to deliver them to the authorities. In order to preserve the retainer, I needed to obtain my client's instructions to do that. Without those instructions, I would have proceeded anyway, which would have terminated the retainer. In the end, I received the instructions I needed and arranged for the tapes to be delivered to the police. They were eventually filed as exhibits at Bernardo's trial. No doubt they went a long way to proving his guilt.

The second issue was whether I could use the tapes to negotiate a deal for my client that would have avoided a public viewing of the tapes. The prosecutors refused to deal, but they revealed a significant concern about the tapes being played in public. At trial, the prosecutors, supported by the families of the victims, applied to Justice LeSage for an order clearing the courtroom when they were played during the trial. I objected, partly for tactical reasons to force the prosecution back to the bargaining table, on the grounds that the *Criminal Code* requires an open and public trial, which meant a public viewing of Karla Homolka's full participation. In a very Solomon-like pre-trial ruling, Justice LeSage ordered that the public would have full access to the tapes, which would be played and shown on monitors in court as part of the trial, except when a victim was depicted. At that point, the public monitors were to be shut off but not the speakers. Counsel could and did make whatever use of the videotapes they wished in presenting their respective cases. The clear implication of the ruling, which I exploited at trial, was that Homolka was not the victim the prosecution tried to portray her as.

After pre-trial motions in April, 1995, the trial commenced with jury selection on May 1, 1995. The defence I advanced was that Karla Homolka was not just an unbelievable accomplice but was in fact the killer of Leslie Mahaffy and Kristen French. Although Bernardo was clearly guilty of abduction, unlawful confinement and sexual assault, his liability in respect of the three homicides was to be assessed as a secondary party. As an unwilling participant in the homicides, he would be guilty of manslaughter. If he was a participant in the murders but not the killer, his liability might only be for second-degree murder. It was the prosecutors' job to persuade the jury that Bernardo had committed a first-degree murder. It was my job to raise a reasonable doubt about that, notwithstanding the sad reality of the three dead girls and what happened to them.

The trial ran through the summer with one week off at the end of July. It attracted large crowds and seating in the courtroom was limited and controlled. Nonetheless, the trial was open to the public, who saw and heard everything except the depiction of the victims on the videotapes. The jury delivered its verdict on the second day of deliberation, September 1, 1995. Bernardo was convicted of two counts of first-degree murder and one count of manslaughter. He was sentenced to life imprisonment without parole for twenty-five years on the murder charges and life imprisonment on the manslaughter.

My retainer ended with those verdicts and sentences. Tony Bryant continued to represent Bernardo, first on his failed appeal and later when he pled guilty to the Scarborough rapes and Henley Island rape allegations. Following those guilty pleas, the Court declared Bernardo to be a dangerous offender. In Canada, persons judicially determined to be dangerous offenders are held indefinitely with a review every few years. To my knowledge, no dangerous offender has ever been released from custody in Canada.

Conclusion

Since the end of the murder trial, I have had no communication with my former client except to speak briefly, years later when I was seeing another client at the penitentiary. I returned to my practice and continued to represent those who put their faith in me. In my years of practice, I have been privileged to represent people charged with a variety of crimes that cover the entire spectrum of criminal offences in Canada, including hundreds of murder cases. The case of Paul Bernardo was not my first high profile case, although his case drew the most media interest.

Like the O.J. Simpson prosecution, the Bernardo trial was covered daily in media across Canada and internationally. Since our laws prohibit cameras in the courtroom, the media reports were comprehensive and were supported with photographs and video footage of me walking to or from the Toronto Courthouse every day. The by-product of this exposure was that people started to recognize me on sight. Complete strangers stopped me on the street to say hello or to shake my hand. No one uttered an unkind word. Perhaps it was their way of thanking me for my efforts or, more broadly, for validating and recognizing my role in the criminal justice system that all Canadians value. In other words, they recognized that we all had a stake in ensuring a fair trial and a just outcome for everyone. Even Paul Bernardo agreed.

John Rosen acknowledges the editing assistance of his daughter Karen Rosen.

Notes 1. Any communications reported or referenced to in this chapter, between Mr. Bernardo and Mr. Rosen, or between Mr. Bernardo and Mr. Kenneth Murray, were all detailed in evidence at the public trial of Mr. Murray in the Ontario Superior Court of Justice: *R. v. Murray*, [2000] O.J. 2188, 48 O.R. (3d) 544

2. When asked by Mr. Justice Archie Campbell, who was appointed to conduct a judicial inquiry into the police failures, what evidence there was against Bernardo on the murders before Homolka provided her KGB statements, the officer reports, "*Absolutely nothing. Other than he was a serial rapist and living in St. Catharines.*" See Report of Mr. Justice Campbell, June 1996. Mr. Justice Patrick Galligan, commissioned to examine the plea bargain, in 1996 reported to the Attorney General that the plea bargain established by the prosecution with Homolka was "unassailable" as the Crown had no alternative but to negotiate it.

3. Murray was later charged and stood trial for attempt to obstruct justice arising out of his handling of Bernardo's videotapes. As a result, there was a full and public discussion of his communications with Bernardo, his communications with me and, to a limited extent, my communications with Bernardo up to and including when I was retained in the matter. In the circumstances, the privilege that ordinarily attaches to such lawyer/client communications was lost.

4. The recital of my discussions with Murray and the characterization of his conduct derives from the judgment of Mr. Justice Patrick Gravely, who ultimately acquitted Murray of attempt to obstruct justice: See *R. v. Murray*, [2000] O.J. 2188, 48 O.R. (3d) 544. At his trial, he admitted that after he and I first met with Bernardo, he returned to the detention centre and got Bernardo to sign typed instructions to remove anything in his discretion from the murder file and place it into the rape file.

Fred Ferguson

THE CASE OF JOHN RYAN TURNER

A leading New Brunswick Crown Prosecutor for twenty-five years, Fred Ferguson QC was appointed to the Provincial Court in 2003 and to the Court of Queen's Bench in 2008. A Life Member of the National Criminal Law Program Faculty, he lectures extensively to legal symposia. He held the Milvain Chair in Advocacy at the University of Calgary, and received the Robert J. Murray QC Award for professional devotion.

ON SATURDAY OCTOBER 5, 1991 I walked to the podium of the theatre inside the James M. Hill High School in Miramichi, New Brunswick to deliver the keynote address to several hundred people gathered for the First Miramichi Conference on Crime. The conference had been organized by local newspaper publisher David Cadogan to address a long-standing and deep-seated problem with violent crime in this eastern New Brunswick community of twenty-two hundred people. Although the Miramichi's reputation for violent crime was long-standing, in the previous two years the murder rate had topped that of Detroit.

The three-man prosecutors' office in which I worked with Jack Walsh and Bill Morrissy was engaged in prosecuting eleven different first- and second-degree murder files at the time. Five of them were the responsibility of serial killer Allan Legere's spree of murders committed after escaping the custody of guards from the nearby Atlantic Institution in the spring of 1989, while serving a life term for the murder of local shopkeeper John Glendenning, and the attempted murder of Glendenning's wife Mary.

I had decided that if this community, that had been beset by serious violent crime since long before I'd arrived there to begin my career as a prosecutor in 1976, was ever going to change, I'd best take the audience back to the genesis of so many violent criminal personalities and speak to them about helping identify children at risk at an early age in the hope that by doing so we might better manage the needs of "at risk" children through early childhood intervention by those trained in the field of child social work and health care.

Little did I know at that time that just across the main highway, running from Moncton to Campbellton along the east coast of New Brunswick, an infant boy named John Ryan Turner, who had just turned one year of age and was living with his parents, Steve and Lorelei Turner, was clandestinely beginning a life of mistreatment and neglect in one of the Canadian Armed Forces military base's single-family dwellings or Private Married Quarters. Mr. Turner was a corporal in the Canadian army. His stay-at-home wife Lorelei had retired from the army earlier. When the case became public almost three years later, the nation would be touched by what had happened to John Ryan Turner in his short life of three years and nine months. Those who read about him or heard about the world in which he'd lived would never forget him.

The Background to the Trial of Lorelei and Steven Turner

There is something odd about how it is that a small percentage of criminal cases take on the name of the victim and not of the accused. It happened only in a handful of homicides that I prosecuted during my twenty-seven years with the Attorney General's office in New Brunswick. Perhaps it is because the manner of death was especially heart wrenching. Maybe it is because the victim was especially well liked, or especially vulnerable, or that great suffering or torture preceded the death. The case of John Ryan Turner's life and death was one of that small number of cases. I believe it was because, as the testimony at the preliminary hearing and trial unfolded, the country realized that this innocent little boy had lived an awful life and died a terrible death. When the case would eventually end, one of the reporters who was covering the case would try to convince me to write a book about it and entitle it: "Unloved to Death." The book was never written.

John Ryan Turner's case would not come to public and then national attention for almost three more years until at 9:00 *a.m.* on May 26, 1994 when Lorelei Turner called the local ambulance service to report that her son John Ryan was non-responsive in the living room of their two-story home. When the EMTs arrived, Steve Turner had returned to his house from work to join the effort to revive his son. The next-door-neighbour, Francine Mallory, was to later testify at the manslaughter trial that when she arrived at the Turner home that morning to see what had happened, Lorelei and Steven Turner were desperately trying to explain their injured and emaciated son's condition to the EMTs. Lorelei said to them, "He wanted nothing to do with me, right Steven?" Steven replied, "He wanted nothing to do with her!" As shall be seen, they were telling words.

Despite valiant efforts, the EMTs could not resuscitate John Ryan and so he was quickly rushed by ambulance to the Miramichi Hospital where a trauma team awaited his arrival. The head of the team was a young emergency room physician, Dr. Charles Gardiner. Upon arrival, it was confirmed that John Ryan had no vital signs and a body temperature of 27.3 degrees C. His normal body temperature should have been 37 degrees C. After valiant efforts were made to revive the young boy he was pronounced dead at 10:20 *a.m.*

While waiting at the hospital for the emergency medical team to try to resuscitate John Ryan, one of the Emergency Room nurses, Claudia MacKenzie, overheard Lorelei repeatedly plead to her husband Steven, "They want to know what happened!" Dr. Gardiner eventually gave brief but riveting testimony at the trial before Mr. Justice Thomas Riordon of the Court of Queen's Bench sitting as a judge without a jury. He described John Ryan as severely emaciated, displaying wasting muscle mass and prominent bone features, particularly at the joints and in the hip and chest area. His body was covered in sores and bruises that were visible on his face, arms, and legs. The corners of his lips were raw. When Dr. Gardiner demanded of Steven Turner that fateful morning how this could have happened, Steven Turner replied that it had just been a phase John Ryan had been experiencing.

Dr. Gardiner would go on to tell the court that he had worked in Zimbabwe before returning to Canada to practice emergency medicine in Miramichi. He explained that the problem of childhood malnutrition in Africa was one that he had frequently encountered before, concluding that he had never, either in Canada or in Africa, seen such a serious case of malnutrition and neglect.

Upon discovering that the Turners had another younger infant daughter, Dr. Gardiner ordered the parents to bring her in for an examination. When examined, the infant was found to be perfectly healthy.

Much later, it was the conclusion of the medical experts that Lorelei had suffered a serious postpartum depression after John Ryan's birth and had failed to bond with him. The dysfunction that grew in the home because of that depressive illness led to John Ryan becoming socially and physically isolated from the rest of the family towards the end of his life and physically confined to his room for much of the time.

Dr. Gardiner also immediately ordered hospital staff to alert the police and the Department of Family and Community Services of his findings. John Ryan's body was taken to Saint John for an autopsy. It was conducted the next day, Friday May 27, 1994, by a renowned forensic pathologist, Dr. John McKay.

New Brunswick has had a pre-charge screening program in place since the early 1970s. Under that regime, after consultation with the police, Crown Prosecutors make the final decision concerning the nature and number of charges to be brought against any person to begin a criminal prosecution. As a result, it was not unusual for Dr. McKay to speak to the prosecutor in a homicide case about the autopsy findings when cause or manner of death was elusive. This was just such a case.

When Dr. McKay called late Friday afternoon to tell the investigators and me what it was he had found, he was perplexed. He could not say with certainty what had been the exact reason for John Ryan's death. He believed it to be malnutrition. He knew that the three-year-and-nine-month-old boy was severely emaciated. At 20.5 pounds, his weight was what one would expect of a healthy eleven-month-old baby. Dr. McKay told me that the body was covered in bruises, abrasions, and pattern bruising in the back and neck, as well as on both of his sides that were consistent with the use of restraint devices similar to those seized by the police from John Ryan's room. He had marks and scars on his ankles and wrists consistent with being tied. There was serious excoriation in the groin area that the pathologist thought at first was possibly the result of sexual assault. Other evidence convinced him that it actually was a case of severe rash even although John Ryan was almost four years of age. There were also large semi-circular indentations at the corners of his mouth indicative of stretching. He had never seen those types of injuries before during his long career. He believed them to be the result of gagging. There was severe wasting of the muscle mass. Most telling was his finding that there had been several fractures of both arms that had healed. He was certain that at least one of those fractures had not been properly aligned before the healing process began. There was no food in his stomach or bowel. His hair was very thin and his head was bruised in several places.

Later testimony from Dr. Michael England, the head of Radiology at the Saint John General Hospital, would confirm that John Ryan had suffered a total of four arm fractures, of which at least three were not medically treated.

It would be seven months before the manner and cause of death would be precisely identified. Dr. McKay consulted many experts in a variety of fields before finding one who accurately diagnosed the case. He found that specialist in his home hospital, the Saint John General — a pediatric neurologist named

Dr. David Meek. Dr. Meek examined the complete police file in the late fall of 1994. As an expert witness Dr. Meek was anything but meek. He was a quiet, unassuming man; measured and thoughtful in demeanour, balanced and fair in his opinions. He was every criminal trial lawyer's idea of an expert who would be an unassailable and compelling expert witness.

In December of 1994, he diagnosed John Ryan's death as a case of non-organic failure to thrive, otherwise known in medical circles as the Kasper Hauser Syndrome of psychosocial dwarfism. The essence of this malady is that the affected child suffers chronic childhood depression that is the product of a constellation of associated causes, in this case the failure to bond with his mother, the physical and social isolation towards the end of his life from almost everyone, and abuse and neglect that resulted in the little boy becoming a physical, psychological, and social dwarf. If not treated, children living in such circumstances eventually die. This, of course, had not been known at the time the manslaughter prosecution was commenced against the Turners.

The charging decision was a great challenge for our office because the cause of death remained elusive at the time the Turners were arrested on the weekend of May 27, 1994. In 1987 the Supreme Court had rendered its epoch decision in *R. v. Vaillancourt*. Justice Antonio Lamer, subsequently appointed Canada's Chief Justice, writing for the Court, decreed that no person could be convicted of murder in Canada under the relatively new *Canadian Charter of Rights and Freedoms* unless, at the time of the causing of the death of another, that person had the specific intent to kill or cause bodily harm that he or she knew would likely result in death while being reckless whether death ensued or not. The judgment had an immediately chilling effect on many murder prosecutions across the country. In this instance we believed that we would not have a reasonable prospect of convicting one or both of John Ryan's parents of murder under the new standard in spite of the compelling evidence of abuse and neglect that was evident. Despite the bizarre circumstances, whether one or both had the specific intent to kill John Ryan was by no means certain.

While this case verged on murder, it was decided that it would be advanced as an unlawful manslaughter case by alleging that the unlawful act of the parents had been their long-term failure to provide the necessities of life to their infant son. We would use the circumstantial evidence of physical abuse to buttress the allegations of profound neglect. On Monday May 30, the Turners appeared in custody in docket court in Miramichi in a packed courtroom to answer to the manslaughter charges. The charging decision was made by Bill Morrissy and me. Bill and I rarely worked together. Indeed, in most prosecutions carried on by our office we rarely had sufficient manpower available to put a second lawyer on any file, including homicides.

Bill was an extremely well-regarded trial counsel. His greatest strength beyond his advocacy skills was his judgment. He was known by counsel who worked with him as "the reasonable man." His skills and abilities as well as his judgment were critical to the charging decision and the prosecution of this case.

The Beginning of Proceedings

On the weekend of May 28, 1995, Officers Pugh and Hansen arrested the Turners for manslaughter at their home on the military base in Miramichi. These two young officers had never been involved in a case such as this one. Nonetheless, they committed themselves from the outset to investigate every possible detail that was imaginable. Their work was first rate from the day they were assigned the file until the last appeal was exhausted. Their effort was tireless.

Upon being arrested at their home, the Turners were immediately explained their rights — both the right to silence and to legal counsel. The first comment from them when they were told that they were going to be held in custody for court on Monday was, "Who will look after feeding the fish." In the face of what both police officers knew from their investigation to that point, including the results of the autopsy they had obtained, the comment astonished them.

Criminal docket court in Miramichi is likely a mirror image of many others across this country. The courtroom is always filled with people accused of everything from shoplifting to very serious assaults and sometimes homicide. A battery of lawyers is always present with their clients and the scene is generally one of disorganized confusion to the uninitiated, but completely comprehensible to those who ply their trade in the trenches in this and other Provincial Courts across Canada. That Monday afternoon, with both Turners in custody, and court about to convene, the two detectives heading up the investigation from the local police department, Randy Hansen and Dan Pugh, arrived with the photographs they had taken at the autopsy the previous Friday. They approached the counsel table with sombre looks on their faces and passed the sheath of photos to me. Up to that moment I had not seen any photographs of the little boy, nor had anyone else in our office.

By that point in my career, some seventeen years out from law school, I had seen just about every kind of homicide possible, many of them too gruesome to recount here. And yet, despite those experiences of professional life, and the information Dr. McKay supplied to me by telephone the previous Friday, I was ill-prepared for what I was about to see. I had never before cried over a case as a lawyer and must say that the only time I ever cried in the twenty-seven years I was a prosecutor was because of that little boy, John Ryan Turner. As I began to leaf through the photographs while standing near all of my colleagues seated at the grand oak counsel table in the storied main courtroom of our historic courthouse filled with people, I began to feel my eyes well up and tears begin to stream uncontrollably down my face. I was too stunned to speak, and even had I not been, I could not have cleared my throat well enough to do so. The innocence portrayed in his face as he lay on the pathologist's gurney, the incontrovertible evidence of long-term abuse and neglect depicted in the photographs, and the thought that he was far too young to die at the hands of another or others, most especially his parent or parents, was overwhelming. I stopped at what became, at the trial, Photograph C-2 #11. I shall never forget that photograph as long as I live. The photograph, taken in the soft indirect artificial light of the examining table in an otherwise darkened room, depicted, close up, his innocent face, scarred and red raw at the corners of his mouth by repeated gagging. His cheeks and forehead were bruised in several places. One of his eyes was blackened. Quickly, I turned away to face the side of the courtroom, away from all eyes. I put the photos away and tried to compose myself for the judge's imminent arrival. Court was about to begin.

My mind began to race. Perhaps, I thought, we ought to have charged them with murder. There were too many bruises, too much emaciation of the body, too many marks that would lead even the most sceptical to conclude that this boy had been bound and gagged, and not just once or twice. Most disturbing were the semi-circular marks at the corners of his mouth that were so prominent, one would have had to have slipped a quarter into each in order to close the gaps. It is often said that the Crown never wins or loses and that justice is always done when reason prevails over emotion, as it always should in a criminal prosecution. I decided that the manslaughter charge would stay. I told myself that no one could have ever deliberately set out to inflict these injuries and neglect their child with the intention that he should die as a result of their actions or inactions, surely no one. Within minutes I had composed myself. Court convened and the John Ryan Turner manslaughter prosecution began.

The summer of 1994 saw the results of laboratory tests completed on a host of seized exhibits returned to the investigators and eventually to our office, with the conclusions of the scientists. Almost every section of the RCMP Crime Detection Laboratory, then located in Sackville, New Brunswick, was involved. Of primary importance was the DNA analysis, a very new science at the time. It was principally concerned with socks found in the boy's bedroom that the investigators believed had been used as gags on him. One such exhibit was a sock 30-inches in length. The DNA expert, Heather MacDonald, recorded that saliva and blood found on the centre portion of that sock, as well as on two others found in his room, was virtually assured to have been his. Hair matching that of the little boy was found on the restraining harness found in his clothes closet, and paint found on the top of the back of a chair used to pry the door of his closet shut was identified and matched to the paint on the closet door. Photographs of the bedroom showed that cloth had been draped over the windows to eliminate light from the room.

By fall, a lawyer had been retained to represent the Turners. On the Family Court side of the case, the Turner's only other child, their infant daughter, had been taken into protective custody by the Minister of Family and Community Services, and a psychiatrist had been engaged to do a court-ordered psychiatric assessment of the parents. Part of her mandate would necessarily involve trying to identify the cause of John Ryan's death. She was Dr. Barbara Ross, a child psychiatrist practicing in the Moncton area at the time. On September 2, 1995, Dr. Ross contacted me to attempt to gain access to medical charts as well as videos of John Ryan taken at home during his life that had been seized and retained as potential exhibits by the police after his death. I arranged for her to have access to what it was she wanted, but recommended that she also take the time to review the police file and expert reports that had been filed up to that date. At the outset of our conversation, she explained that she was tentatively of the view that John Ryan died from some sort of autism-related disorder. However, after I briefed her on the evidence compiled up to that point by the investigators, she appeared ready to alter that view and seriously consider physical abuse as a possible cause. She was told we would need consents from the Turners through their lawyer to allow her access to the police file. Those were never obtained and nothing further was done by her to gain access to what the police had in their hands for evidence.

Dr. Ross' November 13, 1994 report to the court was lengthy and detailed but appeared to rely principally on her interviews with the Turners, the videos of John Ryan in his infancy as well as some information she was able to access through Dr. Makram El-Bardeesy, a paediatrician who had examined John Ryan in August 1992, almost two years before his death. Dr. Ross ruled out the possibility that John Ryan died of Munchhausen by Proxy Syndrome or "overt abuse." Munchausen by Proxy Syndrome involves either abuse or exaggerated or fabricated symptoms of illness in a child reported by their caregiver in order to gain attention. It is a form of child abuse and neglect and can, in rare cases, be lethal.

Dr. Ross concluded that the Turners fell within the normal range of parenting skills. She concluded, "It is my strong belief that this child was not well and that he had a diagnosable medical condition." She then went on to conclude that John Ryan suffered from a pervasive developmental disorder called Rett Syndrome or, in the alternative, "child disintegrative disorder." Both are debilitating degenerative disorders found in children. In conclusion she reported, "Thus my conclusion is that I find no evidence of child abuse having been inflicted upon this child and I believe that he suffered and died from Rett Syndrome."

When I read the report I was astonished by her conclusions and upset that she had not availed herself of the opportunity I had given her to access the police file and expert reports that were available at the time she did her work. Dr. David Meek had still not become involved in the case but the graphic photographs, the crime lab reports, the report of Dr. McKay and other expert reports from health-care professionals were available to provide, what I believed, was a proper basis for an informed medical opinion to be made utilizing the incontrovertible proof that John Ryan had been the long-term victim of both physical abuse and neglect.

After some reflection, I decided to do something I had never done before or afterwards with any witness expert or civilian that had been part of the case for the defence. Even though I knew Dr. Ross had been chosen to provide an independent psychiatric report to the Family Court, her report left no doubt that she would be adverse to the Crown and the Minister of Family and Community Services in either of the proceedings. I called counsel for the Turners and informed him that I intended to telephone Dr. Ross to implore her to read all of what had been accumulated to date through the police investigation.

When I called her, my approach was polite but at times insistent. I told her I believed that she had overlooked crucial information that was critical to the formulation of an informed and accurate medical opinion. I asked her, as well, to seriously consider reviewing the photographs taken at the autopsy that so-well demonstrated that John Ryan had been the victim of abuse and neglect and had been tied, bound, and gagged repeatedly over a lengthy period of time. She firmly refused to do so. Shortly thereafter, she would stand behind that report's accuracy in the Family Court proceeding in support of the Turners' efforts to regain custody of their infant daughter.

In December of 1994, Dr. McKay spoke to pediatric neurologist Dr. David Meek about the case. He agreed to review the voluminous police file. By that time, counsel for the Turners had filed a motion with the court to have me removed from the case for engaging in allegedly oppressive conduct towards Dr. Ross during my telephone call to her. The motion also requested that the proceedings in criminal court be stayed because of my decision to contact Dr. Ross imploring her to reconsider the basis upon which she had rendered her opinion.

Mere days before Christmas, Dr. Meek determined that John Ryan died of the Kasper Hauser Syndrome or psychosocial dwarfism. He was asked to prepare and forward his final report to the police immediately so that it could be used at the motion hearing to try to nullify the defence efforts to stay the criminal proceeding or, in the alternative, have me removed from the case.

I am sure that Christmas in the Dr. David Meek home was one that saw the doctor unfortunately divide his time between his family, the extensive police file he had been poring over, now measured in banker's boxes, and the report he was beginning to prepare. His January 9, 1995 report was lengthy, thorough, and well-supported medically.

Dr. Meek made several important observations. First, he concluded that Dr. Ross was plainly wrong in diagnosing John Ryan as having died from Rett Syndrome. To her principal conclusion he responded, "...I can say with certainty that John Turner did not have Rett Syndrome." Moreover, he was of the view that medical science had still not accepted that Rett Syndrome had ever been proven to exist in boys. More importantly, he firmly believed that John Ryan did not meet the criteria for such a diagnosis. He also ruled out Degenerative Psychosis of Childhood, Dr. Ross' fall-back position.

His diagnosis was that as a result of a failure to bond with his mother at birth, due to her postpartum depression, John Ryan became disconnected from what were, or became, the disordered family dynamics in the Turner home and became, himself, the victim of a deep depression. That condition, he concluded, was likely exacerbated by being forced to spend a great deal of his time confined to his room, harnessed in his bed, and deprived of the nurturing that comes with interaction from family, their friends and his childhood friends and acquaintances. Dr. Meek found it highly unusual that such a syndrome could lead to the death of a child in a developed country such as Canada. He reported that it had been most commonly seen in Europe at the turn of the last century when overcrowded orphanages saw children having very limited contact with, and attention from, adult caregivers. We immediately forwarded Dr. Meek's report to Dr. Barbara Ross.

Within a month of being provided a copy of Dr. Meek's report, Dr. Ross penned a letter to the prosecutor handling the Family Court case for our office. In her letter, she wrote the following opening lines, "I am in the humble position of wanting to write you this letter. I am now very much aware that my clinical opinion as to the cause of John Ryan Turner's death was in error."

By this time Dr. Ross had already testified in support of her original diagnosis at the Family Court trial and in support of the return of the daughter to the Turners' custody. The Court of Queen's Bench Family Division judge, Mr. Justice Jacques Sirois, had rejected her opinion and ordered the infant daughter into the custody of the Minister.

In concluding her one-page retraction, Dr. Ross wrote, "For the record I would like to state that I am very much in agreement with the opinion of Dr. David Meek and I no longer think that John Ryan Turner had Rett Syndrome.... The reasons by which I was able to come to this erroneous diagnosis are multi-factorial." In concluding her short retraction she offered to discuss the reasons she had misdiagnosed the case with the prosecutor if he wished. He declined her offer. Within days the motion requesting a stay of proceedings and my recusal from the file was abandoned. Counsel for the Turners notified the court that he now believed that he was in a conflict of interest by representing both Turners and wished to withdraw from further participation in the case. We were deep into the criminal proceedings. He had been their counsel for six months. The trial was on the horizon and the Turners had no legal counsel.

Within a short time counsel had been found for the Turners. A bright young defence lawyer from Moncton named Barry Whynot took on the case for Steven Turner. Mrs. Turner retained Brian Doucet, an able and forceful defence counsel from Sackville. Both men immersed themselves in the file and went on to give the best representation they could against the formidable case the investigators had built against their clients.

The Trial of the Turners

By the time the trial began, the whole country had become aware of the disturbing nature of the case. Journalists and television reporters from throughout the eastern part of the country converged on Miramichi to cover the unfolding events. The case of John Ryan Turner had gained national status.

The trial judge, Mr. Justice Thomas Riordon, had come from the civil bar to the Court in the late 1980s. He had a reputation as a highly skilled civil litigator, one of the best in the Province of New Brunswick during his long career. By the time the trial started, he had undergone trial by fire as a judge in the criminal courts of Miramichi over the preceding seven years. A veritable workhorse as a lawyer and trial judge, he had by this time handled a long list of difficult criminal jury trials in our community. But nothing could have prepared him for the evidence he was about to be confronted with, or the testimony he was about to begin hearing.

There were in excess of twenty-five expert witnesses scheduled to testify. Each brought a piece to the forensic puzzle. The civilian witness side of the case detailed the sad life of John Ryan Turner from birth to death. At the conclusion of the trial, the evidence would be characterized by him as: "horrific."

The testimony at the trial established the depth of Lorelei Turner's postpartum depression. She was in frequent contact with a number of agencies after her son's birth including the public health office and the mental health clinic. Her family doctor changed during John Ryan's short life and there were referrals to a pediatrician as well as a speech language pathologist. However, one common theme seemed to emerge. Follow-up by Mrs. Turner was never a high priority.

Shortly after John Ryan's birth, the public health nurse reported to Mrs. Turner's doctor, Dr. McNearny, that she was deeply concerned with what she observed at the home. Mrs. Turner told the nurse that she felt no maternal instincts towards her son. She reported that Lorelei Turner felt that when her son cried and she was unable to stop him from doing so, she felt like throwing him out the window. When the doctor confronted Lorelei Turner with the allegations, she protested that the nurse was in a conflict of interest because the nurse's husband was in the military. The nurse was removed from further involvement with the file. Dr. McNearny continued to work tirelessly to change the relationship between the mother and son and deal with the mother's mental health issues. She achieved only some short-term success.

Another concern was raised by the public health nurse in October 1990, mere weeks after John Ryan's birth. She testified that in a telephone conversation with Mrs. Turner, she was told by the distraught mother that she needed help because of the baby's incessant crying. She tried to drive the point home saying, "Do I have to do something to my baby to get someone to help?"

By the time John Ryan was taken for his twelve-month checkup, the public health nurse noted a black eye. Child protection services were notified and a social worker began tracking the case. Homemaker services were put in place with limited success.

In early 1993, an anonymous report was made to the local Child Protection Unit. By this time, several neighbours were aware of high-pitched yelling, screaming, and cursing at the little boy, particularly by the mother. No one saw fit to report it. On one occasion when Steven Turner was mowing the lawn John Ryan became upset with the noise the mower was making. A neighbour heard him ask his wife to take their son into the house. She replied: "No fucking way! He's not going to grow up to be a wimp! Leave him there!" On another occasion, while visiting friends, Mr. Turner became upset with his son and slapped him hard across the face after which Mrs. Turner told him not to cry, as he was not allowed to cry.

The family doctor was by now Dr. Jill Watts. She had been alerted by the pediatrician, Dr. El-Bardeesy, in late 1992, of concerns he had with respect to speech, comprehension, and expressive delays in the boy. He also was concerned that there had been some neglect by the mother and father. On one visit she noted that John Ryan displayed a number of scratches, a cut lip, bruises, and what appeared to be eczema below the nose. Mrs. Turner told her he had fallen downstairs. That was nineteen months before his death and the last time he would see a doctor.

Corporal Cheryl Reulland, who knew the Turners well, testified that in early 1993 she saw Mrs. Turner pushing John Ryan in a shopping cart at the local mall. She had previously seen a serious scrape on the boy's head and had confronted his mother about it. On this occasion she noticed an egg-shaped lump on his head. She anonymously reported it to the local Child Protection Unit team but was told that without any evidence of the cause of the injury the complaint was too unsubstantiated to warrant an investigation. Eventually, when the police investigators began pulling all of the files of the different agencies together after John Ryan's death, it was discovered that the Child Protection Unit's file on the Turner family had gone missing. It was never found despite a thorough search.

By late 1993 even the postman, William Carroll, noted that John Ryan appeared extremely withdrawn on the rare occasions that he saw him. To him, he appeared emotionless and afraid. Lorelei Turner once told him that John Ryan treated her "like shit just like his father does." The last time William saw the boy was in late 1993, five months before he died.

The next-door neighbours had a daughter, Valerie Zimmer. She was a bright and beautiful young woman who had taken time off between high school and post-secondary education to tend to her new baby brother while her parents worked. She saw John Ryan on occasion in his back yard. She testified that as winter turned to spring in 1994, she noticed that the little boy was getting weaker and weaker. Lorelei told her that he had a serious malady and was under the care of a doctor. At first, Valerie believed her. Eventually she grew so concerned that in late April, she had a friend who was a dental hygienist drop by to visit on two different days hoping that they would see John Ryan outside but he was nowhere to be seen. Her hope was that her friend might have a more informed opinion of his state of health because she was a health care professional.

It was obvious to everyone in the courtroom when Valerie Zimmer testified that she was personally devastated by what had happened to John Ryan Turner. Even though she had been led to believe that John Ryan was under a doctor's care, his death confirmed her worst suspicions. I knew that her testimony would be the most difficult for everyone in the courtroom. Although she was completely innocent, she was tormented by what had happened. His death was in no way her fault. Yet, her feelings of guilt were palpable as she recounted her observations to the court. She could not have known that her observations of him mindlessly pushing his little truck slowly back and forth in the back yard of the Turner home hour after hour in exactly the same way had any significance. Later Dr. Meek would testify that what she saw signified, "a poverty of play" consistent with a child in deep depression.

I began her direct examination from the back of the body of the courtroom, standing just in front of the rail separating it from the public gallery. I wanted to stand as far away from Valerie Zimmer as I could because, having interviewed her before the trial, I knew that her testimony would be highly charged and might cause me to become emotional for a second time in my career. I thought if I stood that far away, I might be able to keep my composure. As her memories unfolded she began to cry. It was apparent to all that she carried far too heavy a burden for a young woman her age. She had done nothing wrong. What made it especially difficult for everyone who heard her was that it was clear that no matter what might be said to try to make her believe his death was unforeseeable for her, nothing could change the way she felt about it. As she continued to describe him being underdressed at times for inclement weather, emotionless, and always alone, she became more and more emotional.

Soon I could hear the reporters just behind me softly crying or sobbing quietly and blowing their noses. Everyone in the courtroom was deeply disturbed. Try as I did, I could not contain myself. Quietly the tears began to stream down my face onto my tablet of trial notes. Fortunately, her testimony was more or less a narrative. She "poured out her heart" spontaneously. I did not have to ask her many questions. I glanced up at His Lordship. He was stoic.

The local Anglican priest, Reverend Wilfred Langmaid, had somehow been put in touch with the Turners and had helped minister to them through the trial. He stood alone at their side and I respected him deeply for his commitment to his avocation as a priest. He had described Justice Riordon's courtroom to me as an almost pastoral scene because of the judge's comportment and treatment of everyone in his courtroom. No one could have disagreed with him. However, having pleaded so many cases before him, and knowing him the way I did, I realized that he was in the most difficult position of all during Valerie Zimmer's testimony. He faced the packed gallery from the front of the courtroom. He could not afford to display emotion. He was the trial judge. The rest of us could be allowed at least some quiet emotion. Somehow Ms. Zimmer managed to complete her testimony. Somehow the rest of us composed ourselves. I do not think that she or anyone else in the courtroom ever knew when she left the witness box that my trial notes were covered in tears. She was a powerful witness recounting what turned out to be the last days of John Ryan's life. After hearing her testimony, everyone in the room had a deep sympathy for her, knowing the weight she carried because of that little boy's death.

The final civilian witness was Shannon MacDonald. She had been John Ryan's babysitter when he was only one year of age. By the spring of 1994, she was working at a local pharmacy approximately two weeks before John Ryan died when Lorelei and John Ryan came into the store. The boy was emotionless and pale. His eyes were swollen. She noticed what she described as purplish-blue cuts at each side of his mouth. She hardly recognized him and was shocked at his deteriorated condition. The mother and child did not stay in the pharmacy long. While they did, Shannon tried to alert other staff to make note of his condition in order to compare what she saw with what they might have seen. She was unsuccessful in her efforts to gain their attention. When they left, she decided to go outside to see what had become of them but they had disappeared. She was the last person the investigators found who saw John Ryan Turner alive.

The case for the Crown was concluded with the testimony of forensic odontologist, Dr. Fenton Smith, Dr. John Anderson, and Dr. David Meek. Dr. Smith testified that the bite marks found on John Ryan's arms were self-inflicted, likely in response to his inability to withstand the pain he was living in towards the end of his life. Dr. John Anderson, a renowned forensic paediatrician from Halifax described the symptomology as a classic description of an emotionally and physically abused and deprived child. Dr. Meek pulled all of the testimony of the other witnesses together and gave a final diagnosis that explained in clear, simple terms the complexities of John Ryan's malady.

The case had required me to read thousands of pages of material on the Kasper Hauser Syndrome or psychosocial dwarfism syndrome, Munchhausen by Proxy and other associated maladies. In order to try to understand how it was that Steven Turner could go to work every day and come home to the tragic world his son was living in, Dr. Meek suggested that I read material on the malady *folie à deux.* I never completely understood how it could be that both of these people were so off base, especially Steven Turner who left the house each day to work in an ordinary world with ordinary people. *Folie à deux* is a malady that develops between two people wherein a shared psychosis, believed to be transmissible from one partner to another over time, occurs. None of the doctors were prepared to apply it to the circumstances without more evidence from the Turners themselves. Neither accused testified at the trial. Perhaps the malady, if it was what they suffered from, infected Steven after Lorelei's mental health deteriorated to its darkest depths. Perhaps it contributed to John Ryan Turner's demise.

So many professionals saw this little boy and yet no one put all of the pieces together. In all, 109 interventions by thirteen different agencies touched the lives of John Ryan Turner and his mother from his birth to his death. Many did laudable work to try to tend to their needs. Perhaps it was the new and pervasive professional concern for individual privacy rights and personal autonomy, and the consequent privacy walls installed between different social and medical service providers, that prevented all of them from sharing information, and thus becoming aware of what was truly happening in their distorted world. Whatever else is not clear, it is abundantly clear that for a very long period towards the end of John Ryan's life, he saw almost no one but his parents. He had, by that point, been cut off from the outside world.

The people who touched his life from the community did not put the pieces together either. So many of them each had a piece of the puzzle that was his awful life. Each saw something, but so many felt each observation was at best at least marginally explainable, or that suspected abuse or neglect was unverifiable. Many no doubt felt they lacked the convincing evidence to take action. Some, like Valerie Zimmer, believed that he was being treated by a doctor or doctors.

And so, in the end, the case brought me back full circle to that speech in 1991 when John Ryan was only one year old. He was a child deeply at risk. Sadly, he was not identified as such. He did not live long enough to strike back at the hand that life had dealt him. After what he had been through, no one could imagine the broken or angry young man he might have grown up to be.

Mr. Justice Riordon reserved his decision. One month later when it was rendered, he found both Turners guilty of manslaughter. The nature of his closing remarks made it clear he had great difficulty understanding John Ryan's death. He did not appear to comprehend it any more than any of us did. In concluding his judgment he said

> This is indeed a tragic case, a sad case. What happened over the last six or seven months of John Ryan Turner's life and his death is very hard to comprehend, it is very difficult for me to understand and I think it's very difficult for most people to understand what went wrong and why things went wrong. It is not possible to make any real sense of what happened.

Lorelei Turner underwent psychiatric examination before the sentence hearing. The psychiatrist diagnosed her with a personality disorder but, as with the psychiatric evaluation done before the trial on her, it would not have exempted her from criminal liability. It was disclosed, however, that she attributed to John Ryan the character of an adult and held him to adult standards of behaviour even though he was only a toddler. Her insight was seen as poor and her personality makeup seen as fragile.

At the sentence hearing we asked that the sentence be at the very highest end of the range for this offence. The abuse and neglect were not one-time events. He was a vulnerable, defenceless and wholly dependent child in his parents' care. He had no way to escape from the misery he lived in and the abuse that had been inflicted upon him. Justice Riordon sentenced both of them to sixteen years each in a federal penitentiary. At the time, it was the longest sentence ever imposed in Canada in a manslaughter case involving the death of a child. It may well still be so.

An appeal was immediately launched to the New Brunswick Court of Appeal. It was dismissed in 1997. An Application for Leave to Appeal was then filed in the Supreme Court of Canada. The Rules of the Supreme Court allow exhibits to be filed as an addendum to the Crown's legal brief on the Leave Application. We decided that the most effective way to put the strength of our case before the three-judge panel, that would decide whether the full Court would hear the Turner's appeal, was to file the two books of photographs. One book was of John Ryan's room and what had been found in it. The other book contained the autopsy photographs, including C-2 #11. Counsel for the Turners was thoroughly upset we had done so. Yet, the photographs best depicted what had happened to that little boy. In late 1997 the Supreme Court dismissed the Application for Leave to Appeal.

Shortly after the case was completed, members of the community raised sufficient funds to place a headstone on the grave of John Ryan Turner located in the Riverside Cemetery overlooking the Miramichi River. A fitting memorial is inscribed on the face of it, "In My Father's House I Dwell." If only that statement had been true during his life.

Conclusion

The case of John Ryan Turner provides a glimpse of the thought processes of citizens who may see children at risk and do not act on their observations. It appears, from this and other similar cases, that most right-thinking people set their reporting standards high enough that unless they see overt abuse or repeated demeaning behaviour they are unlikely to report it. Most people assume the best of others. They accept, when people give explanations that even marginally accord with good parenting practices, that they are carrying out those explanations. They are not likely to be sceptical when it comes to child abuse and neglect because it is so foreign to our common values for parents to abuse their children. No one wants to have his or her name associated with a false complaint of child abuse. And yet, identifying children at risk will always be an important aspect of good citizenship. The children of our great country deserve nothing less than our wholehearted support. They are our future. As has been said in so many ways, it takes a man and a woman to conceive a child but it takes a community to properly raise one.

William Smart

THE REST OF THE STORY

William Smart QC is a Fellow of the American College of Trial Lawyers and the International Society of Barristers and was a member of Canada's 1972 Olympic Track and Field team. He has prosecuted and defended in all courts in British Columbia and the Yukon Territory, and in the Supreme Court of Canada. He is a Life Member of the National Criminal Law Program Faculty.

THERE IS NO CRIMINAL OFFENCE more serious than murder and no trial more important for everyone involved and the criminal justice system than a murder trial. Perhaps because the stakes are so high, murder trials often contain dramatic moments and surprising developments. What occurred, however, in the prosecution of the murder of William Henry Terrico was more than just dramatic and surprising, it was extraordinary. Just how extraordinary, I only appreciated fourteen years later when I learned "the rest of the story."

The Murder

Quesnel is in the Cariboo district of British Columbia at the confluence of the Fraser and Quesnel Rivers, mid-way between Williams Lake and Prince George. The City's origins go back to the gold rush days of the nineteenth century. William Henry Terrico ("Mr. Terrico") owned a used auto parts business located on the outskirts of Quesnel adjacent to Highway 97. He lived alone in his home located on his business property. He was divorced and his children, a son and a daughter, were both grown up.

On the evening of December 27, 1989, Mr. Terrico was speaking on his home telephone with his girlfriend. She was in Prince George, approximately an hour-and-a-half drive away. During their conversation, she heard knocking at his back door. Mr. Terrico told her that he would put the phone down, check who it was, and be right back. Seconds later his girlfriend heard the sound of shots from a rifle, smashing wood, and thumping. Mr. Terrico did not return to the phone and she knew something terrible had occurred. She immediately phoned 911 and told the operator what she had heard.

Quesnel RCMP were notified and promptly attended at Mr. Terrico's home. They found two bullet holes in the back door leading into the kitchen, significant blood splatters in the kitchen, and Mr. Terrico's body lying on the kitchen floor. He had been shot two or three times with a hunting rifle and beaten about the head with a blunt object. The blows to his head were later determined to be the ultimate cause of his death. The RCMP discovered that Mr. Terrico's wallet was missing and the kitchen had been ransacked. They also discovered a key piece of evidence — a distinct shoe impression left in the snow on the cement steps near the entrance to the kitchen.

The following day, the RCMP discovered a rifle in a nearby schoolyard across Highway 97. On the rifle was what appeared to be blood, hair, and human flesh around the stock. The rifle was later confirmed to be the weapon from which the shots were fired and the blood, hair, and flesh were identified as originating from Mr. Terrico. The RCMP also observed footprints in the snow near the rifle that they were able to track back towards the crime scene. The footstep impressions in the snow matched the shoe impression they had seen the evening before on the cement steps. Further forensic investigation identified the impressions left in the snow and on the cement steps as having been left by a Nike Air SA running shoe, size 9½.

Two "Persons of Interest"

Within days of the murder, the RCMP identified a seventeen-year-old named Brewer and the deceased's twenty-two-year-old son, William Jay Terrico ("Terrico Jr.") as the prime suspects. Terrico Jr. was identified as a suspect because of the animosity that apparently existed between him and his father. Brewer was identified as a suspect because the RCMP learned that his social worker had purchased a pair of size 9½ Nike Air Span shoes for him from a local merchant sometime prior to the day of the murder. The RCMP interrogated both suspects and obtained a wiretap authorization to intercept their phone calls. Most importantly, the RCMP were able to locate and seize a pair of size 9½ Nike Air SA running shoes from an apartment where Brewer was residing.

Although forensic identification techniques were less sophisticated twenty-five years ago than they are today, the RCMP were able to match the shoe impression left in the snow on the cement step with one of the shoes found at the apartment. The impression left in the snow not only matched the size and model of the shoe, it also matched unique accidental characteristics found on the waffle sole that resulted from wear and tear. This provided strong circumstantial evidence that one of the shoes found in the closet of Brewer's apartment left the impressions on the cement steps leading to the rear door and in the snow leading to the rifle in the schoolyard. The RCMP were also able to establish that the rifle used to murder Mr. Terrico had been recently stolen from the residence of a lawyer in Quesnel.

On March 21, 1990, Brewer was arrested and charged with second-degree murder of Mr.Terrico. The motive appeared to be robbery. While the case against him rested primarily on the nexus between the Nike shoes found in his apartment and the shoe impression left in the snow outside the Terrico residence, the RCMP obtained another critical piece of evidence: Terrico Jr. told the RCMP that Brewer had confessed to him that he had killed his father. Accordingly, Terrico Jr., initially a suspect in the murder, was now a crucial Crown witness against Brewer.

The Trial

After some preliminary applications, the Crown abandoned its efforts to have Brewer raised to Adult Court and the trial commenced in Youth Court in Quesnel on November 4, 1991. James Williams (now Mr. Justice Williams) and I were retained to prosecute the case. Richard Gibbs QC and Brad Chudiak were retained to defend the case on behalf of Brewer. His Honour Judge Philip Govan, an experienced trial judge who usually presided in the Greater Vancouver area, was assigned to try the case. The trial was scheduled to take about two weeks.

Mr. Williams and I led testimony concerning the circumstances surrounding the murder, what Mr. Terrico's girlfriend heard on the phone, the bullet holes in the door and the blood splatters in the kitchen, the finding of the rifle in the school yard and the forensic evidence establishing it as the murder weapon, the autopsy findings concerning Mr. Terrico's injuries and his cause of death, the theft of Mr. Terrico's wallet, the ransacking of the kitchen, and the evidence connecting the Nike Air Span shoe seized from Brewer's apartment to the shoe impressions left on the step and in the snow.

Mr. Gibbs, a highly skilled and respected trial lawyer from Prince George, chipped away at the Crown's case. His skilful cross-examination of Crown witnesses undermined the evidence establishing Brewer's whereabouts at the time of the murder and, thus, his opportunity to commit the murder. He also raised the possibility that others could have had access to and worn the Nike Air Span shoes on the evening of the murder. As a result, Brewer's confession to Terrico Jr. took on increased importance.

At the end of the first week of trial, Mr. Williams and I stayed in Quesnel over the Remembrance Day long weekend to prepare for week two. Our preparation included interviewing Terrico Jr., as well as other witnesses. The extent of disclosure from police to Crown and from Crown to defence was significantly less then than what it is today, but in preparing to interview Terrico Jr., I noticed a brief reference in a police report to Terrico Jr. declining to take a polygraph (lie detector) test. I was surprised and asked Terrico Jr. about it when we met. He told me he had done so on the advice of Mr. Chudiak, one of Brewer's defence counsel.

I was dumbfounded. I had no idea that Mr. Chudiak had ever acted for Terrico Jr., now the Crown's most important witness. Terrico Jr. added that at the time of the polygraph request, Mr. Chudiak had been acting for both him and Brewer.

I was concerned that Mr. Chudiak, a member of the defence team who would be cross-examining Terrico Jr., may have received confidential communications from him that were protected by solicitor-client privilege. Solicitor-client privilege is considered one of the most important privileges in our law and one that is jealously protected and enforced by the Courts.

A Conflict of Interest

I made further inquiries and learned that one of the investigating officers had spoken to Mr. Chudiak on January 9, 1990 and requested that Brewer and Terrico Jr. take polygraph examinations. According to the officer's notes:

Mr. Chudiak advised him that he wasn't really representing Brewer, he was just representing Terrico, that Terrico claimed the police had really done a number on him and he was reluctant to be interviewed or go to the police again and Terrico would not be taking a polygraph because of these concerns.

I also learned that in an effort to encourage Terrico Jr. to take the test, the RCMP had agreed with Mr. Chudiak's request to permit him to read a transcript of the statement Terrico Jr. had given the RCMP when they had interrogated him. Such a request is not usually granted at this early stage of an investigation, but was granted in this case on the belief that Mr. Chudiak was representing Terrico Jr.

Terrico Jr. told me that he recalled meeting with Mr. Chudiak on two occasions and that he probably did so with Brewer. He said he could not recall what he communicated to Mr. Chudiak, but he did recall there were discussions about police harassment and taking a lie detector test. I did not ask Terrico Jr. about the details of his discussions with Mr. Chudiak as I did not want to breach the solicitor-client privilege I was trying to protect. Terrico Jr. also told me that while he was anxious to have the trial proceed, he was, in the circumstances, unhappy to have either Mr. Chudiak or Mr. Gibbs cross-examine him.

It was clear that Mr. Chudiak could not participate in the cross-examination of Terrico Jr. given that he had previously been his lawyer on the very matter before the Court. However, what about Mr. Gibbs, his Senior, who was leading for the defence of Brewer?

I recalled that a few years earlier, my former law partner, Len Doust QC, had run into a similar situation when he was prosecuting a first-degree murder case. He discovered in the middle of the trial that the junior lawyer assisting him had previously acted for one of the accused on an unrelated matter. Mr. Doust ultimately concluded that both he and his junior had to withdraw as counsel and they did. I spoke with Mr. Doust as well as other senior counsel about my situation and concluded, by the end of the weekend, that I must inform the trial judge.

It was now Monday evening of the long weekend and Mr. Williams and I went to find Mr. Gibbs to tell him what we had learned and that we intended to raise our concern with Judge Govan when the trial resumed the next day. We met Mr. Gibbs at a local restaurant. I recall he was in the middle of eating a large plate of ribs as he told us how much he was looking forward to cross-examining Terrico Jr. He stopped mid-bite into a rib he was holding in his hands when we told him what we had learned. He appeared surprised and assured us that he had no idea that Mr. Chudiak had been acting for Terrico Jr. during the investigation. He also assured us that Mr. Chudiak had not communicated anything to him concerning any discussions he may have had with Terrico Jr. We parted company on the basis we would consider the issue further overnight.

The following morning, November 12, we met Mr. Gibbs before court. We again expressed our concern that he, as well as his junior, was mired in an unusual position of conflict that had to be resolved by the Court. We then appeared before Judge Govan and requested a one-day adjournment in order for counsel to consider what we described as "an issue that had arisen". The adjournment was granted and Mr. Gibbs flew to Vancouver to consult with other senior counsel.

On Wednesday, November 13, we again appeared before Judge Govan. Mr. Chudiak was not at the counsel table and Mr. Gibbs told Judge Govan that he would proceed alone for the remainder of the trial. Mr. Williams and I explained the issue that had arisen and set out the facts as we knew them from our discussions with Terrico Jr. and from the RCMP notes. We said that our position was Mr. Gibbs was in a conflict, notwithstanding Mr. Chudiak had withdrawn as counsel. We submitted that both counsel must withdraw and a mistrial should be declared so other counsel could be retained to represent Brewer at a new trial. Mr. Gibbs advised the Court that Mr. Chudiak had not communicated to him any confidential information from any discussions he may have had with Terrico Jr., but even if there had been such discussions, they took place in the presence of Mr. Brewer and, therefore, were not privileged.

Judge Govan disagreed with the defence position and declared a mistrial. In his reasons for doing so, he said, in part,

> ....the maintenance and integrity of our system of justice is more important than any one case or any one counsel. The public must not only think that justice is being done; it must be done publicly, openly, and in the eyes of the public. The death of Mr. Terrico was a loss in this community. The prosecution of a party or parties thought to be guilty and causing that loss is important to the community. But most important of all is that the public reclaim faith in the very process and institution that decides those issues.

The Appeal

Brewer brought an application to the British Columbia Supreme Court for an order quashing the decision of Judge Govan and requiring Judge Govan to continue the trial and allow Mr. Brewer to be represented by Mr. Gibbs. The appeal was heard by Justice Bruce Cohen, a highly respected judge. Justice Cohen had, prior to his appointment to the Bench, been the elected head (then known as the Treasurer) of the Law Society of British Columbia. The Law Society, of course, oversees and regulates the ethical and professional responsibilities of its members. Coincidentally, some years after this appeal, Mr. Gibbs would hold the same position as the elected head of the Law Society.

Justice Cohen dismissed the application on March 11, 1992. He held that the trial judge's decision to discharge both lawyers and declare a mistrial was a reasonable one. He said the fact that Brewer might disclose communications between Terrico Jr. and Mr. Chudiak for which he was present did not permit counsel to disclose them — only Brewer or Terrico Jr. could waive privilege.

Jim Williams and I reflected on whether we should proceed with a new trial. There was, at that time, no charge approval standard or test for Crown counsel to apply when deciding whether to commence or continue a prosecution. The decision was essentially a matter in the discretion of individual prosecutors based on a consideration of the available evidence and the ethical duties placed upon them.

We concluded that the strength of the Crown's case was not what it had initially appeared to be. The evidence establishing that Brewer must have been the person wearing the seized Nike shoes on the evening of December 27, 1989 and, therefore, the person who killed Mr. Terrico, was less clear, and the evidence establishing Brewer's whereabouts at the time of the murder was problematic. While Brewer's confession to Terrico Jr. was an important piece of evidence, Terrico Jr. was a person whose credibility was suspect. Not only did he have a criminal record, he was also the most likely alternative suspect. We had no doubt that Brewer was the murderer; the question was whether we could prove it beyond a reasonable doubt.

We decided that we should stay the proceedings in the hope that one day Brewer might confess to someone else or some other evidence might emerge that would strengthen the Crown's case against him. We therefore entered a stay, thereby stopping the prosecution. We did so despite resistance from some members of the RCMP.

The Rest of the Story

Life carried on and I thought little more of the case until I received a phone call in approximately 1999 or 2000 from an officer with the Historical Crime Unit of the RCMP. He told me that Mr. Terrico's daughter was encouraging the RCMP to renew their investigation of her father's murder and that they were going to do so. He was seeking any information I could provide him about the case. I told him what I could recall. He also spoke with Jim Williams. Neither of us was expecting anything to come from a renewed investigation so many years after the murder.

I heard nothing further until the end of June 2005. Jim Williams phoned and told me to look at a decision that had just been released by the British Columbia Court of Appeal, *R. v. Terrico*. I did so and read what had occurred after I had spoken with the RCMP five or six years earlier.

The RCMP had conducted a further investigation of Brewer. Their investigation included a sophisticated undercover technique known as a "Mr. Big" operation. The operation is expensive, time consuming, and controversial, but often very effective. It is reserved for the most serious of cases — usually murder investigations — where the police have a prime suspect but insufficient evidence to prosecute. It begins with undercover officers targeting the suspect and luring him into a fictitious criminal organization of their own making. Over time, the undercover officers gain the suspect's confidence and often his friendship, and he is shown that working with the organization can provide significant financial rewards. Eventually, firmly ensnared, he is told that to be fully admitted into the organization, the crime boss — Mr. Big — must approve his membership. This leads to a meeting between the suspect and Mr. Big. Mr. Big is, of course, another undercover police officer. During the meeting, Mr. Big brings up the crime the police are investigating, questions the suspect about it, and presses him for a confession. The questioning is designed to send the message that by confessing to the crime, the suspect will gain admission into the organization. In reality, it will lead to him being arrested and charged.

This was the technique the RCMP employed during their renewed investigation, and it was successful — Brewer admitted to Mr. Big that he had shot and killed Mr. Terrico. He said, however, that he had done so at the request of Terrico Jr. He said they had met at a party when Brewer was seventeen and discussed shooting Mr. Terrico. He said Terrico Jr. hated his father because his father had beaten him, beaten his mother, and abused his sister. Terrico Jr. told Brewer that because he was a juvenile he would only get three years if he did the murder and was caught. Brewer said that Terrico Jr. agreed to pay him $25,000 for killing his father but ended up paying him only $10,000.

Brewer said their plan was that he was to take Mr. Terrico's wallet and ransack the house to make it look like Mr. Terrico had been killed during the course of a robbery. Brewer said he panicked when he went up the porch steps to the house and Mr. Terrico came to the door. He said he pulled the trigger, and one shot went through the door. He then fired a second shot. When Mr. Terrico moved, Brewer had no further bullets so he struck Mr. Terrico on the head a couple of times with the rifle and grabbed his wallet and ran out of the house. He said he threw the gun over the fence into the schoolyard and covered it with snow. He said he gave the wallet to Terrico Jr. and they threw it, together with Brewer's pants and gloves, into the Fraser River to dispose of the evidence.

After his confession to Mr. Big, Brewer was arrested and the original charge of second-degree murder that I had stayed years earlier was reinstated. Brewer pleaded guilty to that offence in 2002 and received a sentence of three years in jail. He also agreed to cooperate with the RCMP and to testify against Terrico Jr.

The RCMP commenced an undercover operation of Terrico Jr. and their investigation again included a Mr. Big operation. It was again successful and Terrico Jr. admitted to Mr. Big that he had hired Brewer to kill his father. Terrico Jr. was charged with first-degree murder because the Crown now had evidence that the murder was planned and deliberate, not just a robbery that had gone bad and had resulted in an intentional culpable homicide. Terrico Jr.'s trial was held in adult court before a judge and jury. He was convicted and received a sentence of imprisonment for life with no eligibility for parole for twenty-five years. The Court of Appeal decision that Justice Williams had referred me to in June 2005 was the Court's reasons for dismissing Terrico Jr.'s appeal from conviction.

I was stunned when I read the decision. There had never been any suggestion from anyone that two people had been involved in the murder. The evidence appeared overwhelming that it was Brewer who had committed the murder and that he had done so alone. Terrico Jr. had been merely a potential alternative suspect because of his animosity towards his father. Had I called Terrico Jr. to testify at the trial in November 1991, there would have been two murderers in the courtroom — one in the witness box and the other in the prisoner's box. I had undertaken to prosecute a murder case where the "star witness" for the Crown, had, it later turned out, been the person who had organized and paid for the murder. By hiring Brewer to kill his father, he was equally guilty. Incredibly, years later, both murderers confessed to the crime, at different times, to a Mr. Big undercover police officer. But for the mistrial, the stay of proceedings, and the good work of the RCMP, neither would have been convicted and I would have never had learned, fourteen years later, the rest of the story.

PART THREE

Reasonable Doubt

Richard Peck

AIR INDIA

Richard C.C. Peck QC has practiced criminal law for four decades. He has appeared before all levels of court in Canada. He has authored numerous publications in the criminal law area, and has contributed to legal education programs throughout his career. He is a Fellow of the American College of Trial Lawyers and the International Society of Barristers, and Co-Chair of the National Criminal Law Program.

When my literary friend, Chris Evans QC, and his equally literary partner, Lorene Shyba approached me to write a piece for this book, their instructions were as follows: "*Review your memories and chronicle a case for us that had a weird, disquieting turn or was a significant personal challenge.*"

I quickly fastened upon the "significant personal challenge" aspect of their request and this has led me to write about the Air India case. For all criminal lawyers, whether Crown or defence, every case presents a personal challenge; the longer and more complex the case, the greater the challenge. Prior to November 2000, the longest trial I had acted in as counsel was before a jury and lasted eight months. That case, a matter of drug-related gangland slayings, was very difficult and had left me drained. I wasn't sure that I was capable of conducting another defence of that length. Unfortunately, where stress is concerned, lawyers' memories are short. Little did I know when I undertook the defence of Ajaib Singh Bagri, one of the two original accused in the Air India case, that the experience would cause the eight-month gangland slaying trial to pale by comparison. Air India was a case that would occupy the better part of four-and-a-half years of my life to the near exclusion of everything else.

Every barrister knows that trials involve an intensity of focus that is very exacting; every day of trial requires vigorous concentration. Looking back over a distance of many years, I find that I have little recollection of life outside the Air India case. In short, from the day I agreed to defend Mr. Bagri at the beginning of November 2000 until the verdict in mid-March 2005, the matter consumed virtually every sentient moment of my daily existence. During the final defence submissions in late October 2004, my co-counsel, Michael Code, passed me a note that read, "*I think we have both aged, which has both its good and bad aspects. We are wiser and fuller but we also lost time.*"

Michael Code was right. We had "lost time." We were not alone in this. There were numerous others including Crown Counsel, other members of the defence teams and, I would expect, the trial judge, who would have had similar feelings. We had all set out on a journey such as none of us had experienced before or likely would again.

I have sometimes pondered why I agreed to undertake the defence of Mr. Bagri. Certainly the challenge was part of it; unexplored terrain lay ahead. Yet there was more to it than that. The case involved a massive police investigation that spanned fifteen years and several continents. It was a *cause célèbre* and when the Indictment was filed on October 28, 2004, the news coverage was both national and international. In such circumstances, any barrister worth his or her salt would have difficulty turning down such a brief. As well there was a certain amount of *chutzpah* involved; a sort of "I can handle any case" attitude. The problem is that the ego comes with a distorted lens; you think you are looking at a ski hill when, in reality, it is a Himalayan peak. Ignorance abounds when one does not know what lies ahead. So why would any barrister embark on such a journey? Perhaps the answer lies in the famous response of the British mountaineer, George Leigh Mallory, who, when asked in 1923 why he wanted to climb Mount Everest simply stated, "Because it's there."

The Case

In the morning of June 23, 1985, a 747 passenger jetliner, Air India Flight 182, out of Montreal, commenced a gradual eastwardly descent over the Atlantic Ocean, heading for Heathrow Airport in London, England. Within a matter of minutes, the plane disappeared from the radar screen at Shannon, Ireland, Air Traffic Control. The ensuing investigation, and trial, determined that a bomb had exploded in the cargo bay, rending the fuselage and sending all 329 persons aboard into free-fall from thirty-one thousand feet into the frigid waters off the west coast of Ireland. This descent would have taken approximately three minutes; three minutes of ineffable terror for those persons still conscious — an eternity of falling into the abyss. Subsequent rescue efforts resulted in the retrieval of only 132 bodies. Remarkably, forensic pathology determined that several persons had survived the impact with the water but had subsequently died from drowning.

This constituted an execrable act of aviation terrorism of a magnitude unmatched in history until the infamous events of September 11, 2001.

Related to the tragedy of Air India Flight 182, approximately fifty-four minutes earlier, and one third of the way around the globe, a bomb in a suitcase exploded in the baggage-handling area of Narita Airport in Tokyo, Japan. The suitcase was to have been transferred onto an Air India flight heading for Bangkok, Thailand and then Delhi, India. The explosion killed two baggage handlers, Hideharu Koda and Hideo Asano. The suitcase had arrived on a CP Air flight from Vancouver.

As an aside, but of particular interest, Air India Flight 182 was running close to an hour late due to loading problems encountered in Montreal. Had the flight been on time for its scheduled arrival at Heathrow Airport, the bomb would have exploded after the plane had landed. This would have fit one of the many theories of the case, namely that the intention of the perpetrators was to have the bombs explode at Heathrow and Narita Airports to serve as a warning to the Indian government. Nevertheless, the fact of the delay of Air India Flight 182 made no difference to the manner in which the Crown presented its case. The Indictment contained eight counts. Count Two and Count Four were charges of first-degree murder; Count Two related to the 329 passengers and crew of Air India Flight 182 and Count Four related to the deaths of the two baggage handlers in Narita. An Appendix to the Indictment set out the 329 names of the victims of Count Two.

The Crown's theory was that suitcases containing the two bombs had been delivered to Vancouver International Airport on the morning of June 22, 1985. A Sikh male had purchased two tickets, two days earlier. One was for the June 22nd CP Air Flight 003 from Vancouver to Tokyo under the name of "L. Singh." Baggage and passengers from that flight were to connect in Narita to Air India Flight 301 heading to Bangkok and then Delhi. The second ticket was purchased in the name of "M. Singh" for CP Air Flight 060 from Vancouver to Toronto, connecting to Air India Flight 182 from Toronto to Montreal, then to Heathrow and on to Delhi. In both cases the two bags were loaded onto their respective Canadian Pacific Air Lines flights but the passenger manifests showed that neither "L. Singh" nor "M. Singh" boarded the flights. The Crown's theory was that "L. Singh" and "M. Singh" were simply fictitious names. The bomb in the suitcase on the westbound (Narita) flight exploded in the baggage-handling area at Narita while in the process of being transferred to Air India Flight 301. The suitcase containing the bomb heading east was transferred to Air India Flight 182 and exploded when the flight was in mid-air off the west coast of Ireland.

The theory of the prosecution was based in part on earlier events that had occurred in India in 1984. Over time, friction had developed between Hindus and Sikhs. This led to the Indian Army attacking the Golden Temple in Amritsar, thus defiling the holiest shrine of the Sikh faith. During this attack at least a thousand people of the Sikh faith died. This attack was taken by Sikhs as a sacrilege against their religion. On October 31, 1984, the Prime Minister of India, Indira Gandhi, was assassinated by her Sikh bodyguards. This was viewed as an act of retaliation by Sikhs for the desecration and killings in Amritsar. The assassination of Prime Minister Ghandi in turn led to a violent campaign against Sikhs, resulting in the deaths of thousands. These events fomented the movement for the creation of an independent Sikh state within India to be named Khalistan. The desire for a Sikh homeland in India had for some time been a sentiment shared by many Sikhs, both in India and in the Sikh Diaspora. The Crown believed that Mr. Bagri along with his co-accused, Ripudaman Singh Malik , both residents of British Columbia, were, along with others, responsible for the bombings. The Crown's theory was that these bombings were acts in furtherance of the Khalistan movement by striking at the Indian government through its national airline.

In early November 2000, after being retained to represent Mr. Bagri, I contacted Robert H. Wright QC, who was lead counsel for the Crown on the case. Bob Wright is one of the most senior and respected Crown Counsel in the Province. I had known him for many years and had great respect for his intellect and judgment. Bob had been one of the top students in his class at Queen's University Faculty of Law and had gone on to practice both in the private bar in British Columbia as well as in the Crown office. Due to his good judgment and personal qualities, including a quick wit and unerring sense of humour, he had long occupied a position near the top of the Crown hierarchy and was the key person to whom the Crown turned when it faced difficult matters. The Air India case was one of these.

In the mid-1990s, the decade-long RCMP investigation into the Air India disaster had been reinvigorated under the highly regarded Gary Bass who was then Officer in Charge of the RCMP Major Crime Section for British Columbia. It is noteworthy that under Gary Bass, the RCMP had dedicated approximately two hundred of its members to the Air India investigation by the late 1990s. In

November 1996, Bob Wright was assigned to commence an assessment of the material being gathered and reviewed by the RCMP. By the time the charges were laid in October 2000, Bob, along with several members of the Crown office, had been assessing the case for four years.

When I contacted Bob I requested that he forward to me initial disclosure of the case. He chuckled and said he would be glad to. I quickly discovered the reason for his mirth; within a matter of days a van full of Bankers Boxes arrived at the office. These boxes contained ninety-three three-ring binders entitled "The Case for the Crown." That gave me my first inkling of the enormity of the tasks that lay ahead.

The Bagri Defence Team

In analysing the upcoming tasks, I realized that numerous challenges loomed on the horizon. The first would be to marshal a team capable of handling the complexities of the case and the vast amount of disclosure that would be forthcoming. In my view, the team needed to consist of persons with diverse legal talents, not simply persons who were skillful in a courtroom setting. Having said that, I knew that we would need particularly competent courtroom lawyers given that the trial, including pretrial motions, could last for years as the Crown's initial witness list contained an incredible 1,185 names.

I first approached Michael Code who was then practicing as a defence lawyer in Toronto, Ontario. I had met Michael some years earlier and was well aware of his background. He had articled for the high-profile Clayton Ruby and had spent a goodly number of years working alongside the renowned Marlys Edwardh. He had also done a five-year stint as the Assistant Deputy Attorney General for Ontario in charge of prosecutions. Thereafter, he had returned to private practice. It was widely known in the legal profession in Canada that Michael had a work ethic second to none, coupled with a fierce intellect, enabling him to have successfully argued numerous criminal law and constitutional matters in the Ontario Court of Appeal and the Supreme Court of Canada.

I met with Michael at a conference in Toronto in mid-November 2000 and after considering my invitation to join Mr. Bagri's defence team he eventually accepted, well knowing that this would entail a great deal of travel to Vancouver, where he would be living out of a suitcase for weeks and months on end. Michael took up his role with the vigour and discipline for which he was renowned and dedicated the next four years of his life to Mr. Bagri's defence. His contribution to the defence was of inestimable value. I remain indebted to him for his hard work and support throughout what was an extremely trying process. Of note, not long after the conclusion of the Air India case, he became a professor at the University of Toronto Law School and in 2009 was appointed as a Judge of the Ontario Superior Court in Toronto, where he now sits.

The next person I approached for his courtroom skills was Michael Tammen, now Tammen QC. Mike was well known for his work ethic and fearless advocacy and as being a tenacious cross-examiner; skills ideally suited to the trial that lay ahead.

I also needed a person who could take a complex array of difficult facts and render them into an understandable and articulable form. Keith Hamilton was that person. Not a courtroom lawyer, Keith had spent most of his career in litigation support as well as report-writing for governmental fact-finding missions and Commissions of Inquiry. Keith was known as being meticulous to a fault and an extremely capable writer. A significant portion of "The Case for the Crown" was dedicated to proving not only that a bomb had been responsible for bringing down Air India Flight 182 over the Atlantic but also to identifying where in the cargo hold the bomb had been placed. A distance of some five feet separated the areas in the cargo hold where the luggage from Vancouver and the luggage from Toronto were placed. As the Trial Judge noted:

> A conclusion that the defence evidence raises a reasonable doubt with respect to the Crown's bomb location would fundamentally undermine its theory about the role of these accused in the alleged offences. Thus, while the distance between the two proposed bomb locations is remarkably small, its significance is great.

Keith was assigned the unenviable task of sorting through forensic evidence contained in some thirty-plus Bankers Boxes, all of which were dedicated to these issues. He analysed this material and put it into language that we could understand. As expected, he did a first-rate job.

Ajeet Kang also worked on the team. Ajeet had her own practice and was known to Mr. Bagri. She was of invaluable assistance in a number of ways and worked closely with Mike Tammen on one significant aspect of the Crown's case that dealt with the history of Sikhs and the Sikh faith. The Crown believed that it was essential that the trier-of-fact, whether it be judge or jury, have a thorough understanding of this history to give context to the charges.

I then assigned a series of tasks to associates in my law firm. Indeed, it seemed that at one time or another, everyone in the firm was working on the Air India case with the sole exception of Jeff Campbell who was handling everything else.

Nikos Harris, who had worked with me for many years and is now a lecturer at the University of British Columbia Faculty of Law, was to provide overviews and analyses of the multiplicity of legal issues that we knew would arise during the handling of the case. Nikos possesses an incisive intellect and is widely recognized in the criminal law profession in Vancouver for his ability to synthesize difficult legal issues.

The next person to be assigned to work full-time on the case was Paul Barclay. Paul had articled at the firm and was well known for his organizational skills. One of his primary tasks was being assigned to the issues of disclosure. Over the course of the handling of the case he drafted six hundred disclosure request letters to the Crown which resulted in 2,019 Crown letters in reply, many of which contained dozens, sometimes hundreds, of documents. Paul organized this material into binders and had such a mastery of the material, coupled with a nearly eidetic memory, that he could call up, on request, virtually any document. Paul was also assigned to review the RCMP master file that was housed at E Division Headquarters in Vancouver, and contained 182 linear shelf feet of manila file folders standing on end. It took Paul until May of 2004, and 230 attendances at E Division, to complete that onerous task.

Finally, other associates in my office were assigned a variety of tasks on the file, specifically, Marlene Mann, April Lee and Eric Gottardi. Many of these tasks were time-sensitive and there was often a sense that one was working in a forensic "pressure-cooker." Notwithstanding, everyone did their work at a high level and within the time requirements.

This was the team assembled for Mr. Bagri's defence. It proved to be a highly functional and cohesive unit. This might seem surprising given the nature of the criminal law practice. It is fair to say that there is a "lone wolf" culture among practitioners in our end of the business. For a number of criminal defence lawyers to work agreeably in concert, everyone has to park his or her ego at the door and this was done.

Over the course of the case, the volume of disclosure that we obtained was nothing short of astounding. I have already mentioned the original ninety-three binders of "The Case for the Crown" and the master file, which, with manila file folders standing on edge, occupied 182 linear feet of shelf space. In truth, these two "batches" of disclosure formed only a small part of the material that we ultimately obtained and reviewed. As we encountered areas where we recognized that further undisclosed materials existed, we made further disclosure requests. Much of the additional material came to us in the form of CD ROMs. For instance, material that was not relevant to the Crown's case but might be relevant to the defence case comprised twenty-six CD ROMs. Much of this material was redacted, that is, portions had been blacked-out, and this in turn generated further work for us in having to approach the Crown to reveal these blacked-out passages. We also received eighty-three CD ROMs, again, many of these contained redacted portions, which the Crown had deemed irrelevant. This material, coupled with RCMP and Canadian Security Intelligence Service (CSIS) wiretap binders, forty-two-shelf-feet of four-inch wide, three-ring binders when taken together, came in at several million pages. In short, this avalanche of material came close to overwhelming us. Joe Bellows QC, one of the senior counsel for the Crown on the case said to me, "The sheer volume of the work drove many of the Crown's decisions."

As an aside, after the case was over, I asked Paul Barclay to give me an estimate of the size of the disclosure material if everything was converted to hard copy. His calculation was that the total disclosure would amount to in excess of fifty-five hundred thick, three-ring binders!

There is one further significant aspect of "disclosure" that needs to be mentioned. This relates to physical evidence. In the time immediately after Air India Flight 182 exploded, an extensive search and rescue mission was commenced. It was during the course of this effort that the 132 bodies were recovered. As well, wreckage from the plane was also recovered, including some from the ocean bed, seven-thousand feet below the surface. In 1989 and 1991 there were two subsequent salvage operations and more wreckage was recovered from the deep. Over time, the recovered pieces of the fuselage and other parts of the plane were transported to a warehouse at a secret location in the Lower Mainland of British Columbia where the Crown experts used this material, along with simulated materials, to partially reconstruct the plane. The purpose of this was to assist in a better understanding of the location of the bomb and the resulting forces and effects of the explosion on the fuselage of the plane. In his Reasons for Judgment, the Trial Judge explained the matter in these terms:

> The expert testimony regarding the structural and wreckage trail analysis spanned fourteen days of trial and was both technical and complex. The Court convened for two of those days at the warehouse housing the partial reconstruction. This permitted the expert witnesses to explain their respective opinions with reference to the reconstruction so as to facilitate the Court's understanding of the spatial relationship between the various targets and the damage sustained by them.

It is doubtful that any case, before or after Air India, would contain as much disclosure material. Gary Bass, who went on to become the Deputy Commissioner for the RCMP in B.C., described the investigation as the most significant criminal investigation in the history of Canada, particularly in terms of the number of police involved, the length of time of the investigation, the cost of the investigation, the jurisdictions and the various foreign police forces involved, and the massive amount of disclosure. The technological challenges were also unprecedented both in terms of the partial reconstruction of the Flight 182 aircraft and the conversion of hundreds of thousands of tape-recordings and photographs to digital format for the dual purposes of preservation of evidence and facilitating disclosure.

The police investigation continued throughout the trial which meant that by the end of the trial, in March of 2005, it had been an investigation that spanned the better part of two decades. The investigation continues today.

The next challenge we faced was in actually getting to trial and completing it before we all reached retirement age. This was a task that would require ingenuity, cooperation and a leap of faith, in that a level of trust had to be reached among the lead lawyers for the Crown and defence teams.

We needed to get on with the trial for the simple reason that the accused would not be granted bail. Early in the matter, specifically in December 2000, bail applications were brought on behalf of Mr. Bagri and Mr. Malik. Michael Code and I represented Mr. Bagri while William Smart QC and his partner Jim Williams, now Williams J. of the British Columbia Supreme Court, acted for Mr. Malik. The applications were heard by Associate Chief Justice Patrick Dohm and were spread over many days. His Ruling was delivered in January 2001. We knew it was going to be an uphill battle even though Justice Dohm was known to be a reasonable and practical judge in bail matters. Justice Dohm ruled against us and ordered both accused detained pending trial. In an interview upon his retirement in April 2010, Justice Dohm said that the bail decision in the Air India case was one of the toughest decisions of his lengthy judicial career that had spanned almost thirty-eight years. In any event, the line was now etched in granite. This was doubly so given the fact that we had appealed Justice Dohm's decision to the Court of Appeal with no success. At this point reality struck home; Mr. Bagri would remain in custody until the conclusion of the trial. The challenge therefore was to get on with the matter as quickly as possible in the circumstances while ensuring that the accused had a fair trial.

Finally, and most practically, we needed a courtroom that was sufficiently secure, and large enough, in which to conduct the trial. There was no courtroom in the Province capable of meeting these requirements. One would have to be built. As it happened, when the Vancouver Supreme Courthouse was built in the late 1970s, an area on the main floor had been segregated for the future building of a high-security courtroom. Under the auspices of Justice Dohm, this is precisely what occurred, and the Air India Courtroom, now Courtroom 20, was constructed. Today, the dedicated use of that courtroom is for high-security trials. It should be noted that it was also fitted with the most modern technology available at the time, much of which was lost on the main lawyers for the defence and Crown, all Luddites to the core. The courtroom took some time to build which actually fit in fairly well with the overall timetable of the matter. Crown disclosure had to be substantially complete before the trial could begin. As previously noted, disclosure was ongoing, even after the commencement of the trial on April 28, 2003; roughly thirty months after the accused had been arrested.

During early days, Bob Wright, on behalf of the Crown, approached the defence team with the notion of forming an "administrative partnership." His view was that if the trial was to commence and conclude within a reasonable time there would need to be a great deal of cooperation among the parties. To accomplish this would also require considerable creativity and the "leap of faith" which I previously mentioned. Many of the documents sought by the defence were in the possession of the RCMP, CSIS, the FBI, and policing authorities in Ireland, Britain and India. All of these agencies had documents pertinent to the case but deemed some of the materials either classified or subject to claims of privilege. The way to accomplish disclosure of these materials came through the innovative use of Undertakings, meaning lawyers' solemn promises. This worked with designated lawyers from the defence teams entering into Undertakings not to reveal the contents of the materials that they reviewed unless the Crown agreed or the Court so pronounced. This enabled the defence teams to review the materials and then advise the Crown as to which particular documents they required to be produced. Once such documents were identified, and if the Crown agreed to release them, the defence could use them for trial purposes. Should the Crown not agree, the matter would be arbitrated by the trial judge. This procedure was invoked and was successful to the extent that, after several initial skirmishes based on defence disclosure applications, no further such applications were required. In short, Bob Wright's "administrative partnership" worked. Tens of thousands of confidential documents were reviewed by the defence with only those required for defence purposes at trial seeing the light of day. All other documents were subject to the Undertakings signed by the lawyers and remain so in perpetuity.

Before the trial could be commenced there was yet another obstacle, namely, dealing with pre-trial motions. These involved a variety of legal and procedural issues that, once ruled upon, would define the evidentiary scope of the trial. Mike Code was instrumental in reducing the potential number of these issues into manageable proportions. In the result, about one-half dozen pre-trial motions were argued, and ruled upon, over a six-month period. This became a significant feature in paving the road to trial.

The next task was to solve the problem of the 1,185 witnesses who the Crown initially believed it would have to call should the defence not be prepared to make any admissions, that is, if the defence put the Crown to strict proof. Even if one assumed that the testimony of many of these witnesses would be of short duration, there are only so many trial days in a court year. Inevitably, such a trial would last for many, many years. As matters evolved, the Crown began to pare down its list to only those witnesses who were absolutely essential. In the event of no defence admissions, this reduced the number down to 883 witnesses; a substantial reduction but still far too many. The trial was to be heard by a judge and jury. Our assessment was that no jury could last the length of the trial even with this reduced number. Inevitably, jurors would drop off and we would be faced with a mistrial. Bail would not be forthcoming and we would simply have to recommence before a new jury. The obvious solution was to agree to a trial by judge alone. We knew that such a course of action came with considerable risk, given that the ultimate decision would be left to one person, rather than twelve. Nevertheless, it was a risk that the defence was prepared to assume. In the result, Justice Bruce Josephson was assigned to hear the case. The Rubicon was crossed and the die had been cast.

Justice Josephson had a long judicial history. He had been appointed a Provincial Court Judge in 1975, became Chief Judge of the Provincial Court in 1988, a Judge of the County Court in 1989 and a Judge of the Supreme Court in 1990. His reputation was that of an intelligent and fair judge. He was also extremely experienced in the handling of criminal cases; by the time the trial commenced, he had been a judge for twenty-eight years. Given his background, we firmly believed that our client would receive a fair trial.

The final expedient employed to reduce the length of the trial was admissions of fact. Canadian law provides that an accused person may admit facts in the Crown's case that are then reduced to writing and subsequently read into the record at the time of trial. This may sound like a relatively simple process but the contrary is true. The defence only admits facts when it is satisfied that the Crown can prove the facts so admitted. The exercise of admitting facts can also be useful to the defence particularly where the facts being admitted may advance the defence position but could be difficult for the defence to prove. This was the case in the Air India trial. It was Michael Code who met with the Crown over many days, and hundreds of hours, to work out the admissions of fact. This was a laborious and detailed exercise but it proved very useful.

Batches of admissions were drawn up and circulated to the defence team for Mr. Malik. By this time the lead counsel for that team were William Smart QC and David Crossin QC, highly regarded members of the Criminal Bar in British Columbia; extremely capable advocates whose courtroom abilities are of the first water. They too had to sign the admissions of fact that Michael Code had worked out with the Crown. They did so and through this process of admissions it is estimated that roughly two years of trial time were eliminated. Put another way, there were in excess of six hundred admissions of fact which ultimately reduced the Crown's list to eighty-three witnesses. The trial had now attained manageable proportions.

The Trial

As we approached the commencement of the trial, we foresaw that the case would be a test of strategy, stamina, and perseverance. In short, it would tax our resolve. We were up against some of the best prosecutors in the Province. The Crown had created teams to deal with discrete facets of its case. Each of these teams was led by a formidable prosecutor. As mentioned, Bob Wright QC was the overall, lead prosecutor for the Crown. He was also in charge of the team assigned to the forensic science aspects of the case, which included the nature and location of the explosive device on Air India Flight 182, and the explosive device in the baggage-handling area of Narita Airport; intricate tasks, replete with minute details and involving several, disparate scientific disciplines.

The Crown had created two separate prosecution teams: one team for each accused. Joseph Bellows QC was the lead prosecutor for the team assigned to the case against Mr. Malik. Called to the bar in 1975, Joe had handled many significant prosecutions and was known as a tireless worker with exceptional skill in organizing complex evidence. He was also well known for his meticulous preparation and precise attention to detail in every case he handled, many of which were of a high-profile nature.

The lead prosecutor for the team assigned to Mr. Bagri's matter was Richard Cairns QC who was called to the bar in 1972 and, like Joe Bellows, had a long history of prosecuting high-profile cases. Richard was a clever tactician and skillful cross-examiner. Any trial where Richard was acting for the Crown was a challenge.

If having to face Bob Wright, Joe Bellows and Richard Cairns was not enough, each Crown team was staffed with very seasoned prosecutors including Gordon Matei, Dianne Wiedemann and Karima Andani, to name only a few. Over the course of the trial, no fewer than twenty-one prosecutors appeared in court, with numerous others working behind the scenes. As *Vancouver Sun* newspaper reporter, Kim Bolan, wrote in her article, which appeared after the trial verdicts, the Crown Prosecution Team "...was unprecedented in its size and depth of experience."

The trial began on April 28, 2003 and continued until early December 2004. During that time 230 days were spent in trial. At the end of final submissions, Justice Josephson reserved his decision and adjourned the case to March 16, 2005 for the rendering of his judgment.

This was a trial like no other that I, or my colleagues, had previously encountered. By the time we hit the floor of the courtroom, we had been analyzing disclosure and engaged in intense preparation for thirty months; in other words, two-and-a-half-years of detailed examination of every aspect of the factual matrix of the case and every legal argument that we could foresee arising during the Crown's case. They had been long and tiring months but paled when compared to the months when we were in trial. Seventy-hour work weeks were the norm; some weeks longer. The trial was always on our minds. During that time, holidays became a thing of the past; merely finding a few hours of leisure time a week was a rarity. I think that it was our team's unified approach and commitment to the case that allowed us to maintain personal equilibrium. When new matters arose on the sudden, we were able to divide the tasks amongst ourselves so that the workload was evenly distributed. Even then, we were all fully engaged. As individuals, we became distracted and, occasionally, cantankerous in our daily lives. How our families put up with us is beyond my ken. By the time Justice Josephson adjourned the case we were all exhausted, both physically and mentally. To employ a euphemism, the case had "taken the Mickey out of us."

Trials are complex exercises often involving unforeseen developments. The essence of a trial is the re-creation of past human events through the mechanism of human memory delivered by sworn witnesses. Human memory is notoriously fallible and it is, in part, because of this that we utilize the test of cross-examination to ferret-out the truth. With all trials, the lawyer's challenge is an exercise "in controlling the contingencies of litigation," to quote the words of the venerated legal scholar, Professor John Henry Wigmore. In other words, no matter how in-depth our preparation was, we knew that unanticipated matters would arise as the trial progressed.

In some ways, all trials are the same in that they depend on the testimony of witnesses, findings of fact arising from such testimony, and final verdicts based on facts and law. At the same time, all trials differ, particularly in terms of the consequences to the individuals affected by the outcomes. Although the Air India trial was highly complex, it still came down to the ultimate reliability of a dozen or so key witnesses. All the *ubër* technology of the newly fitted Air India courtroom was not going to change this.

As noted earlier, a portion of the trial was devoted to expert evidence respecting the location of the bomb on board Air India Flight 182, and other complex forensic evidence. However, the core of the Crown's case came down to witnesses who claimed that both Mr. Bagri and Mr. Malik had made statements to them which were of an incriminating nature. Thus, cross-examination became a crucial aspect of the case; the credibility of the Crown witnesses had to be successfully assailed by heaping doubt upon the testimony of these witnesses. As one might readily imagine, this put tremendous pressure on those assigned to conduct the cross-examinations. It was this critical time that taxed the abilities of the lawyers to the greatest degree; if the Trial Judge accepted the credibility of any of the key witnesses, the accused would likely be convicted.

After judgment had been reserved on December 3, 2004, the waiting period began. The next three-and-a-half months became a time during which we were all in something of a daze. We had been drained by the process of the past four years and to now attempt to focus on new cases and tasks was extremely difficult. Although we were able to recover some of our vigour, at the same time the suspense of the looming judgment increased, exacerbated by the fact that the media-reporting of the trial had been consistently negative to the defence. There had been occasions during the trial where we on the defence teams wondered if we had occupied the same courtroom as the media. Clearly, the Fourth Estate was against us. If there was any upside to this reporting it was only that, from time to time, we felt the need to reassess our objectivity.

On March 16, 2005, we gathered in the overflowing Air India Courtroom to hear the decision. The tension in the courtroom was palpable. Members and supporters of many of the victims' families were present in the public gallery as were members and supporters of the accused men's families, albeit on opposite sides of the gallery.

As he began, Justice Josephson read aloud only the concluding portion of his written judgment that was appropriate in the circumstances given that it contained 1,345 paragraphs and ran to 615 pages. As he started speaking, Justice Josephson began with his decision respecting Mr. Malik. This was quickly followed by his decision concerning Mr. Bagri. During the course of delivering his Reasons it was clear that everyone in the courtroom was overwhelmed by the solemnity of the occasion. As well, the suspense that permeated the occasion was incredibly intense. As we had learned throughout the trial, Justice Josephson was impossible to read.

In the end, Justice Josephson found both accused not guilty and discharged them from the Indictment. After almost four and one half years in custody, Mr. Bagri and Mr. Malik left the courtroom as free men.

There is a time-worn adage in the legal profession that *hard facts make bad law.* One way to translate this phrase is to say that the more horrifying a crime, the harder it becomes to adhere to those hallowed principles that distinguish our criminal justice system. Those principles are the presumption of innocence and the requirement that the Crown must prove its case beyond a reasonable doubt. Air India was truly a case of hard facts that would put any judge or jury to the test. In such circumstances, judicial courage is essential and Justice Josephson exemplified this quality. He concluded his judgment with the following, telling words:

> I began by describing the horrific nature of these cruel acts of terrorism, acts which cry out for justice. Justice is not achieved, however, if persons are convicted on anything less than the requisite standard of proof beyond a reasonable doubt. Despite what appear to have been the best and most earnest of efforts by the police and the Crown, the evidence has fallen markedly short of that standard.

Denoument

Thus the matter ended. A brief press conference was held in the pouring rain under a jerry-rigged canopy adjacent to the courthouse steps. Mr. Bagri's daughter, Inderdip, said a few words on behalf of her father, who stood silently beside her, appearing somewhat dazed. They then left, without any fanfare, in the company of family and friends. Mr. Bagri quietly returned to his home in Kamloops, B.C. and resumed his employment as a mill-worker.

The Bagri defence team repaired to my office where we spent some time doing a "recap" and determining how we were going to deal with, and catalogue, the mass of materials which had accumulated over the previous years. Later in the afternoon, we sat and talked over several potables, not in celebration, but with a sense of relief that the journey was finally over. Everyone was exhausted to the core. It had been a long four years with little respite; in a sense, it had assumed many of the characteristics of a forced-march, which had now come to an end. Now there was only one thing for us to do — take a few deep breaths and get on with the next case.

Noel O'Brien

CORPORA DELICTI: THE TRIAL OF JAKE WANNER

Noel C. O'Brien QC of Calgary law firm O'Brien Devlin MacLeod has been counsel in numerous high profile criminal trials across Canada, many of which have been the subject of prominent legal and media comment. He taught criminal law at the University of Calgary and has authored and lectured in his field. He is a Fellow of the American College of Trial Lawyers.

THE ANCIENT AND NOBLE Latin language remains useful within the realm of legal phraseology and is well-equipped to define the essential elements of most crimes. The familiar phrase, *corpus delicti*, literally translates as "the body of crime." In legal terms, *corpus delicti* is referenced as the requirement in law that compels a prosecutor, who seeks a conviction for an offence, to first establish that a crime has in fact been committed. In a murder case, the most obvious method of proof is the production of a corpse. The *corpus delicti*. But the failure of the state to produce a "body" is not always a legal impediment to a finding of guilt. Although rare in number, judicial history has shown that in some cases a conviction for murder can be rendered without a corpse. This is a story about an investigation and trial that involved not just one, but two missing bodies, the plurality of which engaged the phrase, *corpora delicti*.

This is the strange case of Jake Wanner, striking in its peculiarity because the evidence gathered by police would link him to the alleged murder and disappearance of two persons within a very brief period of time. The actual bodies of these alleged victims inexplicably vanished forever under the most bizarre circumstances. It would be left to the prosecution to present a case of murder against Jake Wanner without a corpse. It would be the task of a jury to determine if the absence of a body would impede the proof of the *corpora deliciti*. And as always is the case, it would be left to public opinion as to whether justice was served or denied.

What first struck me when I first met Jake Wanner in the Red Deer Remand Centre in January of 1989 was how out-of-place he seemed within the confines of the local lock-up. His quiet and paternal demeanor seemed inherently inconsistent with the brutality of the facts that formed the allegations of murder that he faced. He was fifty-six years of age, a short and stocky man, whose kindly face was capable of conjuring up feelings of pity and empathy in the observer. His eyes revealed a resignation to his fate, yet at the same time, a form of stark defiance in a belief that it was he who had been wronged by others.

Marital Failure, Blood, and a Locked Door

Jake Wanner met his wife, Winnie, when he was twenty-eight years old. They soon married and quickly had four children, two boys and two girls. The family moved to Alberta to start a new life in 1969. Initially, the family settled in at a small trailer court in Red Deer. It was in these early days that Jake and Winnie met Grant Whitehead and they soon became close friends, often camping, fishing, and hunting together. Jake and Grant even bought camping trailers that were identical to each other. They would joke over the fact that the keys to Jake's trailer also opened the doors of Grant's trailer. There was never a hint that Grant Whitehead and Jake's wife, Winnie Wanner, would someday become lovers.

Jake Wanner flourished in Alberta. He started a welding company and bought a pristine, beautiful eighty-acre farm southwest of Red Deer. It was there that he and Winnie raised their four children. But in the winter months of 1988, after more than twenty-five years of marriage, Winnie had become restless. Jake was not living up to what she wanted her husband to be. He was stubborn and short tempered, and even though he was never violent toward her, she felt an ongoing inherent fear of him. Winnie began to show signs of wanting to move on in her life; without Jake.

Their old family friend, Grant Whitehead, had sensed Winnie's unhappiness and, although almost fifteen years her senior, he began to lure her towards a sexual relationship. By the summer of 1988, Winnie had told Jake that she was moving off the farm to her own apartment. Winnie rented a small unit in the Parkvale Apartments on 45th Street in Red Deer, Alberta. She began spending a great deal of time with Grant Whitehead, more openly and brazenly as the months passed.

It was common knowledge among Jake's neighbours that he was very upset over the breakdown of the marriage. Some were later to say he was furious and in a rage over the loss of Winnie to Grant Whitehead. Grant would claim that Jake used his superior hunting skills to stalk him and Winnie no matter where they went. Needless to say, Jake and Grant were no longer friends.

Willard Nunweiller was a forty-two-year-old truck driver from Medicine Hat. He was a big man, towering over six feet in height and weighing over 235 pounds. He was also a good friend of Grant Whitehead.

On July 18, 1988, Willard Nunweiller came to Red Deer to visit with Grant Whitehead. Grant invited him to stay overnight in his camping trailer. It sat adjacent to the mobile home where Grant lived. The two men enjoyed a number of drinks together on the evening of July 18 and then Nunweiller went off to bed inside the camping trailer. The trailer door was locked. Grant left Willard to sleep off the drink and went over to visit with Winnie at her apartment where he stayed the night. It had been arranged that Grant would meet Willard Nunweiller for breakfast the next morning.

When Grant Whitehead arrived the next morning at his trailer, he noticed a large crowd of people and a heavy police presence. Large pools of blood had gathered around his trailer. Inside the trailer, there were only the gruesome signs of blood splattered everywhere. Willard Nunweiller was gone. Oddly, the trailer door remained locked.

Where is the Body?

Initially the police attention was focused upon Grant Whitehead as a potential suspect in the disappearance of Willard since Grant was the last person to be with him. But Whitehead was quick and certain in his direct accusation of Jake Wanner. He told police that Jake had a key that would fit his trailer. He claimed that Jake had blamed him for the marital failure and that the disgruntled man had been stalking him and Winnie for a long period of time. He immediately surmised that Jake had entered the trailer with homicidal intentions in the mistaken belief that it was Grant Whitehead who was lying asleep inside. Grant Whitehead was convincing in his version of events and immediately the police directed their attention towards Jake Wanner. The RCMP were made aware that Jake, albeit a short man, was powerful in strength and that he was known to have single-handedly lifted the rear axle of a pick-up truck. They surmised that Jake could have easily pulled the 235-pound Nunweiller from the trailer after killing him.

Despite a flurry of police activity and news reports about the misfortunate Willard, his body was not located by police. There was no trace of him to be found other than the pools of blood splattered in and around his sleeping quarters. He simply vanished. The police publicly announced that they had no clues as to his disappearance but privately the RCMP gave considerable weight to the theory presented by Mr. Whitehead. There was a clandestine focus by police on Jake Wanner as the prime suspect in the disappearance of Willard Nunweiller and the police were going to watch him closely.

For several months, Grant Whitehead and Winnie Wanner lived in fear of Jake. They understood that the evidence was not sufficient to arrest Jake for the murder of Mr. Nunweiller but that did not prevent them from believing that their lives were in grave danger. Mr. Whitehead armed himself with a .308 rifle that he carried with him at all times in his vehicle. He gave Winnie a .22 caliber rifle that she kept in her Parkvale Apartment in a small closet near the entrance door. Grant never did believe that the diminutive Winnie would be capable of using it.

Several months passed without a single sign of Willard Nunweiller, alive or dead. On December 31, 1988, Grant and Winnie celebrated the beginning of the New Year. Almost six months had passed since the disappearance of Mr. Nunweiller and they may have let their guard down somewhat. Yet throughout these anxious and uneasy months, one particular RCMP officer made a habit of checking in on Winnie from time to time and provided her with immediate access to police whenever she needed reassurance or comfort for her wellbeing.

On the evening of Tuesday, January 3, 1989, heavy snow began to fall in the Red Deer area. Jake Wanner told his son, Nathan, that he was going out to have an invoice signed by a customer and inquire about some welding jobs in the oilfields around Eckville, Alberta. Nathan recalls him wearing a black parka-style jacket. Jake left at about 6:30 *p.m.*

In the meantime, at around 7:00 *p.m.*, Grant Whitehead placed a phone call to Winnie Wanner. They spoke of a television show that she was watching and Grant promised to come over later on that evening. Everything seemed normal. Mandi Robbins, an eleven-year-old girl, lived in a house directly across from the Parkvale Apartments where Winnie Wanner resided. Later, Mandi would claim that at about 9:30 *p.m.* she saw a suspicious man walking in circles outside the front of the apartment. She observed him carry a very large and heavy duffle bag that he eventually dumped into the front seat of his white truck. She would later testify that she noticed that the truck did not have a tailgate and agreed that the single photograph shown to her by the police of Jake Wanner's white Jeep pick-up truck was the same one that she had seen. The tailgate of Jake's truck was painted black, which the RCMP surmised would appear to an onlooker at night as though the vehicle was missing a tailgate.

True to his word, Grant Whitehead showed up at the Parkvale Apartments at 10:00 *p.m.* He thought it odd that the apartment door was not locked when he entered Winnie's unit. He called out for Winnie but there was no response. He immediately went for the closet where she kept the .22 rifle and noticed that it was standing dutifully in its rightful spot. Grant was numb with fear as he moved towards the small bathroom and into a scene of stark horror. The sliding shower door was smashed. There was dark red blood splattered all over the walls adjacent to the tub. The toilet bowl was full of blood. A long 38-centimeter carving knife was lying on the floor. But Winnie Wanner was nowhere to be seen.

Grant immediately contacted the RCMP. There was no question in the minds of the police as to who was responsible. The investigators rushed to the Parkvale Apartments and met with Grant Whitehead and assessed the scene.

By 11:30 that same evening, Jake Wanner walked into his own home. His son Nathan was there with his friends. Nathan was to later testify that Jake looked "perfectly normal" although he found it odd that Jake was wearing a different jacket than the one that he had on when he left the home. He also thought it odd that Jake decided to do a load of laundry almost immediately upon his return to the farmhouse.

Jake had not been home very long when a procession of RCMP police vehicles, lights lit up and flashing, filed down the lane to his farmhouse. Several officers swarmed into the house and without formal introductions, immediately arrested Jake Wanner for the first-degree murder of his wife, Winnie Wanner. The fact that Jake was already on the police radar for the suspicious disappearance of Willard Nunweiller propelled the RCMP officers into immediate action. There were no other suspects. It was as though the crime was expected to occur and the arrest of Jake Wanner was merely the culmination of the inevitable expectations of Grant and Winnie having come true. No preliminary investigation was warranted in the minds of the police this night.

A subsequent search of Jake Wanner's farmhouse in the early morning hours did not yield much in the way of incriminating evidence except for one thing. A peculiar array of articles of clothing, still damp from a recent washing, were located in the old-fashioned wringer-style washing machine that Jake would normally use for his oily work clothes. In the machine they found his black parka, socks, gloves, underwear and "white shirts." It was undoubtedly an odd combination indeed, found as they were in this antique washer with a glistening new model standing upright beside it. And just as important, was the discovery that some of the items were darkly stained with markings that the investigators immediately took to be blood.

Jake Wanner displayed the demeanor of quiet and soft-spoken men. An external observation of him would undoubtedly leave one with the impression that he would not be the kind of person likely to raise a hand against anyone. But there was also a firm resilience in him that rendered him immovable on matters of importance to him. This trait provided him with a fierce determination to prevail once his mind was made up. For the RCMP, Jake would prove a very difficult person to break.

Once Jake was arrested, he had very little access to the outside world. For the following three weeks he was held in the holding cells of the RCMP detachment. He sat alone, unrepresented by counsel, almost resigned to his fate, and eerily quiet. No one told him to remain silent; it was just in his nature to do so. The police attempted to use his isolation to their advantage, keeping him in the local cells instead of moving him to the Remand Centre as they would normally do during court adjournments. Jake Wanner would be interrogated time and time again without uttering a word that could incriminate him.

Frustration for the Police

Jake did not contact me until several weeks had passed since his arrest. During that time, he had endured a constant barrage of questions from police officers from one day to the next. It was a frustrating experience for even the most seasoned officers. At one point the police interrogators thought that they had Jake's agreement to show them the location of Winnie's body. They placed him in the back of the police cruiser but once inside, Jake would only refute any suggestion that he had made any admission to them.

Frustrated with their inability to have Jake Wanner speak with them, the police resorted to the use of family members to visit the accused man with the hope that he would reveal the whereabouts of Winnie. This included Jake's eldest son, Devon, and his son-in-law, Ed Evans. At best, this tactic led only to a few ambiguous statements from Jake that left the impression that Winnie's remains might be located within twenty-five miles of the city. Jake would neither deny nor admit anything of substantive value to the investigation.

When I ventured into this legal landscape that already had Jake Wanner defying the best of the police interrogators, I immediately realized that this was a man who would not be readily forthcoming to anyone. There was little use in demanding a full account of events from Jake at this stage of the process. It would take a long time to build up trust. But what was eminently clear was the fact that Jake Wanner had felt betrayed by his wife, Winnie, and his friend, Grant Whitehead. The tears appeared to come naturally to him when he spoke of that betrayal. Nevertheless, anyone speaking to him could have detected that he bore an underlying enduring defiance, if not a sense of righteousness, when he spoke of her.

The prosecutor assigned to this case was Crown Counsel, Luc Kurata. I had known Luc for some time prior to this matter. Luc is an affable country-style prosecutor who understood the rural life around Red Deer. It gave him some advantage over lawyers such as me who practice in large metropolitan cities. Luc easily presented himself as a "good ol' boy," the type who would tug on suspenders and rely on a jury's common sense to make out his case and bring home a conviction. He was good at it and those who underestimated Luc's abilities as a prosecutor would soon suffer the consequences of letting down their guard. There was no doubt in Luc's mind that Jake Wanner was culpable in the killing of his wife. There was no doubt in his mind that he was also responsible for the death and disappearance of Willard Nunweiller. But no one was more cognizant of the fact that the prosecution had no bodies to produce as part of its case. He understood the difficulties of proving a murder case in the absence of a corpse and understood that the circumstantial evidence to overcome this defect would have to be powerful and strong.

Crown prosecutors and defence lawyers are often friends. Luc would never let his solemn duty to try to put my client in jail for the rest of his life interfere or conflict with our out-of-court friendship. We both understood that this camaraderie must be left outside the courtroom door. So, it was natural to me that I would visit his home, sit in his dining room, with his motorcycle engine in a thousand pieces on the table, discussing every aspect of our upcoming trial.

Luc Kurata is a pragmatic man. He would readily test his own theories. He believed that Jake had killed Winnie and put her body in a large duffle bag and dragged her to his truck for eternal disposal under the watchful eye of Mandi Robbins. To satisfy his own mind that this could be done, Luc had convinced his own wife, complicit in his theory, to agree to leap into one of his old hockey bags in order to conduct his own personal experiment as to the viability of Jake being able to haul a body out of an apartment building. Coincidentally, both Winnie and Luc's wife were petite women and, satisfied of his own achievements, Luc was convinced that Jake Wanner would have had no difficulty in this gruesome task.

After Jake had spent approximately ten months in custody, I was able to obtain an Order from the Court of Queen's Bench directing that Mr. Wanner be released on bail. This was in part because of the delay in the process of having the matter proceed to trial quickly. However this change in his custodial status also provided the Crown with an opportunity to obtain a Wiretap Order, which enabled the police to place a bug in the house of Jake Wanner. The desperate search for any form of admission would continue.

The police investigators were hopeful that Jake would say something that would be indicative of his guilt. Very little came of it. Perhaps, the most damning piece of evidence arose in the course of a soliloquy by Jake Wanner during which he appeared to be speaking to a photograph of his missing wife. The recorded interception, directed at a mere apparition, allowed one to hear Jake Wanner's own words, spoken in agitation, perhaps even anger, calling Winnie out and blaming her for all of his woes and the circumstances in which he found himself. A dog was heard to yelp in the background.

The jury was never to hear this piece of evidence. It was excluded by the trial judge after a preliminary motion was made attacking its admissibility. The argument was based, more or less, on a technical violation with respect to the notice provided to the defence as required by law. The trial judge ruled that the Crown failed to comply with the provisions of the *Criminal Code* and, as such, this evidence would not be presented to the jury.

As the trial date neared, there were many conversations with Mr. Kurata, the prosecuting counsel. The aim, of course, was to attempt to negotiate a resolution on behalf of Mr. Wanner. After all, he was facing a charge of first-degree murder and although the evidence was circumstantial, he ran a significant risk of being convicted and serving the rest of his life in jail. The focus of these bartering sessions was based upon the underlying fact that Mr. Kurata had no corpse to produce. Although the prosecutor believed that the circumstantial case was a strong one, he eventually agreed to a plea bargain. The Crown would accept a plea of guilty to a lesser charge of manslaughter and make a joint submission for four years imprisonment. To me, this amounted to substantial victory. Instead of spending the rest of his years in jail, Mr. Wanner might realistically serve less than two years taking into account the parole provisions in place. The agreement even went so far as to permit the defence to select a particular judge who would undoubtedly be willing to accept this joint submission on sentencing.

There was only one hurdle to face in accomplishing what I felt to be a resolution weighing heavily in favour of my client. That was Jake Wanner himself. Jake did not argue against the sensibility of the joint agreement. In fact, although the judicial system was foreign to him, he readily accepted that the sentence was a very low one in the circumstances. He would go along with it. The problem arose, however, when I placed before him an Agreed Statement of Facts. This document would require Mr. Wanner to admit that he did in fact take the life of Winnie Wanner. When I placed before him the pages outlining the barest of facts that included an acknowledgment of responsibility in the taking of her life, Jake refused to sign it. He would not admit that he killed Winnie Wanner. He would not admit that he caused her death or her disappearance. The acceptance of the plea bargain may well have made eminent sense to an objective observer, but it would not sit well with Jake if he had to admit publicly that it was he who had taken her life. He would take his chances. The deal was off.

Facing the Judge and Jury

The trial of Jake Wanner was to be conducted by a judge and jury. The judge assigned to the case was The Honourable Mr. Justice Willis O'Leary, a dedicated and intelligent jurist, well known for being fair minded in his approach to his duties. The selection of a jury was uneventful. A jury of six men and six women were chosen in the Red Deer Court House.

Jake Wanner dutifully attended the trial every day, arriving promptly at the appointed hour in his grey suit and tie. He didn't look comfortable, tightly bound in the clothes he rarely resorted to. Anyone could see that he was a country man in a city suit.

Despite the horrific nature of the allegations against him, the irony remained that Jake Wanner was able to project a consistent affable demeanor. This did not surprise me since I recall that each time that Jake came to our office, several legal assistants would often comment on his gentlemanly persona. He appeared as a fatherly figure, quiet, polite, and unassuming. Certainly on the surface, Jake Wanner seemed a very likable man. He did not rub you the wrong way. It would be difficult for anyone meeting Jake for the first time to imagine that he could exhibit the degree of savagery necessary in a man capable of carrying out a premeditated and nightmarish massacre. A cold slaying that ended in the permanent disposal of bodies; corpses so well extricated from this Earth as to be never discovered again. I was hoping the jury would have the same impression of Jake.

When Mr. Kurata made his opening statement to the jury, he knew it was important to immediately bring home to the triers of fact that there was an unusual aspect attached to this case; the matter of the *corpus delicti*. His case would have to proceed in the absence of a body. The prosecutor knew that I would focus on that deficiency. It would fall upon him to emphasize the strength of his circumstantial case that, he suggested to the jury, was overwhelming in its nature.

The Crown had elected not to charge Jake Wanner with the murder of Willard Nunweiller. I believe that this was a strategic decision that, no doubt, had been made for a number of reasons. Although Mr. Nunweiller had not been seen again since his disappearance, the Crown understood that proof of his death could be problematic. He was a bit of a drifter in some respects. It may have been that the Crown felt that if he failed in the prosecution of Winnie Wanner, perhaps evidence would surface at some future time that may implicate Mr. Wanner in the demise of Mr. Nunweiller. He could then prosecute Jake for that crime. It has never been explained clearly as to why the Crown pursued the murder charge solely on Winnie Wanner. The circumstances of the disappearance of Willard Nunweiller could well have created an insurmountable incriminatory coincidence in the minds of the jury which may have lead them to the conclusion that Jake Wanner had killed both people. We will never know.

As the trial of Jake Wanner proceeded, Mr. Kurata advanced his theory that Jake Wanner was furious at the breakup of his marriage and that he clearly blamed his wife Winnie, and her lover, Grant Whitehead, for his loss. The Crown claimed that Mr. Wanner was fearful of losing half of his assets and the family farm. Mr. Kurata called witnesses who testified that Winnie had expressed a fear that Jake would in fact kill her over the marital breakdown. Although we were able to counter the effect of some of this evidence in cross examination, the irrepressible fact remained obvious to those who knew her; Winnie Wanner was not a person inclined to simply vanish on her own accord. That being the case, the Crown surmised that she must be dead.

The prosecution also relied heavily on the evidence of motive. The Crown called Grant Whitehead to assist the jury on this issue. He explained how he became the lover of Winnie Wanner and how Jake's anger at the discovery of this tryst led the two of them to arm themselves with firearms in fear of retaliation from the disgruntled husband. But there were elements of Grant's testimony that seemed troubling. I sensed he was trying too hard to be convincing in his details and overall he did not present as a person who was trustworthy. One was never really sure about Grant, or his role in all of this. He did not play the "victim" very well. But more significantly, he had been caught out in cross examination over some inconsistencies in his evidence with respect to when he saw Jake "skulking" around Winnie's home. He had testified before the jury that he saw him there on the day before the killing yet he had indicated to the police in his initial statement that he hadn't seen Jake for about three months previous to the disappearance of Winnie. He left me with the impression that he was quite desperate to work toward providing that crucial evidentiary link which he hoped would lead to a certain conviction of Jake Wanner. I trusted that the jury would feel the same.

The Crown theory was that the physical and forensic evidence seen in Winnie's apartment established her death and that there could only be one person who would have any reason to kill her. Only Jake Wanner could have had such a motive. The Crown attempted to supplement its case with the evidence of young Mandi Robbins who claimed that she saw Jake Wanner's truck outside the Parkvale Apartments on the snowy night of the gruesome discovery by Grant Whitehead. Mandi was eyeing the scene from her bedroom window across the street and said that she saw a man load a heavy bag into the passenger side of the truck. The young girl testified that Jeep truck was identical to that owned by Jake Wanner. The Crown would argue that the man had to be Jake Wanner caught out in the culmination of his murderous scheme as he was embarking upon the disposal of his spousal corpse.

A heavy snow storm on the evening of January third eliminated any possibility of obtaining tire tracks which might incriminate Mr. Wanner or assist in the location of the body of Winnie Wanner. Adding to the mysterious evaporation of a corpse was the fact that the body was not just hidden, but within a very short time frame, disposed of so effectively that police were never able to uncover its whereabouts. Of course, eventually this would allow me to urge upon the jury the improbability of a man being capable of eliminating any sign of the body of his murdered wife in a time span of less than two hours. After all, the Crown theory necessarily suggested that between the time he was alleged to have been seen loading the body in his truck at 9:30 *p.m.* and his arrival home on his farm during a snow storm at 11:30 *p.m.* he was able to dispose of the body of Winnie Wanner with such a degree of expertise that it would prevent the police from ever discovering even the slightest sign of her remains. These facts suggested that there was either a very well executed preplanned disposal or alternatively, they laid the groundwork for the argument that there was no murder at all.

The RCMP had spent enormous amounts of money digging up dump sites and oil field sites looking for Willard Nunweiller and Winnie Wanner. The two disappearances were indeed perplexing. In a sign of sheer desperation, the police engaged the services of two "psychics" to assist in the location of the bodies. All efforts, physical and supernatural, were to no avail.

Although the prosecution had no body to show the jury, Mr. Kurata turned the jury's attention to the "blood" that splattered the walls and tub in the bathroom in Winnie Wanner's apartment. The water in the toilet ran deep red with blood. The scene was admittedly horrific. The bloody aftermath of what appeared to have been a slaughter, coupled with the disappearance of Winnie, were powerful and potent pieces of evidence in the arsenal of the Crown. Mr. Kurata would rely upon his experts in forensic science and blood splatter analysis in the hope of convincing the jury that Winnie Wanner was dead and that

Jake Wanner was the brutal assailant who led her to her demise.

It was a relatively simple task for the Crown to produce evidence from a forensic analyst establishing that it was Winnie's blood that was discovered throughout her bathroom. But it is quite another thing to attempt to link that blood to Jake Wanner. The clothing that Jake Wanner had curiously placed in the washing machine when he arrived home at 11:30 *p.m.* on January 3rd had been seized by the police. There was solid evidence of staining on those clothes that the original investigators believed was Winnie's blood. However, Corporal Peter McLaren, an RCMP blood analysis expert, testified that his testing for blood remained inconclusive on the stains found on Jake's clothes. He testified that detergent would have effectively eliminated any scientific evidence of the blood. The Crown would be left with a potential inference of guilt based upon the fact that Jake dumped all of his clothes in the washing machine immediately upon coming home that evening. But he could not link any of Winnie's blood to those clothes.

Grappling with the Issue of Corpus Delicti

Inevitably, the prosecutor had to grapple with the issue of the *corpus delicti*. He had to prove that a "death" had occurred. Without the actual body, the Crown would now attempt to achieve this task by providing a graphic recreation of what must have occurred in the bathroom and ask the jury to conclude that Winnie Wanner was surely dead. In this regard, he called a blood stain pattern analyst who would attempt to provide his interpretation of the numerous smudges, drips and splatters of blood and their specific locations all in an attempt to create a clear picture of what must have occurred.

The expert, Sergeant Daniel Rahn, was well qualified in his field. He was also an RCMP officer. He parked himself confidently in the witness box, surrounded by numerous close-up photographs of the blood, and began to explain the meaning of each splatter, stain, smudge and drip. He had personally attended the bloody and gruesome scene in the bathroom of the Parkvale apartment of Winnie Wanner. He acquainted himself with the minutest details of anything forensically relevant. He provided his testimony in a very methodical manner, taking great pains to exhibit scientific objectivity despite his own membership in the investigating police force. He testified in such a matter of fact way that one could be forgiven for concluding from his testimony that the crime could only have happened in the manner he so expertly described.

Sergeant Rahn observed that the bathtub was a small, old-fashioned style with two sliding doors made of Plexiglas. The door would slide from left to right to allow one to enter the tub. He pointed out that one of the sliding doors had the Plexiglas smashed out of it during the violent struggle that clearly took place within the tub itself. For the benefit of the jury, he carefully analyzed the drips and the splatters of blood and explained how each assisted him in re-creating the struggle and the type of violent blows that left these telltale marks. His analysis allowed him to conclude that the assailant must have himself entered into the bathtub with the victim where he struck several blows to the victim's head with a blunt instrument, the skull positioned below the area of the tub taps. He testified that the absence of blood on the floor indicated that the Plexiglas sliding doors on the tub were actually closed at the time of the attack. The attack would have been vicious and violent in every respect, eventually leading to the smashing out of one of the Plexiglas doors. Something in Rahn's description of the detailed picture he painted for the jury did not sit well with me. An inherent inconsistency if you will. I hoped that this may be the very thing that would allow me to plant a seed of doubt in the collective mind of the jury. I would wait for the right moment. I would raise it in closing argument.

When the Crown had closed its case, it was time to make the final decision as to whether Jake Wanner would testify on his own behalf. In my mind, there was no doubt that Jake had to face the jury and give an accounting of the events that brought him here. The circumstantial evidence demanded it. In my opinion, the jury wanted to hear from Mr. Wanner. I could take comfort in the fact that Jake had always been consistent in his denial of responsibility for the death of Winnie. He would come across as a shy and reserved man but I knew he would not be swayed by anyone to admit to something that he had denied for several years leading up to this trial. I had no doubt that Mr. Wanner would never break down in cross-examination. After all, he withstood the lengthy interrogation by police for several weeks after his arrest when he was without counsel. He would not admit to the lesser charge of manslaughter on a plea bargain even if it meant eliminating a risk of life imprisonment. He refused to admit to causing the death of his wife to anyone before this moment. He would not break down now.

When Jake Wanner took to the stand in his own defence, the courtroom was filled to capacity. He was nervous and unacquainted with speaking in front of so many onlookers. He tearfully spoke of his love of Winnie Wanner. He seemed genuine. Despite all of the circumstantial evidence pointing directly towards him, his actual manner of delivery seemed to serve him well. He spoke of the many happy years that he had with Winnie and disputed the allegation that he was motivated by hatred and revenge. He claimed he helped her financially and even assisted in her move to her apartment. He came across sincere in his denial of guilt. His obvious defiance displayed during the course of the cross-examination by the Crown did not seem out of place. I think that a jury would expect that if an accused was truly innocent, he would naturally remain steadfastly defiant in the face of allegations that he killed his wife. For the most part, Jake Wanner held his ground.

There was however one issue of some concern that arose during the cross examination of Mr. Wanner by the Crown. The subject matter of the questions focused on the assortment of wet clothing that the police located in Jake's washing machine in hours after the disappearance of his wife. Mr. Kurata effectively cross-examined Mr. Wanner regarding the reasons as to why he would place his good white dress shirts in the old wringer style washing machine that he admittedly reserved for the task of cleaning his oily old work clothes? And why would he add to that load that curious collage of gloves, coat, socks and underwear? And why would all of these items form one load with his brand new modern washing machine sitting next to it? Why would he wash those clothes so late at night when it was Nathan who normally did the laundry in that household? And why would he come home wearing a different coat than the one his son saw him wearing when leaving the house earlier that evening? I recall Jake not having much to say in response to these questions; nothing much more than a shrug with the forlorn look of a man incapable of coining a lie in the face of an implicit but obvious accusation. All he could muster was a mumbled comment that it was cheaper to do everything in one load. I am sure I heard a few chuckles from behind me. Although his responses did not appear to be convincing, the manner in which he responded seemed to evoke a bizarre form of empathy. It is difficult to understand how sympathy can sometimes arise for even those accused of the most heinous of crimes; but sometimes it just does.

When Jake Wanner left the witness box, there was nothing more for the jury to hear. They were going to have to determine the fate of this man solely on what they had heard over the previous weeks. It would no doubt be a bur densome task for those uninitiated and unaccustomed to this solemn responsibility; to determine if they should condemn a man to languish in a prison for the rest of his life for the crime of murder in the first-degree solely on the basis of circumstantial evidence and in the absence of a corpse.

Mr. Kurata, for the Crown, would argue that the prosecution had a very strong circumstantial case that irrefutably led to the conclusion that Jake Wanner had killed his wife. The jury had never been told of the Nunweiller death and his mysterious disappearance or its potential powerful connection with the demise of Jake's wife. It could not form part of the Crown's argument to the jury. But Mr. Kurata did advance a very convincing argument of guilt, supported, he said, with the evidence of Winnie's disappearance without any rational explanation, the bloody signs evidencing her last moments inside her small bathroom, and the motivation of a vengeful husband. He argued that all of these factors, taken together, pointed to the inescapable conclusion that Jake Wanner was her killer.

Whenever I am called upon to address a jury, I strive to present myself as an advocate who truly believes in the argument being advanced. Where a lawyer hopes to effectively communicate his position to a jury, an element of sincerity is a necessity. This means that the manner of your presentation can be as important as the substance of your argument. It certainly helps if you have a genuine belief in the legitimacy of your argument, but that may not always be the case. In this case, I was torn. In some ways I could readily accept the strength of the Crown's argument but in the end, I always felt this continuing nagging doubt as to the guilt of Jake Wanner. I was hopeful that the jury felt it too. I hoped that I could convey an aura of sincerity in my submissions to them that may work towards creating that same doubt in their own minds.

Naturally I take my role as an advocate very seriously since the consequences of any error on my part can have devastating effects for my client. So when my eleven-year-old son, Chris, asked if he could drive to Red Deer with me to watch the final arguments to the jury, I was naturally reluctant for fear that my focus might be affected. His promise to stand firmly out of the way so as not to interfere with the serious task at hand was convincing. We arrived early at the courthouse on the morning of my submissions to the jury and Chris took his seat, unattended, in the front row. I was delighted that he could observe our judicial system at work and knew he understood that my sole attention would be on my duties in the courtroom.

Remaining Focused

And I did remain focused with the jury. I pride myself in the arduous preparation for a jury address that enables one to deliver a solemn and convincing argument, unaided by notes wherever possible. The world around you disappears when you take to your feet before a jury. Nothing else around you exists but the sound of your own words and the eyes of the jurors staring back at you.

But things were about to take an immediate turn for the worse. I began to present my theory to the jury by first addressing the many arguments that Mr. Kurata would present. As I was about to reach a crucial point in my argument, the presiding judge, Justice Willis O'Leary, interrupted me. "Excuse me Mr. O'Brien" he said. "We are going to have the jury step out". My instant reaction was one of shock. This was a first. I had never been interrupted during a jury address. Any concerns with respect to a jury address are traditionally dealt with afterwards and corrections could be made later in the judge's charge to the jury. But I know Justice O'Leary; this had to be serious. I was compelled to remain mute as the jury filed out of the courtroom.

When the last juror exited the courtroom, Justice O'Leary kindly indicated to me that there appeared to have been an issue with respect to "your son". My son? Apparently Chris began to feel a bit "woozy" with the graphic discussion about blood stains. Lawyers appear well equipped to set aside the effects of the stark horror of the facts of a crime because we tend to focus on the more scientific aspects of the gruesome evidence. Thankfully, an alert sheriff observed Chris turn white-faced as he began to collapse forward towards the wooden rail that separated him from the counsel table. The sheriff caught the ashen lad by the forehead in the nick of time to save us all from yet another bloody scene. He was carried from the courtroom and I remained oblivious to it all until Justice O'Leary spoke up. An ambulance was called.

As the jury convened among themselves, Chris was laying prone on his back outside the courtroom, being attended to by paramedics. The ambulance was quick in arriving. It turned out that he simply fainted and he was shuffled off to a spare room in the courthouse where he was kindly attended to by Luc Kurata's wife, and Crown witness, Nathan Wanner. How ironic indeed, as I plodded on before the recalled jury to conclude my address fearing that all hope of eloquence might be lost in the interruption.

Of course, I laid bare my concerns with the case for the prosecution. First and foremost, there was no body. The absence of a body, I pleaded, did give rise to a possibility that perhaps Winnie Wanner became restless, maybe even fearful, and simply wished to extricate herself from her existing life in Red Deer.

The jury was faced with the stark question; was Winnie Wanner really dead? The issue had to be grappled with. It could not be avoided. Despite strong evidence to suggest that she probably was, the real point of the trial was to determine if this jury could be convinced of her death beyond a reasonable doubt.

It is always difficult to know for sure what factual seed you plant in the mind of a jury may blossom into a reasonable doubt. I am convinced it can arise from the smallest piece of evidence, sometimes innocuous in its nature. In Mr. Wanner's trial I took a chance that the jury may find a reasonable doubt anchored to the testimony of the expert blood spatter analyst, Sergeant Dan Rahn.

Sergeant Rahn's evidence was that the assailant had been inside the tub engaged in a brutal and vicious attack on the victim. The blood splatter spurted some ninety-eight centimeters up the walls surrounding the bathtub and the numerous drips, stains and splatters were analyzed by the expert in a manner that enabled him, according to his testimony, to paint a true picture of Winnie's savage death. The attacker, he said, had entered into the bathtub itself and the sliding doors were shut closed while he delivered the murderous blows. The scenario was so violent in the close quarters that one of the sliding Plexiglas doors was smashed out.

However a closer look at the crime scene photographs of the bloodied bathtub revealed a curious image. Standing untouched along the lip of the bathtub adjacent to the wall were several bottles of shampoo, body lotion, water softeners and a razor. The spattering of blood on these articles themselves and the corresponding splatters on the adjacent wall beside them, made it clear that not a single one of these items had been disturbed. Not a one had been knocked over. Sgt. Rahn admitted that this was so in cross examination. It was a question that had to be posed to the jury; how could it be possible that during the course of a murderous struggle of such a violent nature inside the small confines of a bathtub, that not one of these articles would have been disturbed or toppled over? An alternative explanation did exist; that it was a staged scene? If the jury had a doubt about this, they would be forced to acquit.

With the arguments of both counsel completed, Justice O'Leary gave his usual fair charge to the jury and sent them on their way to decide the ultimate fate of Jake Wanner. In the meantime he remained on bail throughout the deliberations of the jury and displayed a remarkable calm as he left the courthouse to await the verdict. The prosecutor, Luc Kurata, and myself, with our jobs now completed, prepared ourselves to wait it out.

It was late evening when Luc and I were in the Barristers Lounge in the Red Deer courthouse. It was not uncommon for defence counsel and Crown counsel to have a well-earned drink or two after a long-fought trial while the jury ruminated about the guilt or innocence of the accused. While we waited, a stocky RCMP officer approached Mr. Kurata seeking a private consultation. Luc left with him only to return a few minutes later to advise that the RCMP had located some "bones" in an area not far from Jake Wanner's farm. Along with the bones the police also had located some "eye drops" which were similar to those known to be used by Winnie Wanner. The bones had been sent to Edmonton for a preliminary forensic analysis.

What more could happen? This trial just continued to take a different course at every turn. Both Luc and I had thought that the case had been finished but now we faced another complicated issue. We debated amongst ourselves as to whether or not the case was in fact closed to any further applications or whether the Crown could re-open its case or even seek a mistrial. The verdict had not yet been rendered, he argued. In my view, the case was now in the hands of the jury and that no further evidence could possibly be admissible.

Needless to say, I was truly in a panic internally, although I tried not to let it show. We spoke of the possibility of speaking to the trial judge to get some direction on the matter. Then, without advance warning, the same police officer entered the Barrister's room. His face told me that he clearly bore important news. He did. The bones were not those of Winnie Wanner. In fact, they were not of any human being at all. They were "deer bones". Relief swept over me. Jake Wanner was not even aware that all of this was going on as he awaited the verdict back home on his acreage.

I am sure that every defence counsel always remembers the specific details of where he was and when it was that he is called back to the courthouse because a verdict has been reached by the jury. This case is no different. I sat in the small lounge in the Courthouse. I recall contacting Jake by phone and meeting him as he entered the building. There was a large number of media taking his photograph as he walked in. It was a strange feeling rushing into the courtroom with him knowing that there was a possibility that he would never see freedom again. It crossed my mind that Jake was a stubborn and silly man in some respects, because he didn't need to risk his life had he accepted the original plea bargain. He would not be facing the prospect of serving a sentence of life imprisonment without parole for twenty-five years, had he only accepted my advice to take the plea to the charge of manslaughter which would be accompanied by a very low sentence. I guess it could be said that Jake, in his own way, was a very brave man to place his trust in the judicial system.

I recall that these things were in my mind as the jury filed out. The process always seems so long when the jury is polled, each and every one of them, to ensure that all twelve are sitting in their rightful seats before the verdict is announced. It is time consuming and excruciatingly painful. I looked straight into the faces of each of them, six women and six men. All of them stone faced for fear of tipping their hand. There was nothing more that could be done. It was fate now.

After what seemed to be an eternity, the clerk asked the jury if a verdict had been reached and if so, "so state by your foreperson." Up onto his feet rose the foreman, a small piece of paper being shuffled in his hand. From his mouth sprung forth the most powerful and significant words that he probably ever uttered to anyone in his life. He declared, "Not Guilty." Those same words were to be the headlines of the *Calgary Sun* the next morning. Jake Wanner had gambled and had won.

A Continuing Mystery

Jake Wanner died recently. His obituary indicated that he loved to fish and camp and spent the winters in Arizona. He was a good dancer and regularly attended the local dances and was well liked by the ladies in attendance. He came to see me several years ago in my office. I had not spoken to him in the intervening years since the trial had taken place. He told me what he had been doing to keep busy during the course of his retirement years. He never mentioned Winnie Wanner. He never mentioned the trial.

I admit that as a defence lawyer, you develop a habit of coming to a certain conclusion, one way or the other, as to the guilt or innocence of your client. It is not an opinion which is really relevant during the course of our challenge to defend the accused. But nevertheless, we are human and we do formulate a view as to what really occurred. But Jake Wanner's case is very different. I have never really been quite sure, in my own my mind, exactly what had happened. There was something about the evidence of Mr. Whitehead that made me uncomfortable, yet there was nothing that I could find in my preparation to suggest that Winnie Wanner would be the type of person to simply disappear on her own. And then there was Jake himself, who vehemently refused to accept a minimal sentence and eliminate the risk of life imprisonment on the basis that he could not sign off on a document in which he would have to admit to killing his wife. The blood splatter analyst testimony did create some concern in my mind and perhaps in the mind of the jury also. Strangely though, the fact remains that Winnie Wanner and Willard Nunweiller have never been seen since. And now, the only person who might know what had occurred is also gone.

Shortly after Wanner's death, I received a phone call from one of the RCMP officers involved in the original investigation. He wanted to ask me whether, in light of Jake's death, I could shed some light on the whereabouts of either of the missing bodies. I think I was a bit taken aback by the question itself. Did he really think that I had this information locked up in my head all of this time. Or perhaps he was just curious like me. As I told the officer, I suppose it will just have to remain a mystery.

Joel Pink

THE ANTIGONISH BEECH HILL MURDERS

Joel E. Pink QC has been a criminal lawyer for forty-four years in Halifax, Nova Scotia. He was a Faculty Member of the National Criminal Law Program for thirty-one years, President of the Nova Scotia Barristers Society, and taught at Dalhousie School of Law. He is a Fellow of the American College of Trial Lawyers and The International Society of Barristers and co-editor of From Crime to Punishment, *now in its eighth edition.*

WAS JUSTICE DONE in the case of *Her Majesty The Queen in the Right of Canada v. John Alexander MacKenzie*? As it was related to them by an experienced trial judge, a jury of his peers used common sense to decide on a verdict, applying the basic principles of law — presumption of innocence, burden of proof, and proof beyond a reasonable doubt. It is not for me, or anyone else, to question whether that jury was right or wrong.

The accused, Johnny MacKenzie, had some troublesome years in Ontario where he'd accumulated a few minor criminal convictions like assault, theft under $200, and discharging a firearm. After serving some jail time, he decided to turn his life around, returning to his native Nova Scotia to embark on a new beginning. His dream was to be a homeowner in the area where his parents and grandparents had once lived, in Antigonish County. In August 1986, he bought two acres that had once been used as a garbage dump by some local residents. There was a clear patch of land, on which he placed a mobile home trailer. It was only later that he realized his dream had turned into a nightmare.

Living within a few kilometres were Johnny's neighbours; John Boucher and brothers Joey and Edmund Deon. Because he had impeded on their territory by setting up a trailer where they used to go four-wheeling, these neighbours relentlessly harassed him and violated his peace. They dumped garbage on his property; tore up his front lawn and garden; bulldozed his driveway; threatened to kill him; broke into his trailer and chained the back door so he couldn't get in; placed stolen goods on his property and then reported him to the RCMP; dragged his dog behind an ATV until dead; and killed his cat, leaving its remains on his back steps. The police did not react and I was lead to believe that they did not like going to the Beech Hill Road because of the unexpected and that when they were faced with a complaint, the other side would deny it.

Johnny, a meek and mild man, pleaded with all three men to stay off his property and leave him to live in peace. They ignored and laughed at him, making his life so miserable that it could have driven most people to move away and give up their dream. Johnny, however, never gave in to their cruel acts and refused to be forced out by these three men. The harassment became so intolerable that he slept on his trailer floor with prayer beads, hoping that bullets being fired in the vicinity of his trailer would not hit him. He also turned to alcohol to calm his nerves and for the six weeks prior to June 23, 1989, he never saw a sober day.

He spent the day of June 23, 1989 drinking heavily with his friend, William Cogger. According to a Forensic Toxicologist, Johnny's blood/alcohol concentration at 4:30 *a.m.* on June 24, 1989 read as high as 330 milligrams of alcohol per 100 milliliters of blood; a number that means he was four times over the legal driving limit.

Between 3:30 and 4:00 *a.m.* on June 24, 1989, Lorraine Boucher, wife of John Boucher, heard gunshots. Not realizing the significance of the sounds, she drifted back into a sound sleep until morning, without her husband beside her. A neighbour, Daniel Girrior, also heard three shots at 4:17 *a.m.*, another two shots at 4:58 *a.m.*, and approximately thirty seconds later heard two more shots. On each occasion that he heard the shots, he testified before a Supreme Court judge and jury, he looked at the clock in his bedroom. According to Mr. Girrior it was not unusual to hear gunshots in Beech Hill at any hour of the day or night.

William Cogger, Johnny's friend, stayed over for the night in Johnny's trailer. He woke up between 4:30 and 4:45 *a.m.* and, according to his watch, he saw Johnny sitting at the kitchen table with a beer in his hand.

In the early morning hours of June 24, 1989, Lorraine Boucher discovered the body of her husband on their front lawn and called the RCMP. The RCMP responded to the scene immediately and they discovered John Boucher, deceased. Upon further investigation, the body of Edmund Deon was discovered in his bed, dead from gunshot wounds, and at the house diagonally across the road, Joey Deon was found in his truck, fatally injured from a gunshot wound. He died from his injuries a short time later.

The RCMP sent in a veteran and experienced investigator, Sergeant Robert Peebles, to assist Constable Kevin Cleary from the local detachment in the homicide investigation. Sergeant Peebles arrived at the scene at 10:45 *a.m.* and was directed to the residences of John Boucher, Edmund Deon, and Joey Deon. It was quickly determined that John Alexander MacKenzie was likely their prime suspect because of his many reports of harassment against the three men.

The police spent the entire day gathering evidence at the scene. During the day, Johnny's well was drained and the RCMP located a pair of shoes and a 22-calibre gun, which later proved through forensic testing to be the murder weapon used in the shooting of the three men.

At approximately 7:30 *p.m.*, the RCMP obtained a search warrant for MacKenzie's trailer. They found a 22-calibre rifle but determined that the gun had not been fired. As a result of this information, Corporal Kenneth W.L. Diamond and Sergeant Peebles proceeded to the residence of George Levangie on the South River Road, Antigonish County, where they located Johnny at 8:41 *p.m.* The RCMP described him as a person "who had been drinking heavily." They immediately placed him under arrest for the murders of John Boucher, Edmund Deon, and the wounding of Joey Deon. He was given the police caution, read his rights under the Charter, and then escorted back to the detachment. A statement was not taken from him at this time due to his level of intoxication. Johnny was remanded to the Antigonish County Correctional Centre.

At 9:46 *a.m.* on June 25, 1989, Sergeant Peebles and Constable Cleary summoned Johnny from his cell and he was taken to an interrogation room in the superintendent's office at the Antigonish Correctional Centre. Sergeant Peebles advised him of his right to remain silent, to instruct counsel, and that if he could not afford a lawyer he could contact Nova Scotia Legal Aid and counsel would be provided for him. After the interview, at 10:15 *a.m.* he made a request to phone his sister to see if she could contact a lawyer for him. The phone call was made, and Sergeant Peebles was informed that a legal aid lawyer would be arriving shortly. The legal aid lawyer arrived at 10:37 *a.m.* Between the hours of 10:15 and 10:37 *a.m.*, Sergeant Peebles did not remove himself from the interrogation room. The police knew that Johnny was a talkative person and would converse freely if the opportunity was presented. He did.

In Nova Scotia, if one is charged with murder he/she at the time has the right to request counsel of his or her choice. Johnny did not wish to accept the services of Nova Scotia Legal Aid. He requested me, and I received a call from Nova Scotia Legal Aid requesting my services on June 25, 1989.

The RCMP charged John Alexander MacKenzie with three counts of first-degree murder. Shortly after I was contacted, I was informed that Johnny had made a statement to the police between the hours of 9:46 *a.m.* and 10:37 *a.m.* and that he had made an earlier statement to his friend William Cogger.

The question was: How was I going to maneuver around the admissions that Johnny made in his statement to the police — admissions to William Cogger, the murder weapon and the shoes in his well — and still try to establish the legal defences of provocation and drunkenness?

The case was a legal nightmare. There was no room for maneuvering. The Crown was not interested in discussing a guilty plea to manslaughter; they thought they had an airtight case. This was the case to put to the test the three basic principles of law: the presumption of innocence, the burden of proof, and proof beyond a reasonable doubt. These fundamental rights guaranteed under our Charter would be confidently put to a jury who would make every effort, under the terms of their oath, to reach a verdict that was fair, just, and in accordance with the evidence and the law.

The presiding judge was the late Honourable Justice Alexander Murdoch MacIntosh, judge of the Trial Division of the Supreme Court of Nova Scotia, an experienced trial judge. During the *voir dire* to determine the admissibility of the statements, the police painted a picture of John MacKenzie as a sober individual who was fully aware of his surroundings and willing and eager to talk. Even after he requested a lawyer, Johnny kept on talking without any promises, inducements, or threats from the police. As far as the Crown was concerned, any statement made by Johnny was freely and voluntarily given.

As defence counsel, I had to portray a different picture; a person who was an alcoholic, who had not been sober for six weeks and was extremely hung over. My task was to try and present the theory that any information elicited from Johnny was not from a person with "an operating mind." It was at this point that I decided to throw in a possible *Charter* violation — the right to remain silent (after the police were informed that counsel was on their way).

After hearing defence evidence tendered at the *voir dire* from a forensic toxicologist, a psychiatrist, and John Alexander MacKenzie, the trial judge ruled that Johnny's conditions were consistent with symptoms of alcoholic withdrawal.

The learned justice was unable to accept the opinions of the experts about the lack of ability of the accused to appreciate the consequences of making incriminating statements to the police and giving up right to counsel. He did, however, accept the evidence of Sergeant Peebles and Constable Cleary that the accused was sober and alert and aware of what was going on, so the statements made between 9:46 *a.m.* and 10:05 *a.m.* were admissible, those subsequent to that time, not admissible.

The Crown had thrown the first pitch and it was a swing and a miss for the defence. However, there has to be three strikes before you are out. I never gave up hope. You just never know as a case unfolds where there might be a new development that may be beneficial to your client. Most importantly, Johnny had the benefit of having his case heard by a jury who I felt would be sympathetic towards him.

What was the jury going to hear as a result of the judge's ruling on the *voir dire* in regards to his statement? The learned trial judge's ruling allowed the jury to hear the content of the statement that Johnny made to the police between 9:46 *a.m.* and 10:05 *a.m.* It was transcribed as follows:

> I think they're dead. They never leave me alone, the cocksuckers. I told them to stay away from my property but that cocksucker, John Boucher landed up the other night … when Bill Cogger trying to let on, he dropped a rock on his foot. He came looking for beer. When he left around 3:00 *a.m.* that fucking Joey Deon came to the door. I told him to fuck off, that I was asleep. Then I guess it started bugging me and I snapped and I went down and shot them. First down to John Boucher's place and I couldn't see him. Then he came out and started shouting: "What are you doing around here?" I said: "I came to kill you, you cocksucker, and I shot him."

Constable Cleary said "How many times?" and Johnny replied:

> I don't know perhaps five. I figured I shot one I might as well do them all. Then I went up to Joey Deon's rapped on the door. I heard a moan. He was in the truck, drunk so I put two in the cocksucker. Then I went up to Eddie's. He wouldn't open the door so I put three in him through the door. Then I went in and finished him off. I was going to shoot myself but I wanted another drink so I ran home.

Constable Cleary then asked: "What did you do with the bullets?" and Johnny replied: "Threw them in the woods." He also stated, "I put them in the well and dress shoes in the well." Some of the facts as related in his statement could be proven to be inaccurate, for example, how many shots were fired.

How was the defence going to overcome the comments made to William Cogger at 4:40 *a.m.* on the day in question? The following is an excerpt from William Cogger's testimony at trial when he was asked by the Crown Attorney about his conversation with Johnny:

> Q. And what can you say – any conversation with him?
>
> A. Not too much right then because I didn't stir too much. I just woke up. I got up on my elbow and I could see John sitting at the end of the table.
>
> Q. Did you have any conversation with John MacKenzie?
>
> A. Well, I got up — no. I don't know when he … it'll be quarter to five or something like that and he came in and told me that he got the three sons of whores last night.
>
> Q. Okay, what did you say to that or was there any further conversation?
>
> A. No there wasn't too much more conversation. I told him I didn't want to hear about it at all. But I just figured it was just a dream or something he was reacting. He is a pretty good storyteller and he acts the stories out.
>
> Q. How many times did he tell you this?
>
> A. Oh maybe twice before I faced him. I went eye to eye with him and I said: "John, tell me this is not the truth or say something to that effect," and he said, "No, brother it's not true."

On cross-examination I somehow had to minimize William Cogger's evidence. I asked William Cogger the following questions on cross-examination:

> Q. My learned friend asked you about a conversation you had with John MacKenzie in the morning. As I understand it, after he made some initial comments, immediately thereafter, he, in fact, told you he didn't know whether or not it was a dream. Is that not true?
>
> A. He did, yeah.
>
> Q. And then when you pushed him a little further, he said, "No brother it's not true."
>
> A. That's correct.
>
> Q. In fact, John MacKenzie, when he has been drinking has been known

to talk a lot of nonsense. Would you agree with that sir?

A. Story after story.

Q. In fact you've told the jury about other problems that he may have been having, that he said on some other occasions he was going to shoot them, and then he was going to take his own life, he was drinking at that time, wasn't he?

A. Oh, every, every time he told me that.

Q. But you didn't take him seriously?

A. I told him one time — an occasion, John that would be a very poor trade.

Q. And in fact, you did not take him seriously?

A. I did not no, no.

Q. Let's face facts, Mr. Cogger when you are drinking and drinking to the state that you were drinking on this particular day, your memory of the events are clouded and you cannot honestly say for sure what John MacKenzie told you during the early morning hours of June 24, 1989.

A. No, not really. I could recollect some stuff but it's possible that a lot of the stuff he said I can't remember. I didn't.

Q. John MacKenzie was, or is a private person who likes to be alone and to basically be with nature. Would you agree with me there?

A. Yes very much so.

Q. And in fact, during the afternoon of the 23rd you in fact together with John took some peanuts and went down to feed the squirrels?

A. Yeah he has a squirrel station down in the woods just a little ways down and he feeds them.

Q. He not only had a squirrel station but he also had a calf, a little baby calf?

A. Right.

I figured now that some of the bluster had been taken out of the direct examination and I would have to deal with my client's statement to William Cogger during my final address to the jury.

Another hurdle that the defence had to overcome was the evidence of Lorraine Boucher, the widow of John Boucher. She portrayed her husband as a well-liked man who was a good neighbour and would never cause harm to anyone. She portrayed her husband as a good friend of Mr. MacKenzie.

I had to discredit her without allowing the jury to feel sorry for the grieving widow. Throughout her evidence she was tearful. Lorraine Boucher would not succumb to my suggestion that Eddie and Joey Deon and her husband were best friends. All that she would state is that they were casual acquaintances but on the other hand Joey and Eddie Deon were good friends of John MacKenzie. I started my cross examination by stating:

> Q. Would you agree that friends would not harass one another and then use the trailer — their tractors to dig up another's driveway?
>
> A. That's right.
>
> Q. Would you also agree with me that friends would not tear down one's gate that was erected to keep persons off of one's property?
>
> A. That's right.
>
> Q. Would you agree that one would not take another animal such as a cat and kill it?
>
> A. Yes.
>
> Q. Would you also agree with me that another friend would not take a friend's dog, drag it behind an All Terrain Vehicle, and kill it because the All Terrain Vehicle outran the dog and then dumped it on ones lawn - would you not agree that would not be a friend?
>
> A. Right.
>
> Q. If in fact, Mrs. Boucher, either your late husband, John Boucher, Joey Deon, or Edmund Deon did any of these things, would you not agree they would not be acts of a friend?
>
> A. No, I'd say they'd be acts of an enemy.

Twelve men and women would apply common sense to the issues, I felt. I kept reminding myself of the three basic principles of law: presumption of innocence, burden of proof, and proof beyond a reasonable doubt.

I tested Johnny during the *voir dire* and he did not make a good impression on the trial judge. That was most unfortunate; however, the real test would be whether the jury would believe him or be left in reasonable doubt after hearing his evidence.

Johnny did testify before the jury and he presented his evidence in a credible manner. He testified before a full courtroom. In fact the Sheriff's Department brought in the Fire Marshall to enforce the fire regulations and the overflow of spectators were escorted from the courtroom. The following is a portion of Johnny's testimony:

Q. Now Mr. MacKenzie, what was your condition as you eventually went to sleep on the floor that night?

A. Well I passed out, sir, from that moment I hit the floor to – I – the next — I was awaken at 3:05 *a.m.* with a lot of kicking and banging at my door. I looked at my clock, I have a little battery electric clock on a mantelpiece to see what time somebody would be coming bugging me. I could tell by the time who was there actually, because none of my people never came at that hour of the morning. it was 3:05 *a.m.* that morning – the morning of the 24th.

Q. Who was it?

A. It was Joey Deon. I told him to go away we're sleeping, leave us alone. And he slammed the door. There was talking and cursing going on and then he — I laid back on the floor, I didn't get up and I didn't look out the window but I did hear people's voices, I did hear bottles rattling and I did hear motors revving up and I did hear tires spinning and gravel flying in my driveway and I don't know how long this took place, maybe ten minutes, but they eventually left.

Q. What effect did this, of course, have upon you?

A. Well I – like I said I never got off the floor. I tried to get back to sleep because Bill Cogger and I had plans at seven in the morning. We were going to go down to St. Augustine's Monastery to the Shrine, and we were going to meditate and pray and I was — I had no intentions of staying drunk that day. I was going to sober up because I had to be to work Monday morning, sir. So while I was trying to get back to sleep on the floor I — I was thinking of all the problems that I was having, all the persecution with these people and I could not get back to sleep. So I did get up, and I said I'll go to sleep now and I grabbed a mickey of rum I had, Captain Morgan light, and I drank four good big mouthfuls in me and then I opened up a bottle of MacEwan's Ale and I used that for a chaser and then I went and laid back on the floor thinking I'd be — I'd go to sleep now. I continued to stay awake and these things of harassment and torture kept running through my mind, so I said there is one alternative to this, I've got stronger alcohol than rum. I went into the washroom and dumped out a good shot of Aqua Velva, which I know is seventy percent alcohol and I put some juice in it – out — out of the kitchen with it and I put juice in it, and I drank it down very fast so I couldn't smell it and taste it and I opened up a beer for a chaser and I laid down on the floor at that time, Sir. …

Q. What happened after you took the swig of Aqua Velva?

A. Well after I took this Aqua Velva, I opened up a beer and I laid down on the floor and the next thing I can honestly remember is waking up on the floor. I don't know how much time was evolved. I had a cap on my head. I had a coat – a small jacket on me and I had the idea that I had seen bodies on Beech Hill Road that night.

Q. What bodies did you see on Beech Hill Road that night?

A. Well to the best of my knowledge I – I thought it was a dream and I thought I seen John Boucher, Joseph Deon, and Edmund Deon. I thought – this is what I thought I seen, Sir.

Q. What is the next thing you seen, Mr. – the next thing you saw Mr. MacKenzie?

A. The next thing I – well this was disturbing to my mind. So I got up off the floor and the first thing I seen was a 22 pistol was laying on counter and I had – if it hadn't been given back to me or not I wasn't sure. The last time I seen it, it was taken from me and Lorraine – before I entered Lorraine Boucher's car. So I – I went to the fridge and I — I sat down and I was thinking, the gun is there and I think – I think I've seen bodies. If I walked by bodies and if the gun is here, it looks very much, whether I'm guilty or innocent, I'm going to be blamed anyway, because I'm the number one suspect, kind of the feuds that we've been having on Beech Hill. So I saw William Cogger kind of make a turn on the chesterfield. I went over and I talked to him. I told him what I – what I dreamed. He said, "You're absolutely crazy," he said, "you never left this house," he said. Well I said, "I pray to God I didn't Bill," but I said, "the pistol is on the counter and I don't remember seeing the pistol for the last twelve days. I was fighting with Boucher to get the pistol back." And over that conversation with Boucher, he said, he was talking to Corporal Seewald, and Corporal Seewald said, "Yes he knows MacKenzie got the pistol." He said, "I'm going up to Ray MacKenzie's place to get the pistol." Boucher told me this, and he said, "Lorraine is not giving you back the pistol until the police raid your place and until you sober up off this drunk." So I told this to Billy Cogger and I said "There's the pistol and I think I seen bodies. I walked by bodies. I'm going to definitely be first number one suspect." So I said, "Bill, do you think it's wise that I get rid of the shoes and pistol if I walked by bodies?" He said, "I – I — it's up – I don't know John." He thought I was fooling. He said, "It's up to you." Then he said, "I guess so." So I was in no state of mind to reason. If I thought I saw bodies, the most reasonable thing to do would be to phone help — help for these people but I did. I don't remember throwing the gun and the shoes in the well. I didn't know I put them there until the RCMP told me in the Antigonish lockup.

Q. Tell me, sir, in the early morning of June 23rd, today, do you have any recollection of shooting John Boucher, Edmund Deon, and or Joey Deon?

A. I have no recollection whatsoever of shooting these men and I examined it in my conscience very much since. That is why I insisted to be put in the Nova Scotia Hospital. It was my idea to go there so I could talk to a psychologist, psychiatrist to see if such a thing did happen. I did see the bodies some way or another. I've talked to these people and I've still – I've been told by professional people that I don't. …

Q. Okay. The question is, do you have any recollection today?

A. No, I do not, sir. And I do not have the nature to kill people under any circumstances, animals or humans.

The Crown did not call any rebuttal evidence to refute Mr. MacKenzie's evidence about the gun. It was then left for me to try to convince the jury that there was a reasonable doubt about who in fact fired the shots.

It is not the role of the defence counsel to judge his or her client's story but this is the role of the jury. It was my task to present to the jury a case that would leave them in reasonable doubt as to Johnny's guilt. If the jury was convinced beyond a reasonable doubt that it was Johnny who fired the shots, then the jury would still have to deal the issue of provocation, drunkenness, and the offence of manslaughter. That is exactly how I approached them: decide the first issue. If you should conclude that John MacKenzie fired the shots, then you may proceed to answer these other questions.

Going back to the first question of 'Who did it?' I said to the jury,

It is not a matter of looking at the evidence and saying to yourselves:

> In light of all the circumstances, who else could have done it? That is not the issue. The issue is: Has the Crown proved beyond a reasonable doubt that, in fact, it was John MacKenzie who shot the three men?
>
> In light of the evidence that you have heard in this Courtroom, can it be said that the Crown has met that burden. The Crown has called two witnesses in which they will try to tell you, that from their evidence you can conclude that it was in fact John MacKenzie."

I reviewed the discrepancies in timing: shots were said to be heard by one witness, against the other witness's assertion that MacKenzie was in his trailer at those times, drinking.

> Accepting what both of these Crown witnesses said, can it be said beyond a reasonable doubt so that you can say that you are sure that it was John MacKenzie who shot these three men?
>
> How did the gun get into the trailer? Well, that is not for us to answer, that is for them to prove. Surely they can prove that it was that gun that in fact killed those three people, but they still have to put John MacKenzie behind the gun with his finger on the trigger before you can say that, in fact, he committed any type of homicide.

Still in the context of the first question for the jury, when dealing with Johnny's statement I decided to remind the jury that once a statement has been ruled admissible it is in the same position as any other evidence and that they may accept it or reject it in whole or in part.

The same can be said about any statement that Johnny made to William Cogger. It was the jury's prerogative after examining all of the evidence to decide whether they will accept the evidence in whole or in part or not at all. The opinions of the judge, the Crown, or defence are not pertinent. At the end of my address I declared,

> As I commenced my address so I will end it by stating that the mere fact that John sits before you does not mean that he must be guilty. There is no burden upon John to prove that he is innocent. The burden is solely upon the Crown and that burden never shifts.

I completed my jury address by stating:

> Ladies and gentlemen of the jury, when you listen to His Lordship's instructions concerning reasonable doubt and you hear his instructions regarding the Crown's burden of proof, these are not empty slogans. They are the foundations of the Criminal Justice System in Canada. They are what our system offers my client as a way to answer such a serious allegation, a way to make a defence. Not only because of the great impact a conviction would have in these circumstances on my client and those close to him, but also because it is necessary for the law to recognize the errors and inaccuracies and the misconceptions that sometimes result. When we try to judge the truth of what a person says or what we try to infer, where there are gaps in the evidence as there clearly are here, then the words "reasonable doubt" will have a significant meaning. Listen carefully to His Lordship's instructions.

I was hoping for a favourable jury charge by the trial judge. In his fair and well-balanced four-and-a-half-hour address, the late Honourable Justice Alexander Murdoch MacIntosh made many pertinent remarks that a jury could use in deciding whether the Crown has proven their case beyond a reasonable doubt, emphasizing that they must, "Use your own common sense in judging the weight you give to the evidence."

The jury returned at 4:30 *p.m.* on the first day of deliberation to re-hear the evidence of William Cogger, Lorraine Boucher. and Daniel Girrior The jury deliberated for two-and-a-half days and at 2:23 *p.m.* on the third day a verdict was reached.

The townspeople crowded into the courtroom. There were people outside waiting for the verdict.

> Clerk: Members of the jury have you agreed upon your verdict?
>
> Mr. Foreman: We have.
>
> Clerk: What's your verdict on the first count?
>
> Mr. Foreman: The verdict on the first count is not guilty.
>
> Clerk: What is your verdict on the second count?
>
> Mr. Foreman: The verdict on the second count is not guilty.
>
> Clerk: And what is your verdict on the third count?

> Mr. Foreman: The verdict on the third count is not guilty.
>
> Clerk: Members of the jury, you have found the accused not guilty, are you in agreement?
>
> Body of Jurors: Yes.
>
> The Crown Attorney then requested the jury to be polled.
>
> Clerk: Your verdict on all three counts?

Each Juror responded "not guilty."

Those in attendance applauded and the judge, without thanking the jury or discharging the accused, said: "Well, the Court stands adjourned."

Johnny was free to return home. Upon his exit from the courtroom, townspeople clapped and cheered for him.

Johnny was given a ride home and in the car he thanked me for my assistance but said that it wasn't my work that had him acquitted, it was God's wishes. I accepted his words without comment. We shook hands and I returned to Halifax to wait and see if the Crown would appeal.

The date of the acquittal was April 20, 1990, and on May 17, just three days before the thirty-day time limit, the Crown appealed the verdict. There were eleven grounds of appeal. The appeal was heard on February 13, 1991, before a panel of three justices of the Nova Scotia Court of Appeal: The Honourable Justice David Chipman, the Honourable Justice Gordon Hart, and the Honourable Justice Gerald Freeman.

On April 11, 1991, the Court of Appeal handed down its 108-page decision. The majority allowed the Crown appeal and sent the matter back for a new trial. Justice Freeman dissented. Johnny gave us instructions to appeal the matter to the Supreme Court of Canada. Having a dissent in the Nova Scotia Court of Appeal gave Johnny the automatic right to appeal. On April 22, 1991, I filed a Notice of Appeal based on questions of law from the dissenting judgment of the Honourable Justice Gerald Freeman of the Nova Scotia Court of Appeal.

After oral argument, the Supreme Court of Canada reserved its decision until January 5, 1992 when Justice Gérard La Forest in his decision wrote,

> In my view it is acceptable for a trial judge to focus the jury's attention on the vital issues of its inquiry. Perhaps the jury should not be directed to compartmentalize their deliberations, but at the same time it is unrealistic to view a jury's decision as some epiphanic pronouncement of guilt or innocence; rather, the jurors engage in a

> deliberate process of evaluating the evidence presented to them.... As in this case, where a statement by an accused at trial is entirely at odds with a previous out-of-court statement by the accused, and the jury believes the statement at trial, or is left in reasonable doubt that it is true, then the jury must reject the out-of-court statement; the accused must be given the benefit of the doubt. In arriving at that conclusion, the jury should, of course, give consideration to the evidence as a whole.

Chief Justice Lamer in his judgment concurred with Mr. Justice La Forest.

> An analogy I often use in charging juries, especially in cases where the Crown's case was circumstantial, was that of a fisherman's net. The evidence presented at trial by the Crown seeks to establish factual propositions. Once established, facts may be used to infer other facts. In this way, established factual propositions intertwine to construct a net of such propositions. If a factual proposition is established as a mere probability or likelihood, and not beyond a reasonable doubt, it cannot be used to infer any further facts. The interweaving of facts breaks down and there is a hole in the net. A net with a hole, however small, is no useful net at all since there remains a critical factual proposition which is not consistent only with an accused's guilt. Thus, a fact which is not established beyond a reasonable doubt can play no part in the jury's decision to convict, either as a fact on which they rely to find an essential element of the offence, or as a fact used to infer such facts.
>
> Therefore, while it is a misdirection to instruct juries to 'reject' evidence, to tell juries to reject factual propositions which the Crown's evidence does not establish beyond a reasonable doubt is to state the law correctly. In the circumstances of this case ... there was only a single determination of credibility to be made. If they believed the accused's exculpatory evidence at trial, they must of necessity have disbelieved his inculpatory statements to the police. It must be remembered, though, that the accused need never establish his or her versions of events beyond a reasonable doubt; that standard only and always applies to the Crown. The accused must only raise a reasonable doubt with his or her evidence, even where he or she bears an evidentiary burden.

The judgment of the Supreme Court of Canada upheld the instructions of Justice MacIntosh and stated that he was not in error in his charge to the jury on statements attributed to the accused. The Supreme Court of Canada allowed Johnny's appeal and reinstated the acquittal of the jury.

I chose this murder case for this book not because I was successful before the Supreme Court of Canada but because this case encompasses every basic principle of law that we learn in the first-year criminal law course. Regardless of the charge, never forget that these three basic principles of law always apply; presumption of innocence, burden of proof, and proof beyond a reasonable doubt, and if at any time there is any doubt that doubt must be found in favour of the accused. This case also highlights the importance of the jury as triers of fact where opinions of the Trial Judge, the Crown Attorney, or even the Defence counsel are irrelevant. Questions of credibility and the weight to be given to any evidence is for the jury to decide.

Patrick Fagan

BOYS WILL BE BOYS

Patrick C. Fagan QC commenced law practice in 1988, after ten years of RCMP service. He was appointed Queen's Counsel in January 2008. He has defended a number of high profile cases at all levels of Court in Alberta, in other Canadian jurisdictions, and in the Supreme Court of Canada. Mr. Fagan raised five children during his policing and university years, two of whom have joined him in practice in his Calgary firm.

Every now and again for no good reason the Universe, in its infinite wisdom, decides to reach out and drive a stake through the heart of an entire community. On Friday, May 25, 2001, such would be the fate of the unsuspecting residents of Chestermere, Alberta.

Chestermere is located on the south side of the Trans-Canada Highway approximately twenty kilometres east of Calgary at one of those welcome bends in an otherwise razor-straight prairie road. According to official reports, there were 3,742 people living in Chestermere as of May 2001. While it is certainly true that most Chestermere residents work in Calgary, all have chosen to live in a small town. They have done so for the same reason given by small-town residents since the dawn of urbanization — quality of life.

The defining geographical attribute and pride of Chestermere is a pristine spring-fed lake of modest proportion and depth around which the community has steadily grown. One cannot help but notice the vivid contrast created by this placid natural endowment and the not-so-distant, imposing skyline of downtown Calgary.

Shortly before 2:00 *p.m.* on May 25, 2001, upwards of seventy high school students gathered at John Peake Park on the northwest shore of the lake. There, only a few hours before commencement of graduation ceremonies for the Class of 2001, they would all witness a killing.

For Tyler Trithart and Ben Caron, life in Chestermere was looking good. Both boys enjoyed the love and support of a caring family, close friends and all the good times that a small town can offer a couple of testosterone-fueled sixteen-year-olds.

Tyler had a passion for vintage cars and dreamed of being an automotive mechanic. He also had penchant for adopting stray animals, which encompassed, to the delight of his two younger brothers, a lame duck. The Trithart boys were counting the days until the family left for the trip of a lifetime — Disneyland. Things were tight but Tyler's parents, Fern and Nolan, were working opposite shifts to make it happen and Tyler was picking up the slack by babysitting his brothers.

As for Ben, he had a new part-time job, a girlfriend, honours standing in his recent Grade 11 report card and he had just attained, as had Tyler, what is for every red-blooded Alberta male the holy grail of adolescence — a driver's licence. Ben dreamed of being a peace officer and, like Tyler, seemed to take genuine satisfaction in helping others. Ben was the Caron's only son.

Tyler didn't have a steady girlfriend as of May 25, 2001. He did, however, have a bit of a crush on a girl called Meghan who he had known since grade four. As chance would have it, as of May 25, 2001, Meghan was Ben's girlfriend. The boys would be inexorably drawn into a protracted heated argument over Meghan during which ill-conceived and bravado-laden threats were exchanged. Honour (that is, teenage peer pressure) would demand satisfaction and by 11:00 *a.m.* rumours of a pending fight seized the sanguinary imagination of the student body. Neither boy was a fighter and neither boy really wanted to fight. None of that mattered, the die had been cast.

The unspoken venue of choice for pugilistic endeavors was and always had been John Peake Park; the agreed time of engagement was 1:30 *p.m.* At least an hour before the scheduled event, jacked up diesel trucks, sedans and minivans brimming with titillated progeny started to arrive at the park. It would be an epic way to kick off grad weekend and the consensus was that it just doesn't get any better than this.

As with all social events of consequence, nothing ever goes quite according to plan. Minutes before the much-anticipated arrival of the two hapless combatants, the police appeared on the scene. They had noticed the gathering and had driven up to enquire as to the reason. Their concerns were immediately allayed by a posse of familiar and disarming bright-eyed locals: "Just hanging out officer," "Nope, no drugs and no alcohol," "Yep, we will be careful at grad tonight," "You have a nice day now officer." By the time the patrol car taillamps faded in the distance, Ben and Tyler were eyeing each other from across the park.

According to witnesses, as Ben and Tyler walked towards each other, the crowd closed in behind them chanting *"Fight, Fight, Fight."* Both boys looked like they wanted to be somewhere else. A simple word from anyone in the crowd might have turned the tide. On this day, however, there would be no reprieve. This implacable assembly had come to see a fight and by God there would be a fight.

What happened next is not entirely clear. Yes, there were sixty to seventy eye witnesses but as any experienced trial lawyer will tell you, it tends to be much more difficult to prosecute a case with a multitude of witnesses than a handful. Some say that Tyler's hands were at his side when he squared off with Ben and that he was sucker punched; others say that both boys had their fists clenched, wound up to hit each other and Ben managed to land the first blow. Some say that after the first punch Tyler collapsed and that Ben struck him repeatedly in the head as he lay helpless and bleeding on the ground; others say that it was not until Tyler started to get back up to continue the fight that Ben hit him three or four times to end it. Some say it was a five-second fight; others say the fight lasted several minutes.

Regardless of the precise physical dynamics of this schoolboy scuffle, by 3:50 *p.m.* on May 25, 2001 two lamentable facts were beyond dispute. Tyler was in a body bag enroute to the Calgary Medical Examiners Office and Ben was under arrest for second-degree murder.

Later that day I attended the detention centre where I was greeted by security personnel. The first words out of the mouth of the attending guard were "we heard what happened, damn shame but that boy doesn't belong here." I was escorted down the hall to a secure area where Ben was waiting.

Ben looked like a wretched, slimmed-down version of that Sam character from *Lord of the Rings*. There was no strength in the boy's grasp as he shook my hand and although he feigned a degree of stoicism it was obvious that he had been crying. He was soft-spoken, respectful, contrite, and utterly lost. The old guard was right, the boy didn't belong there.

Priority One was to secure, if at all possible, Ben's timely release from custody on reasonable terms. Initial media coverage, sensational and highly adverse to the defence, no doubt contributed to the Crown's decision to vehemently oppose Ben's release. Front-page news boldly, and erroneously as it turned out, stated that Tyler died from massive head injuries suffered in a fight during which he was hit with about ten punches as he lay helpless on the ground. The same paper ran a simultaneous article reminding the public, as though somehow related, that two innocent teenagers had been stabbed to death in Calgary several months prior.

I scheduled the bail hearing for the following week. At those proceedings the assigned prosecutor, Ms. Darlene Oko, endeavored to persuade the judge to detain Ben by personifying the outrage of the public. Ms. Oko argued that if Ben were released, public confidence in the administration of justice would be seriously undermined. His Honour Judge Steve Lipton was not persuaded by Ms. Oko's submissions, nor was he about to be influenced by a notoriously fickle and misinformed court of public opinion. Judge Lipton ordered the release of Ben on reasonable terms.

Now that Ben was back in the care of his parents, we could relax somewhat and try to approach this murder prosecution from a position of strength. Over the course of the next few months we achieved two significant objectives. Firstly, we successfully applied to have Ben's case transferred from adult court to youth court. Secondly, we managed, without giving anything away, to convince the Crown to reduce the charge from second-degree murder to manslaughter. Both achievements would serve to ameliorate Ben's sentence in a worst-case scenario.

As I poured over hundreds of pages of Crown disclosure I was repeatedly drawn to the same unpalatable conclusion. The odds of success at trial were remote in the extreme and the safe route was a negotiated resolution. True to form, Ms. Oko adopted a hard line on sentencing. Specifically, in exchange for a timely guilty plea to manslaughter, the Crown would seek a period of secure custody (that is, jail) of two years. The Crown made it equally clear that if we didn't take the deal, then 'when', not 'if' Ben was convicted, they would seek the maximum.

To convict Ben of manslaughter the Crown would have to prove beyond a reasonable doubt that Ben caused the death of Tyler by means of an unlawful act. The unlawful act that the Crown needed to prove was assault as defined in *The Criminal Code of Canada* which reads, "A person commits an assault when without the consent of another person he applies force intentionally to that other person directly or indirectly."

The critical question from a defence perspective was whether we could rely upon Tyler's consent to engage in the fight as a defence to manslaughter. When an assault is committed and causes the death of a person, the assailant is criminally liable for manslaughter. It also follows, however, that where consent acts as a defence to the assault, it will also act as a defence to manslaughter, based on that assault. Although the defence of consent is very limited and somewhat convoluted in Canada (and there are subtle but important differences between consenting adults and consenting young persons) the general rule of thumb for a weaponless fight is that it is not available as a defence where an accused intended to apply force causing serious hurt or non-trivial bodily harm. I sincerely doubt that the eminent jurists who chose to so limit the defence of consent have ever been in a fight.

Consent was the only potential defence available to Ben and it did not look good. It was abundantly obvious that Ben killed Tyler. He repeatedly struck Tyler in anger and one or more of those blows caused his death. It was equally clear that Tyler did not deliver a single blow during the fight. The defence equation was further exacerbated by the fact that several punches were delivered after Tyler was on the ground and, according to some witnesses, while he was helpless. If the evidence at trial unfolded as the Crown expected, it would require no quantum leap in judicial reasoning to conclude that Ben intended to cause more than non-trivial bodily harm.

Our first potential break in the case appeared in the autopsy report. The report identified the immediate cause of Tyler's death as a sub-arachnoid hemorrhage due to a vertebral artery tear occasioned by blunt facial trauma. In plain English, a blow to Tyler's face tore a vessel in his neck about the size of a single strand of spaghetti. Blood from that tear tracked up into the base of Tyler's brain, created pressure and shut down his essential bodily functions. According to the autopsy report, other than bruising to the face no significant injuries were noted.

Arguably, what we had here was a freak, albeit deadly, injury. Although prospects of success remained dismal, this forensic revelation cast a new light on the case. With much trepidation, we rejected the Crown's offer of resolution, entered a plea of not guilty and scheduled the matter for trial.

The trial was held in Chestermere Provincial Court before the Honourable Judge Gordon Clozza. In my years at the defence bar I don't recall the faces of colleagues brightening when fixed with knowledge that Judge Clozza would be hearing their case. Although Judge Clozza had a legal mind of the first order he didn't cotton much to fancy legal argument and he had a reputation for dispensing frontier justice despite the obsequious maneuverings of legal counsel. My sources confirmed, however, that Judge Clozza was a man who had taken the time to live a bit before seeking a judicial appointment and he would know the difference between gang violence and a schoolboy fight. Furthermore, he was not the type of judge to be bullied or otherwise influenced by public pressure. All in all, I considered Judge Clozza to be a pretty good draw.

A couple months prior to commencement of the trial, prosecutorial conduct of the matter was transferred from Ms. Darlene Oko to Mr. Danny Elliott. At first blush, one might consider this to be a favourable development for the defence. Mr. Elliott was, however, a highly experienced trial lawyer with a peculiar talent for always presenting himself as the proverbial voice of reason. He was tough, soft spoken, and careful to choose when and where to take a stand. Mr. Elliott was, in brief, a very dangerous adversary.

Chestermere Provincial Court proved inadequate to facilitate the throng of would-be spectators seeking entry to the trial proceedings. Latecomers who were granted entry found themselves relegated to standing-room status against the walls flanking the Bench while others sat cross-legged in the aisle separating the rows of church-like pews. Members of the media, upon noting that Ben would be seated with me and my junior associate Greg Dunn at Counsel Table, scrambled for a strategic vantage point in the accused box.

At no time during the week of proceedings that followed was Judge Clozza required to caution the audience concerning their decorum. From start to finish there was a religious-like solemnity observed by all in attendance. Any hint of lowbrow levity that may have existed was buried along with the body of Tyler Trithart.

Several minutes before commencement of the trial, Mr. Elliott and I met with Judge Clozza in his private chambers. At that time Mr. Elliott gave Judge Clozza an overview of where the Crown was headed and concluded his unofficial commentary with "damn shame, he's a nice kid but it's manslaughter, pure and simple." After suppressing an impulse to nod in agreement I uttered several words destined for the legal archives, "Well, I guess we'll just see what happens, eh."

Within a couple of days, Mr. Elliott established beyond any reasonable doubt that Ben killed Tyler by punching him in the head. He also made it abundantly clear that Tyler never threw a punch during the so-called fight and that he was struck repeatedly by Ben after being knocked to the ground. As for the issue of intent, Mr. Elliot led direct evidence that just prior to the fight, Ben removed the sweater his mother knit him and replaced it with a t-shirt. The next morning's newspaper headlines echoed the theory of the Crown on the critical issue of intent: "Accused Dressed For Blood."

Consent remained the only legal means by which the case for the Crown could possibly be undermined and an acquittal achieved. It was a solitary narrow window of opportunity that could vanish with sufficiently adverse testimony from any witness in direct or cross-examination. My job was to keep the defence of consent alive. The plan adopted to achieve this objective, always susceptible to instantaneous revision or abandonment, was a five-fold challenge: to establish that death was caused by a freak injury; to establish that the freak injury was the result of the timing of the blow and the position of the victim rather than the application of excessive force; to establish that the freak injury was caused by the first punch and that the punches on the ground would not have contributed to Tyler's death beyond the *de minimus* (negligible) range; to delicately but effectively impugn Tyler's character by portraying him as the instigator of the fight which took his life; and to present Ben as a non-violent small-town boy of exceptional character and promise.

As the trial ensued, matters initially unfolded pretty much according to plan. With the invaluable assistance of forensic pathologist Dr. John Butt, we managed to transform the Crown's forensic pathologist into a witness for the defence. He concluded by agreeing with the defence that the injury was freakish in nature and even if sustained on the steps of an emergency ward, hospital staff could not have saved Tyler's life. As there were no visible injuries or symptoms to remotely suggest a tear to the vertebral artery, the injury was, in essence, a death sentence.

Few moments create more grey hairs for defence counsel than the decision as to whether or not to call an accused to testify. One well-placed question by the Crown can destroy all progress and any hope of an acquittal. Despite painstaking preparation of one's client, the emotionally charged nature of the experience and the fact that avenues of attack are limited only by the ingenuity of one's opponent can reduce the most intelligent and promising witness to imbecility. Some cases, however, cry out for an explanation that can only be given by an accused. Come what may, this was just such a case.

Ben took the stand and testified under oath before his family, Tyler's family, neighbours, teachers, classmates, and strangers. He did well in direct examination and cross-examination seemed to be going just fine. That is until Mr. Elliott asked Ben who owned the punching bag hanging in the garage. I hadn't seen that one coming; Ben was on his own. The Crown also questioned Ben about boxing lessons from a friend and a series of other potentially damaging questions but in the end Ben seemed to do okay.

My relief as Ben finally turned to leave the stand dissipated when Judge Clozza stated that he had a question of his own. While judges do have the discretion to question witnesses, most either resist the temptation entirely, or indulge sparingly. They tend to defer to experienced barristers in their much-more informed selection of questions and wisely confine themselves to their appointed task of deciding the case. Succinctly put, a good judge knows his or her limitations.

Well, as it turned out, Judge Clozza had at least a dozen questions for Ben. Mr. Elliott could have asked the same questions but he was far too experienced to do so. Mr. Elliott knew that any defence counsel worth his or her salt would have prepared an accused *ad nauseam* in anticipation of this particular line of questioning and he was not about to walk into the trap. Judge Clozza, bless his soul, stepped in with both feet.

As I sat contemplating my final submissions, Mr. Elliott approached and handed me a couple of pro-defence cases dealing with consent, shook my hand and wished us luck. Later that morning, Mr. Elliott stood as agent for Her Majesty the Queen and did his duty. He aptly described the case as the tragedy of Tyler and Ben. Tragic for Tyler for obvious reasons and tragic for Ben because he was facing a manslaughter prosecution. Mr. Elliott submitted to Judge Clozza that the only logical, reasonable and just decision open to the Court was to enter a conviction as charged. After pausing for effect, Mr. Elliott sealed his closing submissions by reminding Judge Clozza that it was manslaughter, pure and simple.

The next morning Judge Clozza walked into the courtroom with his verdict; there was no sound from the gallery as Court convened. Ben, resigned to the uncertainty of his fate, sat quietly with his tightly clasped hands resting on Counsel Table. I swear I could hear his heart beating through his chest. After the obligatory recital of facts and law, Judge Clozza ruled that he had a reasonable doubt as to whether Ben intended to cause more than non-trivial bodily harm, that consent did operate as a defence, and that Ben was not guilty.

The media would tell of how the gallery, still bursting at the seams, exploded with emotion at the verdict. They would also tell of how Ben stood hesitantly, turned and embraced his lawyer. What the media did not capture is how Ben's father approached me at Counsel Table. The tough old prairie veteran never uttered a word. With tears streaming down both cheeks he simply looked me straight in the eye, shook my hand and nodded. As I returned the gesture, he put his arm around Ben and took him home.

It is said that in a person's journey from adolescence to maturity there is no single occurrence or defining moment that marks the transition. Rather, the process is said to occur over time through the culmination of experience. The great novelist Joseph Conrad described the zone separating adolescence from maturity as an ever-shifting shadow line. For Ben, there was no shadow line. One moment he was building a deck with his Dad and the next moment he was under arrest for murder, handcuffed, searched, body swabbed for DNA and imprisoned. In an instant he was placed beyond the loving reach and influence of his parents, his pastor, his teachers and at the mercy of an enraged public seeking retribution. Ben's loss of innocence, his transition from boy to man, was swift and irrevocable.

Defence counsel do not generally have the luxury of indulgence or reflection in the result of their professional endeavours and I'm not entirely convinced that it is an advisable exercise in any event. When I lifted Ben's file from archives I read for the first time the victim impact statements and, as a father of five children, I felt the pain and sorrow that permeated every page. While I was pleased to learn that Fern and Nolan Trithart were ultimately successful in raising enough money for a family trip to Disneyland, it was heart wrenching to discover that they were compelled to use those hard-earned funds to bury their boy.

I have, of course, broken my own rule not to indulge in reflection and, as predicted, the experience has proven to be emotionally draining. Having done so, however, I have concluded that the successful defence of Ben Caron was sufficient justification for becoming a trial lawyer and for perhaps existing at all. At the time of Ben's trial, I was retained to defend five other homicides. I have no immediate desire to conjure up the names, faces, and emotion associated with any of those proceedings. As I am still, as they say, in the breach, I think I'll keep those files locked in archives for now.

With typical Canadian idealism and naïveté, talk abounded as to how we as a society can prevent the tragedy of Ben and Tyler from happening again. The short answer is, we can't. Most young men, at least in Alberta, don't join dead poet's societies where they sit around giving each other goose bumps by reading from Frost and Shelley. Boys have always fought and they will continue to fight. Despite all distorted belief and misguided efforts to the contrary, boys will be boys.

Brian Beresh

IN DEFENCE OF LARRY FISHER

Brian Beresh QC, founding partner of Beresh Aloneissi O'Neill, Edmonton, has practiced criminal law for almost forty years. He is a past president of the Criminal Trial Lawyers Association and an original director of the Canadian Council of Criminal Defence Lawyers. A former Bencher of the Law Society of Alberta, he has taught advanced criminal law at the University of Alberta Faculty of Law for twenty-five years.

THE RIGOURS AND DEMANDS of criminal defence work are well-known to those who seek to make it one's life calling and devotion. We defenders live in daily fear that clients might wrongfully be convicted, particularly of circumstances where no realistic chance of an appeal exists. None of us wants that to occur on our watch, but none of us are in control of the facts or potential inferences that can be drawn from them.

Saskatchewan has long been known as a province that can serve up, without much notice, some of the coldest weather on the planet. January 31, 1969 started and continued as one of the coldest recorded days in Saskatoon's history with the thermometer hovering at the minus-forty-degree mark. A thick fog blanketed the city, and citizens were warned to take precautions if going outside.

In January of that year, Gail Miller was a twenty-year-old nursing assistant at Saskatoon City Hospital. Her morning shift started at 7:30 *a.m.* and her routine was to leave her boarding house, located at 130 Avenue O, at about 7:00 *a.m.* and walk south on that avenue for about three quarters of a block to 20th Street where she would catch her bus to the hospital. She wore a nurse's uniform and a heavy black coat to protect herself from the elements.

Gail Miller was raised in the farming village of Laura, southwest of Saskatoon. The Miller family consisted of nine children. Ms. Miller studied at Saskatoon's Kelsey Institute, did a practicum in Swift Current, and eventually settled in the "big city" of Saskatoon. By all reports, despite her new residence, she maintained her small-town roots and attitude. Ms. Miller was last seen alive by a roommate at approximately 6:40 *a.m.* on January 31, 1969. About 8:30 that morning, a young student, Mary Marcoux, on her way to school, discovered Ms. Miller's body in an alley between Avenue N and Avenue O. Significantly, her body was not found on the direct travel portion of the alley, but off to one side of it.

In Saskatoon the alphabetized avenues, which run north and south, increase as one travels in a westerly direction from downtown. The location of the body was approximately one block from her boarding house and not on the route she would normally take to catch her bus. An examination of the scene revealed to the Saskatoon police that Ms. Miller was found facedown in the snow with her panties down around her ankles, and her dress was down around her waist, but her coat was properly on her body, although unbuttoned in the front. Once the body was removed, a blood-soaked blade of a single-edged paring knife was found and police quickly formed the opinion that it was likely the murder weapon. Interestingly, a few days later, police discovered another knife not far from the body. It was a double-edged hunting knife, which could not be identified by any of the neighbours as belonging to them. Mysteriously, this knife was lost by the police, and therefore could never be tendered as evidence in any of the proceedings.

Dr. Harry Emson, a senior pathologist, conducted an autopsy and recorded fifteen slash marks to Ms. Miller's neck and upper chest. In addition, he noted four stab wounds on her front, four on her back, three around the collar bone, and one on each of her sides. The location of the stab wounds were found to be consistent with cuts found on her coat. No cuts were found on her dress. Although her clothes were dishevelled, Emson found no evidence of forcible intercourse. He placed the time of death at about one hour before she was found at 7:30 *a.m.*-ish and clearly between 6:45 and 7:30 *a.m.*

During the night of January 30/31, 1969, David Milgaard, who the police described as leading a "hippie lifestyle," had travelled with friends from Regina to Saskatoon. At some point on the morning of Gail Miller's death, Mr. Milgaard went to visit a friend, Shorty Cadrain, who lived at 334 Avenue O South, approximately a block and a half from Gail Miller's residence and about a block and a half from the location where Ms. Miller's body was found.

He remained there for a number of hours before leaving the city to travel to Calgary. Residing in the basement of the Cadrain home was Larry Fisher, a construction worker, and his wife Linda. The two men had no contact during the time that Milgaard was at the home.

The police continued their investigation and on May 30, 1969, David Milgaard was arrested and charged with the murder of Gail Miller. He was defended by leading and eminent counsel, Calvin Tallis QC. The prosecution selected the friendly, but tenacious, T.D.R. "Bobs" Caldwell QC to prosecute the case. After a jury trial, Milgaard was convicted and all subsequent appeals were unsuccessful. By all indications, by late 1971, criminal proceedings relating to Gail Miller's death appeared to have been concluded.

I met Larry Fisher in early April 1980 while I practiced in North Battleford, Saskatchewan. Little did I know that I would continue to act for him until early April 2012, some thirty-two years later.

On March 31, 1980, in North Battleford, Mr. Fisher was charged with attempted murder and rape of an elderly woman who was attacked late at night following her return from a social event. I was retained to represent him on those charges. On June 11, 1981, Mr. Fisher pled guilty to both charges, and escaped a dangerous offender application by agreeing to a ten-year jail sentence. This conviction added to his existing record for multiple sexual offences that spanned from October 21, 1968 to May 28, 1971.

I left Saskatchewan to establish a practice in Edmonton expecting never to hear from Mr. Fisher again.

In November of 1971, David Milgaard's application for leave to appeal to the Supreme Court of Canada, in relation to his conviction for murder of Gail Miller, January 31, 1969, was dismissed. Mr. Milgaard subsequently filed two applications for a review of his conviction with the Federal Minister of Justice, pursuant to section 690 of the *Criminal Code*, on December 28, 1988 and August 14, 1991.

Mr. Milgaard's mother, Joyce, a robust and sincere advocate, commenced an active campaign in support of the reviews of her son's conviction. This included the famous Winnipeg public exchange between her and then-Prime Minister Brian Mulroney on September 6, 1991, which eventually led to the Federal Minister of Justice referring Mr. Milgaard's case for review to the Supreme Court of Canada on November 28, 1991. This would be only the third time that the Supreme Court of Canada would hear such a reference in the history of this country. The Reference process is intended to be a review conducted by a single judge or multiple judges to determine whether or not the criminal justice system had erred in the particular case under review.

By the time the reference was directed, Larry Fisher's name played prominently in the Milgaard team's theory of "the other guy." From comments made by the Milgaard team, there appeared to be little concern about the reputation of Mr. Fisher. Mr. Fisher retained me to represent him at the Supreme Court Reference and on December 20, 1991, he was granted standing to participate.

By the time the Reference commenced on January 16, 1992, my impression was that the media, previously critical of Mr. Milgaard's attempts to have his case reviewed, seemed to have largely shifted support in favour of Mr. Milgaard and appeared to me to be looking for fresh blood. Some journalists were interested in the "facts" but many simply wanted to find a villain.

Although I had appeared in the Supreme Court of Canada a number of times before the Reference on other cases, I knew that this encounter would be different and extremely challenging. Evidence was scheduled to be called before the five judges on the Reference Panel, all of whom we were advised would strictly preside over the rare event.

As I prepared for the Reference, I was also concerned that the "division of camps" (Milgaard vs. Fisher) would test the relationship I had with Milgaard's lawyer, Hersh Wolch QC. Hersh and I had co-defended prior to that, and I considered him to be a very close friend. I confess with hindsight that although Hersh and I had our differences throughout the lengthy process, our friendship to this day has remained firmly intact. Subsequent to the inquiry, Hersh and I each spoke at a legal conference in Saskatoon where, during the preliminary introduction of each of us, our friend Morris Bodnar QC suggested that he did not find it unusual for Hersh and I to be sitting together in the audience as we were probably comparing cheque stubs from the Department of Justice. That Department had funded our involvement in the Supreme Court Reference.

Feeling somewhat like a fish out of water as I prepared for the Reference, I contacted the late Arthur Martin QC, then a member of the Ontario Court of Appeal, and asked to meet with him, given that he had been counsel on the 1966 Steven Truscott reference to the Supreme Court of Canada. It had been the last reference of this nature that the Supreme Court had heard. The only other reference heard by that Court was in the Wilbert Coffin case in 1953 arising from Mr. Coffin's conviction for having killed three American hunters.

Justice Martin kindly and generously invited me to his Toronto home where we spent a number of hours together discussing the procedure followed and evidence led in the Truscott Reference. I was humbled to spend those hours with such a unique and wonderful person. I will forever remember how patiently he answered my numerous questions and what a sincere gentleman he was. It was an honour to be in the presence of such a true professional who devoted his practicing life to criminal law. He was also the only person I have ever met who had the entire Canadian Criminal Case series on display in his living room. As a result of that meeting, I developed what I thought might be an effective strategy in representing Mr. Fisher's interests at the reference. What the meeting did not prepare me for was how to handle a hostile and aggressive press corps.

Although Mr. Fisher's status was that of an intervener on the reference, the Supreme Court very fairly permitted him a broad standing given the direct and indirect suggestion that he was the "true culprit." An intervener in this process is not considered a direct party, but has substantial standing to represent the intervener's interests as they might specifically arise in the Reference.

A small example of this occurred when Brett Morgan, a lifetime con-artist, testified that Mr. Fisher had made prison statements to Morgan tantamount to confessions of his involvement in the Gail Miller death. I recall Morgan, in the witness box, dressed in prison garb, dramatizing the context of the "confessions" in his evidence led by Counsel for the Department of Justice. I was fortunate to have substantial historical information about Mr. Morgan's past and for about one hour, cross-examined him relying heavily upon that material. I exposed much of his past deceit and treachery.

I vividly recall during my heated cross-examination of Morgan in the main chamber of the Supreme Court of Canada that was reconfigured clumsily as a trial courtroom (a setting which vividly struck me as being akin to the setting in the movie *Breaker Morant*), Chief Justice Antonio Lamer clearing his throat and quietly saying to me as he looked over at Justice John Sopinka, "Mr. Beresh, I think we have your point." The truth is I was just starting to feel my stride, but I humbly accepted his wise direction, and quickly concluded my questioning of Morgan.

In its final decision, the Supreme Court of Canada did not accept or rely upon any of Morgan's evidence. The Chief Justice's diplomatic direction to me clearly signaled that I had established that Morgan was a stranger to the truth.

As a side note, which may have been predicted from what was discovered in my cross-examination of Morgan's past, Morgan, while at the Reference, developed a romantic relationship with one of the many journalists present covering the historic event. I found this quite bizarre as he was in custody when he testified. That relationship continued, and subsequently the journalist was instrumental in assisting Morgan to gain his early release on parole on a conviction of manslaughter. They were subsequently married and he eventually killed her and was convicted of her murder. While serving that sentence, he died in jail.

The exuberance of the Supreme Court Justices, to leave no stone unturned on the Reference, for me, struck its highest point when Mr. Fisher testified denying any involvement in the Miller death. Following the questioning by all counsel, he was questioned closely by Chief Justice Lamer, formerly a renowned defence lawyer. As he pressed Mr. Fisher suggesting that this was the moment to "get any matters he wished off his chest," Mr. Fisher adamantly denied participating in Miller's death. Finally, the Chief Justice's last attempt was to question Mr. Fisher as to whether or not he was prepared to take, after Court retired, a polygraph test in relation to his evidence. The question silenced the courtroom until Justice Sopinka leaned over to the Chief and, I suspect, told him that he ought to withdraw the question before Mr. Fisher responded. The Chief Justice quickly stated "That's all, thank you Mr. Fisher."

The reference concluded with the Supreme Court's decision released April 14, 1992, with recommendations seriously affecting Mr. Milgaard's status. It found that the new information placed before them could reasonably affect the verdict and suggested that the conviction should be quashed and a new trial directed. As history reveals, on April 16, 1992, the Province of Saskatchewan decided to stay the proceedings against Mr. Milgaard and not order a new trial.

In my view, Mr. Fisher was not seriously implicated in Gail Miller's death by the Supreme Court's decision. With hindsight, what we had not been properly prepared for was the daily media scrum where the media attempted to further investigate evidence heard during the day's proceedings. Their questioning was vigorous and unrelenting. Given that this was not in the courtroom, there were no established boundaries as to which questions were appropriate. I formed the impression early on, from the questioning, that the media had sympathy for Mr. Milgaard, but none for Mr. Fisher.

What followed the Reference were numerous allegations by the Milgaard team that there had been a cover up by the Saskatoon Police Service. In addition, about two years after the Reference, May 26, 1994, Larry Fisher was released from custody in relation to the North Battleford conviction. On July 18, 1997, it was publicly announced that David Milgaard was exonerated by DNA evidence.

On July 25, 1997, Larry Fisher was arrested and charged with the murder of Gail Miller and the RCMP became involved in a reinvestigation of the Miller death. A fight ensued as to who would be responsible to cover Mr. Fisher's legal fees. Mr. Fisher requested that I represent him. Saskatchewan Legal Aid refused to appoint me to act for him, as I was no longer the "Saskatchewan Prodigal Son," that is, a resident of Saskatchewan. I was personally disappointed with that decision, but it was consistent with Legal Aid's approach in other cases.

Fortunately, I brought a timely application before Mr. Justice J.D. Milliken in Saskatoon with the result being that a unique remedy was granted in what is now referred to as a "Fisher Order" assuring adequate remuneration for legal fees in a case which, by then, was approaching three decades in age. It was a higher rate than generally allowed by Saskatchewan Legal Aid. Unfortunately, the Supreme Court of Canada's decision in *Her Majesty the Queen v. The Criminal Lawyers Association of Ontario et. al.* released August 1, 2013, casts serious doubt on whether such a remedy will be available in the future.

After it became publicly known that I had agreed to represent Mr. Fisher's interests, I recall that a number of my colleagues and judges privately suggested that taking this case would not benefit my career. I reflected on those observations as many of them came from individuals for whom I had a lot of respect.

Their view was that Mr. Fisher's lengthy sex offence record, and Milgaard's exoneration, clearly placed the cloak of guilt on Mr. Fisher's head and that this case was a loser. They sincerely believed that defending this case was not a "career builder." I disagreed as I saw the *modus operandi* in the Gail Miller death as being distinctly different from Mr. Fisher's former crimes. In addition, it struck me that for all the time we spend publicly declaring that the rights of every citizen must be protected, I would be a hypocrite to refuse Mr. Fisher's case for the reasons they suggested.

The preparation of Mr. Fisher's defence was more difficult than any other case that I have defended in almost four decades. Despite the public exoneration of Mr. Milgaard, the Saskatoon Police Service officers who had initially investigated David Milgaard collectively maintained their conviction that they had "gotten the right guy" and were eager when requested to assist in my defence of Mr. Fisher. The lead Milgaard prosecutor maintained his personal belief in Milgaard's guilt, and agreed to, and did, testify in Mr. Fisher's defence.

On the opposing side, Mr. Fisher's former wife now aligned her story to implicate Mr. Fisher. In addition, the prosecution now found itself in the awkward position of having vigorously opposed Mr. Milgaard's Section 690 application (on the basis of his alleged guilt) now having to do an about-face to vigorously prosecute Larry Fisher for the same crime but not as parties to an offence. The awkward position was accentuated by the Province of Saskatchewan eventually calling its own inquiry into the wrongful conviction.

That decision caused endless problems for the prosecution who were forced to oppose any suggestion during the Fisher trial that someone else was responsible for Miller's death. That was particularly evident when the prosecution attempted to limit the evidence of Milgaard's lead prosecutor, Bobs Caldwell, when he was called in Mr. Fisher's defence. It was my duty to pursue all possible defences.

This ethical dilemma was likely highlighted to the prosecution in its review of a transcript of Mr. Milgaard's defence trial lawyer's evidence in the Supreme Court of Canada Reference where he provided numerous reasons why he felt that he could not call Mr. Milgaard in his own defence, including what, in his opinion, was incriminating evidence.

Of particular concern, in my preparation for Mr. Fisher's trial, was that certain evidence or leads found by the Saskatoon Police Service were not adequately investigated and evidence was not properly maintained. It also appeared that in 1969, investigative leadership on this file was absent. In addition, over the years other events complicated preparation. Some witnesses had died, others moved on with their lives and were not interested in revisiting the past; particularly in relation to what some witnesses considered to be a "closed case."

Of interest in this very unusual case was that the Milgaard lead trial prosecutor had insisted that the trial exhibits be maintained at the Saskatoon Courthouse, despite the fact that all periods for potential appeal had expired. They were maintained in a "shabby" condition — sitting open in a shopping cart — and the Saskatoon Courthouse exhibit area had been the subject of three break-ins in the interim.

As I viewed the case, there were three severe challenges to succeeding in Mr. Fisher's defence. The first was that substantial publicity over the prior two-and-a-half decades highlighted Mr. Milgaard's innocence and exposed Mr. Fisher's potential involvement. The second was Mr. Fisher's related and lengthy criminal record. The third was DNA evidence (potentially) implicating Mr. Fisher.

Selecting a location for a fair jury trial in Saskatchewan where, in 1999, the population was 1,027,780 was a difficult choice. I hired a professional polling agency to test various judicial districts in Saskatchewan to try to determine which may have been the least-affected by pretrial publicity. This was complicated, as unlike other change-of-venue applications, the issues being probed were not simply the potential effect of pretrial publicity regarding the crime or the suspect. This now involved a major historic event, which had been in the news for decades. We decided to probe the public's feelings about Milgaard's believed innocence and Fisher's believed guilt. In addition, it did not help that Carl Karp and Cecil Rosner had released their 1998 book *When Justice Fails: The David Milgaard Story*.

The results of our polling were not encouraging for a trial anywhere on the planet. After much discussion and thought, we settled on Yorkton, Saskatchewan, even though it was only forty-four miles from Langenburg where Mr. Milgaard had lived with his family for a number of years. It was also only ninety miles from my hometown and I thought that I would have a good sense of how rural eastern Saskatchewanians might view the case. Twice during the trial, I made reference to my hometown of Kipling hoping to gain some trust and respect, but I am not sure, given the final verdict, that I succeeded.

In my view, a major significant event occurred which directly affected Mr. Fisher's ability to present his case fairly. On May 17, 1999 Saskatchewan Justice Minister John Nilson announced that a settlement had been reached with David Milgaard in relation to compensation and that the province would pay Mr. Milgaard ten million dollars. At the time, this was the largest Canadian settlement ever obtained by a wrongful-conviction complainant. The Province ensured that the settlement received substantial media publicity.

According to many expert legal observers, this event cast serious doubt on whether Mr. Fisher could succeed in his defence by pointing the accusing finger at Mr. Milgaard. What was particularly troubling about the timing of the announcement was that Mr. Fisher's trial date had been scheduled before the May 17, 1999 announcement date, and was well-known to anyone involved in the process, particularly to bureaucrats in the Saskatchewan Government. I have no doubt, from my discussions with individuals directly involved, that the Milgaard team would have accepted a delay in announcement and payment of the compensation until the conclusion of Mr. Fisher's trial on the clear understanding that a reasonable rate of interest would be paid during the interim. Mr. Fisher's trial commenced only five months after the announcement of this major settlement.

I believe that Mr. Fisher's defence faced three major hurdles. Firstly, the pretrial publicity greatly affected the outcome of this trial and could not be overcome by the change in venue of the trial or the trial judge's instructions to the jury. Not only was Mr. Fisher constantly referred to as "the serial rapist," but a dreadful photograph of him in a cell area portrayed him as a sadistic character. I could not conceive of a tactic to overcome or at least neutralize this publicity.

In addition, CTV had produced a "docudrama" about the Milgaard story. My reasonable view of the production concluded that CTV had exonerated Mr. Milgaard and clearly indicted Mr. Fisher in the Miller death. Fortunately, the trial judge agreed with its prejudicial effect and banned its broadcast until the conclusion of the trial. Unfortunately, damage had already been done as the advertising trailer for the "docudrama" had broadcast a number of times.

The second hurdle, Mr. Fisher's prior-related record, caused, in my view, the most significant challenge at trial. In a pretrial ruling, the trial judge held that some of Mr. Fisher's prior sexual misconduct would be allowed into evidence pursuant to the similar fact rule. These events included sexual assaults of young women who were strangers to Mr. Fisher.

Mr. Fisher had pled guilty to all of those crimes, which left little for the defence to contest at the Miller trial. We decided that the best tactic would be to try to highlight the dis-similarities of those crimes from the Miller case.

It was then my view, and it remains to this date, that the similar-fact evidence rule can easily be misused and can easily lead to wrongful convictions. The character bias it creates prevents even reasonable jurors from being able to objectively assess the facts of the case they are trying. The negative "halo effect" created by past misconduct is very difficult, if not impossible, to overcome in our trial settings.

Although I lost the argument that a judge's instructions to a jury, as to the proper trial use of similar fact evidence, was not sufficient protection, I am heartened by Barrett J. Anderson's 2012 *Yale Law Journal* Article "Recognizing Character: A New Prospective of Character Evidence." Professor Barrett concluded at page 1391:

> Studies have demonstrated that jury instructions do not provide a satisfactory remedy when improper character reference is presented to the jury. That fact strongly suggests that the "halo effect" cannot be cured by informing people that they are likely to use character proof wrongly.

I sincerely do not believe that Mr. Fisher's prior crimes met the test for admission pursuant to the similar fact evidence rule. The third concern in the Fisher case, the presence of DNA, in my view, was not as large a factor as we had originally contemplated. There was substantial evidence of potential contamination of the most important exhibit, as a previous sample of DNA had been obtained from Mr. Fisher. Since that trial, the scientific community and the legal community have enhanced knowledge about how easily contamination can occur.

What struck me, and has disturbed me about how the "goal posts" can shift or change given a new context, was evidence at Mr. Fisher's trial. A couple of examples remain clear in my memory. The first related to the Crown's concern about potential exhibit contamination given its desire to introduce DNA evidence at the trial. In 1969 and 1970, that had not been a live issue at the Milgaard trial. By 1999 the Crown was most concerned about any bodily substances found on Gail Miller's clothing and particularly sensitive to any possible defence argument surrounding contamination (a "1969 DNA Genius"). Contamination can occur innocently where airborne material from one item can transfer to another, or by items coming into physical contact with one another.

I vividly recall one of the lead investigators testifying at the Fisher trial that at the autopsy, conducted by Dr. Emson, as each piece of Ms. Miller's clothing had been removed from her body he ensured that it was placed in separate plastic bags. When responding to the prosecutors' questions, he meticulously went through each piece of clothing and how he had separated them so as to avoid any potential contamination.

In cross-examination, I asked him to clarify the procedure and again step-by-step he testified that each piece of clothing was separated and that they did not come into contact with one another when removed from the body. I then confronted him with the 1969 photographs taken during the autopsy process. These photos were poor quality, grainy, and only black and white. I had noticed in the photographs a vague black object on the floor, which struck me as being unusual given a hospital's normal desire to maintain sanitary conditions. As a result of that curiosity I had retained a firm in San Diego, California to enhance the photos to the point at which I could identify that the black object was a clump of clothing heaped together on the floor.

When confronted with the enhanced photographs, the officer was forced to resile from the stated and firm position he had taken in examination in chief, which in my court submission had been a clear fabrication designed to address the real DNA issue at Mr. Fisher's trial. No subsequent investigation was ever conducted into this conduct.

The second trial example was Linda Fisher, who had been residing with her husband Larry in January of 1969. She testified that she had a clear recall of her husband returning home early in the morning on January 31, 1969. She claimed that he was unusually dressed as though he had been at a nightclub. When shown the paring knife found underneath Ms. Miller's body, she also identified it as one which had come from her home.

What struck me about her evidence was that the clothing she described Larry to be wearing would not be suitable for minus-forty-degree Saskatchewan weather and that the paring knife she identified could be one found in thousands of households in Saskatoon around that time.

What was significant about Linda Fisher's evidence was that she did not become involved in the case until the late 1980s, by which time she had separated from her husband and taken up with another person. In addition, she did not report any of these concerns or observations until the late 1980s when she received a flyer in her mailbox indicating a $10,000 reward for any information, offered by the Milgaard family.

The Fisher trial lasted approximately seven weeks with A.L. Johnson from Regina leading the charge for the prosecution. He fought vigorously, but was an honourable opponent. Following Mr. Johnson's jury address and my jury address, a reporter covering the trial headlined an article describing the event as "Two Prairie Boys Dueling It Out on a Fall Afternoon in the Courtroom."

On November 22, 1999 Mr. Fisher was convicted of murder and his subsequent appeals were unsuccessful.

I later represented Mr. Fisher at the Saskatchewan Milgaard inquiry held in Saskatoon, before Mr. Justice Edward MacCallum. That inquiry concluded with the *MacCallum Report* being released on September 26, 2008.

With hindsight, I believe that this is the most challenging case I have ever tried. The circumstances were so unique and so bizarre that I seriously believe there was not sufficient evidence to convict Mr. Fisher when properly applying the proof beyond a reasonable doubt standard, as described by the Supreme Court in *R. v. Starr*.

What will likely remain a mystery forever, and disturbing for me in defending this case, are these unanswered questions:

1. How was it that both Milgaard and Fisher, total strangers to each other, and each convicted of the same murder, could have been in the same small bungalow in Saskatoon on the same night hours after Miller's death without having contact with one another?
2. How could Gail Miller have been sexually assaulted in a major way (at minus-forty degrees) in a frozen alley and stabbed multiple times without any signs of a struggle or blood being present in the snow immediately surrounding her body or in the alley?
3. How was it that if Ms. Miller was sexually assaulted and stabbed in the alley, which was the Crown's theory, that the coat she was wearing had numerous stab wounds but clothing worn by her beneath her coat was undamaged?
4. How was it that the blade of the paring knife, believed to be the murder weapon, was found underneath Gail Miller's face-down body when she had suffered stab wounds to her back, given the Crown's theory that the final physical assault to her was the stabbing in her back in the alley?
5. What happened to the second "hunting" knife that was lost by the police and why was this never explained?
6. Given that it is more likely that her body was dumped in the alley from

a vehicle, how could Mr. Fisher be implicated when it was proven that he had no access to a vehicle at that time?

7. Why did the Milgaard lead prosecutor, Bobs Caldwell, insist that the Milgaard trial exhibits be kept, regardless of the passage of all appeal periods, given that none of the exhibits could realistically be considered to be "trophy exhibits?" Notwithstanding his stated strong belief, do Caldwell's actions reveal a potential doubt he may have had about Milgaard's guilt?
8. If Linda Fisher's evidence is accurate that she saw her husband early on the morning of Friday, January 31st, why would he be dressed at that point in clothing not suitable for the climactic conditions outside and not in his construction work clothing?
9. Was Linda Fisher's evidence affected by her initial interest in the $10,000 reward offered by the Milgaard Investigative team and/or her clear anger toward her former husband? Cross-examined by me at Fisher's trial, she did not accept that either of these factors affected her evidence.
10. Would Mr. Fisher's defence more likely have succeeded if the trial would have been held in another Judicial Centre?
11. Would the verdict have differed if the case had proceeded by judge alone, rather than judge and jury?

For me, these issues remain unresolved and have caused me serious concern about whether or not justice was done in this case, or whether as occurred in 1969/70 the state needed to find someone responsible for this horrendous crime.

In the end, I have no regrets for accepting the task of defending Larry Fisher's interests. Contrary to my detractors' initial advice, my involvement in the case did not affect my legal career adversely. In fact, some have argued the opposite.

PART FOUR

Collateral Damage

Mark Brayford

DEMOCRATIC FREEDOMS UNDERMINED: ROBERT LATIMER

Mark Brayford QC, a partner with Brayford Schapiro in Saskatoon, is designated in criminal law by Best Lawyers in Canada. He has appeared in the trial and appellate courts of several provinces, and in the Supreme Court of Canada. He is Vice-President of the Canadian Council of Criminal Defence Lawyers, and a former president of the Canadian Bar Association (Saskatchewan Branch) and the Saskatoon Criminal Defence Lawyers Association.

William Penn, one of the fathers of Pennsylvania, was tried in England in 1670 for preaching the banned principles of the Quaker Religion. In spite of his being obviously guilty, the jury refused to convict. The judge attempted to coerce a conviction, holding the jury without food and water. Eventually four jurors were jailed for nine weeks. On appeal, Bushell's Case (1670), as it is known, ruled against the imprisonment, confirming that jurors could not be punished for bringing in a "perverse verdict." This case is widely credited with establishing the principles of jury nullification. Tyrants will always be circumscribed in their power if citizens have the right to a jury trial.

At first blush, the seventeenth-century trial of William Penn might seem a surprising analogy to the 1994 and 1997 trials of Robert Latimer, but Latimer's trial was, arguably, the single greatest assault on democratic freedom in Canada during the last century.

In Penn's case, the jurors brought in a verdict that was against the law and the evidence, a phrase referred to as jury nullification. Jury nullification is a critical safeguard to prevent injustice from unfair laws or unfair prosecution.

Simply put, jurors are our ultimate safeguard, given their absolute power to acquit if they view it would be unfair to convict.

As in Penn, so too it seemed that the jurors in the Robert Latimer murder trial disagreed with where the law and the evidence were taking them. Their questions to the trial judge, and subsequent comments, indicated that they were about to engage in jury nullification and acquit Robert Latimer. As a result of an accidentally misleading answer from the trial judge, the jurors did not use jury nullification to find Robert Latimer not guilty. The Latimer jurors were erroneously lead to believe that they would have the right to exercise some compassion on sentence if they convicted. It seems clear that this is why the jurors did not engage in jury nullification. This misunderstanding by the jurors about their power to exercise compassion at the time of sentencing fundamentally undermined the protection of jury nullification, but the Supreme Court of Canada did not find this to be reversible error. Robert Latimer was deprived of the ultimate safeguard.

Background

Robert Latimer was a Saskatchewan farmer who, along with his spouse Laura, lovingly raised their twelve-year-old daughter, Tracy, alongside their other children. Tracy was Robert and Laura's first child. As is typical, they loved her unreservedly and were fiercely protective of her. Tracy was born in a small rural hospital, where a broken fetal heart monitor masked the fact that Tracy's brain was being starved for oxygen throughout her birth.

In many cases such as these, where it is obvious that a child has suffered profound brain damage through the birthing process, a decision would be made not to resuscitate the child. This was not the decision of Robert and Laura. They set about the task of loving and caring for Tracy in an effort to give her the most normal life they could, despite the fact that her intellectual and physical abilities would never progress beyond that of an infant.

From birth, Tracy's body was racked with seizures, hundreds of seizures, which were destroying the limited intellectual capabilities that she was born with. As often happens in these cases, the brain was sending scrambled messages to the various muscles and limbs of Tracy's tiny body such that she spasmed severely. Her tiny body was literally trying to twist itself apart.

By cutting and severing, and inserting steel rods, medical specialists attempted to resist the contractions sufficiently that Tracy could keep breathing. Regrettably, these surgeries, and the lengthy rehabilitation periods following each of the surgeries, were horribly painful as it was not possible to use appropriate pain medication. Any significant attempt at pain medication only served to cause further chemical imbalance, exacerbating the debilitating seizures. In spite of, or perhaps as a result of, the profound difficulties that Tracy had to endure, Robert and Laura loved Tracy so much they would do anything for her. As is normal with parents, their child's pain was their pain.

As Tracy approached her teenage years, the excruciating pain was rapidly escalating. Tracy was enduring pain that became more and more inhumane. The proposals for further pain management by severing, cutting, and amputation, without the ability to use appropriate painkillers, started to sound more and more barbaric. It was at this point that Robert felt it had become inhumane for Tracy to be put through any further horribly painful and never-ending mutilation.

The Painless and Silent Killer

After weeks of tormenting himself as to the best way to terminate Tracy's suffering, Robert decided to use the painless and silent killer, carbon monoxide, which would initially put Tracy to sleep and ultimately cause her death. Out of compassion for Laura and the other children, Robert attempted to endure this burden entirely on his own.

On October 24, 1993, while the family was at church, Robert used the exhaust from a vehicle to cause Tracy's death, and then returned Tracy to her bed to make her death seem as natural as possible. It is noteworthy that every single day that Robert had fed Tracy her meals, it was only as a result of his careful attention during her eating that prevented Tracy from choking to death. Clearly, if Robert had simply wished her to die of natural causes, on any day he could have allowed her to simply choke on her food. Robert was not prepared to force Tracy to endure such a horrible death as choking, simply to shirk what he knew was his responsibility as a loving father.

As Tracy had died at home, a doctor and a police officer were called. Although it was patently obvious, given the exhaust smell, Tracy's doctor accepted that Robert's thinly veiled subterfuge was the appropriate way to deal with the situation and was prepared to sign off on the death being from natural causes. Unfortunately, as luck would have it, the police officer that attended did not take the sympathetic view of the small-town physician. Some would say that it takes a particularly big person to exercise the right amount of discretion at the right time. This particular officer exercised no sympathetic discretion, and criminal charges ultimately came about. This was the same police officer who later assisted the Crown prosecutor in improperly tampering with the jury-selection process in an apparent attempt to obtain a jury that would be more favourably predisposed on the issue of euthanasia. This officer was not criminally charged for his conduct, however the Crown prosecutor was. At the trial of the prosecutor, it was held that he did not intend to commit a crime and he was found not guilty.

Robert Latimer went to trial in Battleford, Saskatchewan on a charge of first-degree murder. He was convicted on November 16, 1994 of second-degree murder and sentenced to life imprisonment without parole eligibility for ten years. Following the first trial, there was an appeal to the Saskatchewan Court of Appeal that unsuccessfully attempted to exclude the statement of Robert Latimer where he completely explained his involvement in Tracy Latimer's death. Although this first appeal was unsuccessful, former Saskatchewan Court of Appeal Chief Justice Ed Bayda dissented on the issue of sentence, holding that the sentence was cruel and unusual punishment contrary to the *Canadian Charter of Rights and Freedoms.*

At this point, the case was then on its way to the Supreme Court of Canada when it became known through gossip in small-town Saskatchewan that five of the twelve jurors at the trial had improperly had their views solicited by the RCMP in relation to euthanasia prior to being selected to sit on the jury. The appeal process previously was focusing on the admissibility of Robert's confession, as without his explanation of what happened, there would not have been sufficient evidence to convict him.

Once this procedural impropriety in relation to the jury was learned, it was immediately acknowledged by then Deputy Minister of Justice, Brent Cotter, that this was completely unacceptable. The Crown joined with the defence in requesting that the Supreme Court of Canada order a new trial, when the Supreme Court did not agree with the defence that Robert's confession should be inadmissible.

The Sympathy of Canadians

At Robert's second trial, the anguished decision that Robert had made attracted the sympathy of the majority of Canadians to Robert's plight, and his unwillingness to watch Tracy suffer inhumanely. After his conviction, when it was being publicly discussed that Robert Latimer was now facing a mandatory life sentence, the trial judge, the Honourable Mr. Justice Ted Noble, indicated that the sentence had provoked an unprecedented public reaction as they were apparently outraged at the severity of the punishment. An Angus Reid poll indicated that seventy-three percent of respondents supported the proposition that Robert Latimer acted out of compassion and should receive a more lenient sentence. Thousands of people signed petitions, wrote letters, and made financial contributions supporting Robert Latimer.

Tragically, a small minority of Canadians, some of them within the disabled community, viewed Robert's act of love as some sort of a threat to disabled people generally. The suggestion that Robert may not have had Tracy's best interests at heart, or that Robert and Laura, who had so steadfastly cared for Tracy, were not friends of the disabled community, was one of the cruellest cuts.

At the second trial, given Robert's full confession as to what had transpired, there were only limited options as to how the jury could resolve the case in favour of Robert Latimer. Robert's only real hope rested on the principle of jury nullification: even though in law Robert's actions constituted murder, the jury had the right to refuse to convict if they believed it would be unjust to do so.

Years ago, there had been similar cases where it was simply explained to the jury that they should do the right thing in spite of the law if they were convinced that it would be unfair to convict the accused. More recently, however, the Supreme Court of Canada had forcefully rebuked Morris Manning QC for encouraging a jury in the Dr. Henry Morgentaler abortion prosecutions to engage in jury nullification, *R. v. Morgentaler.* But for jury nullification, Dr. Morgentaler might have spent his life in jail, and the impetus for changing the *Criminal Code* abortion provisions might not have occurred.

Given the constraints dictated by the words of the eminent Chief Justice Brian Dickson, and the concurring judgment of Mr. Justice Jean Beetz on this point, it was not legally possible for counsel to explain to the jury that they possessed the power to set Robert Latimer free in spite of the law, if that was the right thing to do.

Arguably in Morgentaler, the Supreme Court of Canada was just setting an acceptable balance with respect to jury nullification by preventing the defence from discussing the matter with the jury: if the jury came to the conclusion on their own that something was so blatantly unfair that they should not convict, so be it. It was suggested that to allow defence counsel to actually encourage jury nullification would upset the delicate balance of when this legitimate safeguard performed by juries would occur.

Very regrettably in this author's view, to whatever extent this delicate balance was justified, it was unnecessarily devastated by the Supreme Court's comments regarding jury nullification in Latimer.

Misleading Remarks

During the jury deliberations in the second Latimer trial in 1997, the jury was obviously considering jury nullification, and asked the trial judge if they could have a say on sentence if they convicted. An unintentionally misleading answer caused the jury to believe they would have more power at the time of sentencing than they actually would. It is apparent that the jury wanted Robert Latimer to receive a lenient sentence, and that they would not have convicted if they were correctly told of the inflexibility of a murder sentence.

The jury then returned a verdict of guilty, only to be horrified, as was evidenced by things the jurors said, to find that they were going to be required to participate in a sentencing where Robert Latimer would get life in prison with no parole for at least ten years.

These developments occurred at the end of the trial where the jury was obviously upset by this sentence. A request was made of Mr. Justice Ted Noble to grant a constitutional exemption pursuant to the guarantee against cruel and unusual punishment as contained in Section 12 of the *Canadian Charter of Rights and Freedoms*. Showing great courage and compassion, Mr. Justice Noble reduced the parole eligibility and prison sentence from life imprisonment to one year of custody and one year of house arrest, based upon a recommendation by the jury where they refused to follow the law and refused to recommend parole ineligibility for ten or more years. At this second trial, it was Mr. Justice Noble's unintendedly misleading remarks that prevented the jury from performing the most important function that a jury can ever be relied upon to perform, that of jury nullification. Robert Latimer's case cried out for jury nullification to reach a fair and compassionate result.

Ultimately, when the Latimer case came before the Supreme Court the second time, it was held that misleading the jury so that they did not engage in jury nullification was not a reversible error. The Supreme Court affirmed the conviction and increased the sentence to life imprisonment with no parole for ten years.

It seems that the Supreme Court must have viewed itself as speaking for the vulnerable, when one considers the manner in which they handled this appeal. It is the author's view that they were tragically mistaken. We suggest the majority of Canadians were clearly supportive of the compromise achieved by the jury and Mr. Justice Noble, and it was with profound sadness by many that the law was viewed so inflexibly by the Supreme Court.

With the greatest of respect, it is the author's view that the Supreme Court, in attempting to do what they thought was the right thing, completely undermined jury nullification. It is jury nullification that protects each and every one of us from unfair laws, and the unfair application of those laws. As long as we know that we can be tried by a jury of our peers, no matter how tyrannical or unfair a government might become, we could previously always look to a jury for our salvation. A government's ability to oppress the people is completely undermined if fair-minded people can engage in jury nullification. As Lord

Devlin said in *Trial by Jury* (1966), Hamlyn Lectures: Eighth Series, at page 164:

> The first object of any tyrant in Whitehall would be to make Parliament utterly subservient to his will; and the next to overthrow or diminish trial by jury, for no tyrant could afford to leave a subject's freedom in the hands of twelve of his countrymen. So that trial by jury is more than an instrument of justice and more than one wheel of the constitution: it is the lamp that shows that freedom lives.

It is against this backdrop of the Robert Latimer trial that we encountered this unexpected assault on democratic freedom by castrating jury nullification. Unfortunately, a trial that seemingly had nothing to do with freedom or democracy did significant collateral damage to one of the most fundamental safeguards of freedom and democracy.

We can look at freedom of speech, freedom of religion, freedom to vote, or even such sacred concepts as proof beyond a reasonable doubt, and none are more of a cornerstone to our democratic freedom than the right to be tried by a jury of twelve of your peers who can choose not to convict in the face of tyranny.

Some might feel that the fervor with which the author argues for the inviolability of jury nullification in protecting our freedoms is overblown. It is to those people that I repeat the often quoted line "I love my country, but I fear my government."

Epilogue

As bleak as the story seems to this point, events have unfolded that are both optimistic and heartening. Although in the author's view the Supreme Court engaged in buck passing with the suggestion that perhaps Parliament could pardon Robert Latimer, this did not happen. Instead, Robert served his time in a penitentiary and is now on parole in the community, a decade later. Thankfully, the harshness of the law that was brought against Robert Latimer did not break this principled and compassionate man. He was there. He knew what he believed was the right thing to do, and he selflessly did what he knew had to be done to protect his daughter from inhumane suffering.

With respect to the collective freedom of all Canadians, where does this leave us with respect to jury nullification and oppressive laws or prosecutions? Surprisingly, but commendably, the Supreme Court swung the pendulum back somewhat in *R. v. Krieger.* The Court held in Krieger, a case involving a medicinal cannabis grower, that no matter how clear the law or the evidence, it must still be left up to the jury to decide whether to convict or not. Defence counsel were still not permitted to argue for jury nullification.

Then, in events that could never have been predicted at the time, the Internet came along and completely resurrected jury nullification. The ability to manage the knowledge of jurors has been completely usurped by the Internet. The days of chastising defence counsel for explaining jury nullification to twelve people in the courtroom have been overshadowed by the ability of the public to completely control the information highway to the jury. There is little a trial judge can do to stem the flow of information about jury nullification that can occur on the Internet during a trial.

While it may be a somewhat premature forecast, it seems that it is inevitable that jury nullification will become a principle that is directly explained by the trial judge to all juries so that jurors are not inappropriately encouraged by misleading Internet information to engage in unprincipled jury nullification. Even before the evolution of the Internet, jury instructions had evolved this way in some jurisdictions within the United States. Given the almost complete inability of judges to manage the flow of information from the Internet to jurors, at least up until the point at which jury deliberations start, and the jurors are sequestered, it seems that the regressive effect on jury nullification in Robert Latimer's case will almost certainly be undone by the Internet.

Marie Henein

SPLIT-SECONDS MATTER

Marie T. Henein LL.M is one of Canadian Lawyer Magazine's "Top 25 Most Influential Lawyers", and a Fellow of the American College of Trial Lawyers. She has argued major cases at all levels of court, lectures extensively in her field, and co-edits criminal law publications. Recent honours include the Law Society of Upper Canada's Laura Legge Award and delivering the Bernard Cohn Memorial Lecture at the University of Windsor.

THE COUNTLESS SMALL DECISIONS that we make every day are mostly of no moment. Turn left or right. Cross the street now or wait a minute. But these seemingly inconsequential choices sometimes put you in the path of people who alter your life. In mere moments, the most mundane decision can completely change the course your life will take. Criminal cases often come down to those moments — minutes or seconds that are life changing. And I find that I spend much of my career as a criminal lawyer dissecting those moments. A word that provokes; a perception that ignites fear and the rush to self-defence; a simple turn that puts you in the path of an incendiary chain of events. Irreversible fractions of time.

For Michael Bryant, the former Attorney General of Ontario, a couple of small decisions would change everything. The decision not to stop at a book-store, as planned. The decision not to make a left turn one street early. These two inconsequential choices would put him directly in the path of a very angry, intoxicated and aggressive man named Darcy Sheppard. Darcy Sheppard lived a tragic life whose end was years in the making. That is the heartbreaking reality. But as of August 31, 2009, the irreparable damage to Mr. Sheppard had been done and unfortunately, it had left a person who was troubled and often violent. That was the Darcy Sheppard who Michael Bryant would encounter that night.

The next twenty-eight seconds of their one-and-only interaction would be life-altering for all involved. Darcy Sheppard would suffer a fatal head injury after falling off Michael's car, striking his head on a sidewalk curb. Michael, the former Attorney General for Ontario, would find himself, for the very first time, on the other side of the law — an accused, charged with criminal negligence causing death, and dangerous driving causing death. His political star and personal life were irreparably impacted.

Let me share this: as a general rule, I don't like talking about my cases. In part because I think it violates deeply private and personal relationships forged when one is dealing with people at their most vulnerable, and in part because I figure, quite frankly, who cares? There is no false modesty here at all. My ego is more than healthy. I just don't like the public dissection of a case for mere sport. But I think there might be some important lessons here. There certainly were for me.

On the night of August 31, 2009, Michael and his then-wife, Susan, were celebrating their twelfth wedding anniversary. They had driven in his old black Saab convertible for a takeout shawarma dinner at their favourite restaurant and then down to the Beaches in Toronto for a walk, and to exchange small gifts. It wasn't a fancy or particularly eventful night. Finally, they stopped for some dessert in Greektown on Danforth Avenue. As they continued their drive towards their home along Bloor Street, they stopped at a red light at Yonge and Bloor. They were in line behind several cars, waiting at the red light. A cyclist, later discovered to be Mr. Sheppard, was at the corner of the streets. He appeared to be tormenting another driver, randomly throwing garbage in the street, moving pylons around and maneuvering his bike to block cars from moving. Michael did nothing. He did not interact with the cyclist. They did not talk and when the light changed, the cyclist disappeared from view.

Michael and Susan continued to drive along Bloor Street. They debated stopping at a bookstore but decided not to so that they could get home to their two young children. From Yonge and Bloor to the pedestrian lights at Bloor, there continued to be no interaction with Darcy Sheppard. He was nowhere in sight. Michael was not giving the cyclist a second thought.

Michael stopped at a red light, only moments away from home. At the stop light, his car was sandwiched between a vehicle in front of him and another behind him. As the light turned green, the vehicle in front started to move through the green light. Michael also started to move with the flow of traffic. As he was moving, Sheppard raced down the centre line, passing numerous vehicles at a high speed. But when he came to Michael's vehicle, he did something unusual. Surveillance-video evidence would reveal that Darcy Sheppard suddenly slowed his speed dramatically as he approached Michael's door and appeared to deliberately veer close to the driver's door. The video would also show that Sheppard leaned in towards Michael's vehicle and appeared to either swing or throw something in the direction of the driver's head. We would subsequently learn that Mr. Sheppard had a particularly unusual animus for people driving what he believed were fancy cars. Startled, Michael moved the vehicle to the right, away from Darcy Sheppard. Michael was shocked and slammed on the brakes to stop the car. The car stalled.

Darcy Sheppard did not continue driving by. He swerved his bike directly in front of the Saab to stop Michael from moving forward with traffic. His anger was now unequivocally focused entirely on the occupants of the Saab. Sheppard was described by independent witnesses as being in a rage, menacing and tormenting the driver. Independent witnesses confirmed that Michael did not interact with the cyclist, did not say anything, and appeared not to even be making eye contact with Darcy Sheppard.

Sheppard was in a violent rage. The defence investigation would reveal that the source of his rage had nothing to do with Michael Bryant. By this point in the evening, Sheppard had already been in a number of altercations. Earlier that day, he had been frightening drivers and actually grabbed a steering wheel of another driver. Approximately half an hour before encountering Michael, Sheppard had some form of altercation with his girlfriend. He had physically assaulted a stranger on the street with a bike lock. And just moments before, at Yonge and Bloor, he had tormented another driver. We discovered that Michael was Darcy's fifth known aggressive encounter that evening. As one independent witness described Darcy Sheppard that evening, he was violent and looking for a fight.

Michael and Susan were completely exposed. The car top was down, the windows were down, a vehicle was behind them and Darcy Sheppard was in front of them. There was nowhere to go. They were terrified and panicked. So much so that Michael was now wholly unable to control his car — he could not even start it. As the video evidence showed, the standard-transmission car stalled repeatedly. After several seconds, Michael managed to get the car started and caused it to lurch forward, unintentionally striking Sheppard and causing him to fall on the hood of the car. Within a split second, six-tenths of a second to be exact, Michael immediately slammed the brakes on again. This entire sequence of events took twenty-eight seconds.

After braking, Michael reversed, swerving to avoid Sheppard and to get away. But Sheppard would not let him go. He threw a backpack containing a large metal bike lock at the windshield area causing it to bounce either on the windshield or the hood of the car. He ran at the car and jumped onto the driver's side of the car. Michael believed that he was trying to climb into the car. An independent witness observing the incident described Sheppard as putting his body into the car and grabbing either the steering wheel or the driver. Forensic evidence would in fact confirm that Sheppard's body was well into the car.

During that drive, Michael tried to stop the vehicle to push Sheppard off. Sheppard wouldn't let go. Michael wasn't strong enough to push the six-foot-one-inch Sheppard off. During one of these attempts, Sheppard said, "You are not getting away that easy." Darcy was deep into the vehicle, with his entire upper torso leaning into the driver's space. At some point, Sheppard was laughing. Michael was desperately trying to control the steering wheel but had difficulty doing so. At this point, there were only two options. Stop the vehicle and be attacked by Darcy Sheppard, or risk driving into oncoming traffic. At that point, driving into oncoming traffic, exposing himself and his wife to a head-on collision was the only way to get away from Darcy Sheppard's attack. He chose the only option he thought he had. He drove headlong into the oncoming traffic lane with Sheppard still hanging onto the vehicle and attempting to get in. All of a sudden, Michael felt he regained control of the wheel and the cyclist was no longer in view.

He drove to safety just around the corner to a hotel and called 911. If there was any question as to what was in Michael's mind at that moment, there can be no doubt when one hears his 911 plea for help. He asks the police to come because he has just been attacked. It is the call of someone terrified for his life. It is the call of someone who has just been attacked.

The police arrived promptly and placed him under arrest — within an investigative span of minutes and in full view of the media.

Reading this has taken you much longer than the twenty-eight seconds this event took. Twenty-eight seconds, and Michael finds himself in the criminal justice system. Twenty-eight seconds, and he does not get home to his children that night. Twenty-eight seconds, and Darcy Sheppard loses his life. I think that today, if you were to ask Michael what he would have done differently that night, he would tell you he wishes that he would have just stayed home.

For me, much of the work on this case would begin within hours of the arrest and most of it turned on the facts. I have to confess that this attention to factual detail didn't come naturally for me. Graduating from law school, I was convinced that the only thing that mattered was the law. Facts were a necessary obstacle — but I didn't care for them much. Maybe it's the arrogance of young graduates — you assume that you know the real play, you know what happened. You size things up quickly. Or maybe it was just my own naïveté that led me to that view as a young lawyer. But a few trials and appeals later, you learn quickly that the facts are everything — they are the essential fabric of any case, trial or appellate. They not only frame the legal debate, the right facts can drive the case in the direction you want. All of which is to say, I'm glad that Michael Bryant came to me when I had already been twenty years at the bar. There were important lessons that I needed to learn first.

I am now a firm believer in the importance of developing a clear narrative; facts are easier to analyze when there is a beginning, middle, and end, and when there is an internal cohesion to the defence version of events. A clear narrative naturally makes conduct understandable, or at least excusable. In 1992, Professors Pennington and Hastie from the University of Colorado published important findings on the way that juries make their decisions. Their analysis was based on case scenarios given to mock juries. Their hypothesis, called the "story model," is that jurors impose a narrative story organization on trial information and meaning is assigned to trial evidence according to its plausibility when incorporated into their chronology of events. In addition, they theorized that the story that the juror constructed in no small part "determines" the juror's decision. Their research revealed that the willingness to accept a story is determined by its coherence — and this means consistency, completeness and plausibility. The jury's verdict was significantly affected by how easy it was to construct a story from the evidence presented.

Further, the *order* in which evidence was introduced impacted on the verdict. The story that was easier to construct and presented first dominated the jury's decision-making with respect to the strength of evidence and the credibility of witnesses and their confidence in reaching a verdict. In other words, the accepted narrative has an impact on the decision reached. The adopted narrative also impacts on the consideration and assessment of individual pieces of evidence. The evidence doesn't drive the story. It is the other way around. The story drives the consideration and assessment of the evidence.

But the difficulty in any case with a great deal of media attention is that the narrative is written for you, often before you've even said a single word to your client. Lawyers spend a great deal of time discussing how to interface with the media — when it is appropriate to comment, and when it will be beneficial to your client. My experience is that the media are rarely there to be persuaded by you; you are, after all, quite correctly, viewed as a partisan spokesperson for your client. Often, once they come to you for comment the media already have a settled view of the case and there is precious little you can do to persuade them to see it otherwise. Trying to control the media is, I think, usually a waste of time. They will write what they wish to write, as they should. They may love you or your client one day, and dislike you the next. And you will have very little to say about it.

I was informed that the Bryant case had generated more national media stories than any other criminal case before it. I don't know if that is true, but it certainly felt like it. Having been involved in a number of high-profile cases previously, nothing came quite close to this. My office went on a media lock down after I discovered that journalists were attempting to contact my family to find out about his lawyer. As one friend who was interviewed told me, the journalist asked him to disclose something negative about me. Fortunately, he didn't.

In Michael Bryant's case, the narratives were changing daily with the news cycle. A story of road rage. A story about justice for the rich and justice for the poor. A morality play of how the rich and mighty fall. A Canadian Chappaquiddick. Our own bonfire of the vanities, in which nothing is as satiating as the spectacular demise and equally spectacular resurrection of a public figure. The redemptive quality of the experience often feeds the media frenzy. Or perhaps it is the other way around. In this case, there were more narratives than you could count. City politics, stories about bicycles, cars, and bike lanes. Stories about the tragedy of substance abuse. Stories about the lives of bike couriers. The stories were endless.

The video, which played on every news station and was analyzed by armchair quarterbacks everywhere, was the result of retail video surveillance on the stretch of the road where the encounter happened. In fact, there were a number of retail cameras in the area, all seized by the police, which showed much of the brief encounter. Although at first blush it was troubling, the video surveillance would become the most critical piece of evidence for the defence.

I think one of the great gifts that the study of law provides is that one is trained to suspend judgment. We start with a wicked cynicism but learn to put off taking a decided view. Things are never what they seem at first. This case was no different. That much I knew by the time Michael Bryant walked into my office. It wasn't what it seemed. This wasn't road rage at all. How many people do you know who would be in such a rage that they would literally run over someone they did not know? Someone who they've never interacted with before, driving the wrong way into oncoming traffic? That alleged scenario in this case was nonsense. A narrative that we refused to accept.

It could have been any one of us driving home in that car on August 31, 2009. From popular culture's obsession with crime, we get desensitized to the ordinary, prosaic character of most alleged incidents of crime. You can't blame the public for being fixated on the strange, the unusual, the deviant, but that has very little to do with real life. The reality is that for those of us who live our days in criminal law, tragedies are rarely expected, or intended, or even remotely sensational. We weren't buying the narrative that the newspapers were selling or to which the police had committed.

So we began by examining the decisions that were made that night, step-by-step, 1/100th of a second by 1/100th of a second. We needed to deconstruct those twenty-eight seconds plus the seconds that came before, and the seconds that came after. The story of what was revealed that night has been recounted in many places, so I will not belabour the facts. It is enough to say that this was not a case of road rage.

Darcy Sheppard had lived a sad and unfortunate life. His challenges were hard to overcome, no matter how much support and love he had. In the end, they overtook him. He became an often-violent man, struggling with alcoholism and drug abuse. And as a bike courier, he seemed to have developed an obsessive anger towards what he perceived to be rich people in fancy cars. We discovered numerous independent witnesses who had been victims of his rage. One of them had called the police during one of Mr. Sheppard's assaults, as Sheppard threw a brick at him through his truck window. Another witness had had his entire attack photographed, unbeknownst to both him and Sheppard, as Sheppard attempted to climb into his vehicle, grab the steering wheel and spit all over the car. In the end, Michael Bryant was just one of many who had been unfortunate to cross Mr. Sheppard's path when he was raging. And as he tried to climb into Michael Bryant's car and as he raged, Michael Bryant tried to get away; driving into oncoming traffic to do so. The incident was tragic. And sad in every way. And not a crime.

I think it is often easy to approach a case, in whatever context, by letting the other side dictate the framework or the parameters, or worse still, the narrative. As defence lawyers, often our instinct is to take a defensive posture to cases. To be reactive rather than proactive. In criminal law, the prosecution has the burden of proving the case. And one approach is to take the prosecution case, the pre-constructed narrative, and attempt to poke holes, to effectively deconstruct it. There is nothing wrong with that approach. It is part of every defence to be reactive.

But the other approach is to be proactive. This is a very different technique. It requires one to build an affirmative defence. It starts by clearly having a sense of one's own narrative. Then one sets about unfolding it. Usually, this isn't based only on the client's version of events. Sometimes that is all one has: the classic he said/he said, diametrically opposed versions of the same event. But where there is more, one should take advantage of it.

In Bryant, we had the video that captured a portion of the events as analyzed by a forensic analyst. The result was that the seconds could be broken down even further. We chose an analyst who was routinely retained by the prosecution. From the point of view of both the prosecution or the defence, there is no value to simply hearing what one wants to hear. Buying experts doesn't buy you a whole lot; it certainly would not have achieved the result we set out to achieve. The results of the analysis were powerful, debunking many stories that had been floating around. It refuted eyewitness evidence — evidence that any experienced counsel will tell you has, notoriously and scientifically, often proven to be unreliable.

The other significant evidence that supported the defence narrative of an unprovoked, irrational, and extremely frightening attack was the observation of the independent witnesses. It would have been one thing to attempt to describe a confrontation. It was another thing for several witnesses to come forward with stories of encounters that bore a striking similarity to the events that Michael Bryant described. And it was even more powerfully probative to have photographs of these other events. The impossibility of coincidence became very powerful. The fact that people across different walks of life would have strikingly similar encounters with Darcy Sheppard was powerful evidence. What emerged was that these were not run-of-the-mill, ordinary roadside encounters. Mr. Sheppard's unprovoked attacks routinely involved unrelenting pursuits, violence ranging from spitting at drivers to grabbing steering wheels, trying to get into cars, and smashing car windows. The discovery of these witnesses was a combination of the willingness of people to contact us, and a painstaking review of prosecution disclosure, reviewed in teams of two by the defence.

In a few months, we had amassed a formidable amount of independent evidence that pointed in only one direction; to Michael Bryant's innocence. The question was what to do with it? The obvious and usual answer would be to wait and unveil it all at trial. Lawyers are guarded by nature, and keeping one's hand close to one's chest, trial by ambush *per se*, seems to be deeply ingrained. But it is not always right.

The starting point for me was that I was dealing with Rick Peck and Mark Sandler, both outstanding criminal defence lawyers and both tough-as-nails as prosecutors. They were also extremely independent-minded and fair.

Prosecutorial powers cannot be differentially invoked by the state depending on whether the target is a public figure or an ordinary citizen. This is something that our Supreme Court has repeatedly stated is fundamental to our law. As Justice William Binnie stated in *R. v. Shirose*: "It is one of the proud accomplishments of the common law that everybody is subject to the ordinary law of the land regardless of public prominence or governmental status." Justices Beverley McLachlin and John Major put it this way: "High profile matters, by their nature, attract strong public emotions. In our society, the Crown is charged with the duty to ensure that every accused person is treated with fairness."

The principle is a good one. While there is no question that in this country our prosecutors act with the utmost integrity and fairness, it is impossible to ignore the fact that with profile comes greater intensity, scrutiny, and resourcing of the prosecution. Everyone is looking. Everyone is scrutinizing. And this isn't lost on any of the participants. Certainly not the prosecutors or the defence lawyers. People always ask criminal lawyers if they can defend someone who they think is guilty. That is the easy job. Any lawyer will tell you that it is the innocent who are the toughest to defend. High-profile cases are equally paradoxical. The great thing about high-profile cases is that they are high in profile. And the bad thing about high-profile cases is that they are high in profile. In Michael's case, I had both issues to contend with.

In my career, I can think of no case in which I had agonized so much over the strategy. I consulted with colleagues, I listened to their views and, in the end, made the decision I thought was right, together with my client. I opened up our file, exposed our full defence to prosecutorial and police scrutiny, even allowing my client and his wife to be interviewed before the trial began. It was the toughest decision I've had to make in my legal career. There are numerous reasons why there is no obligation on the defence to provide disclosure to the Crown. But in Michael's case we were offering the police and the prosecution a full kick at the can, a no-holds-barred preview. They could dismantle it, shore up their case or, as I hoped, come to see the case in the way that I saw it.

Taking the important evidence gathered by the defence and providing it to the Crown unconstrained by any conditions or restrictions could have been either a great success or a magnificent failure. In the end, as I weighed all my options, I returned to the same feeling. The evidence would not change. It could not weaken. I was that confident in it and to put Michael through what would have surely been the trial of my career was unconscionable if there was any hope of ending it early. In the end, there could be only one reason to take the full-disclosure approach, and that was the complete, unwavering and unequivocal confidence in the strength of our case and in the firm belief that the objective facts, when fully exposed, pointed to one and only one conclusion: Michael's innocence.

That twenty-eight seconds would take months of review. We met with the prosecution and I made a day-long presentation to them. Our witnesses were interviewed, Michael was interviewed, our video expert met with the prosecution team for a day. No statement or report was left unreviewed. The Crown retained their own experts to review the findings. There were no half measures.

And in the end, it was the right decision. The prosecution concluded that there was no reasonable likelihood of conviction. I believe that there was no other reasonable conclusion. Some of the best lawyering often happens outside the public view. I have come to believe that I could have done no better at a trial than I did out of the view of the public in this case.

I am breaking my rule of no case comment, because I can think of no case I have been involved in where the public and legal community's interest was so intense. And while I stopped reading the newspaper articles because I found it too distracting, I couldn't get away from the legal community's oft-expressed sentiment. The truth is that Michael Bryant was well-loved by the legal community. Many identified with him, many knew him personally, and many were utterly grief-stricken over his situation. The pressure to get the right result was, to be honest, overwhelming at times. Nothing in law school gets one ready for this amount of scrutiny. One's failure will be as notorious as one's success, and the legal community, just like the public, loves both stories equally voraciously.

C.D. Evans

WEIGHING MORALITIES OF A VICTIMLESS CRIME

C.D. Evans QC is a Fellow of the American College of Trial Lawyers and held the Milvain Visiting Chair in Advocacy at the University of Calgary Faculty of Law. He is a Life Member of the National Criminal Law Program Faculty. Called in Alberta and NT, he has argued in the Supreme Court of Canada and other jurisdictions. Mr. Evans authored two legal memoirs.

NORMALLY THE CRIMINAL LAWYER doesn't indulge in weighing moralities of a criminal prosecution; rather, our job is to defend without judgment. How was it then that the case of Charles Vernon Myers *versus* Her Majesty the Queen became an exception in my books? Because I liked the man and I thought he was being piled on.

On the law and order hand, it is all very well to play up the Robin Hood aspects of the series of events, and cheer The Exile in his impertinent nose-thumbing, but on the other hand the average citizen takes a dim view of escaped prisoners.

The Backstory, Part One

I was called into service when the fugitive Charles Vernon Myers was nabbed in 1987 on the occasion of his second return from exile. The call came from his son Richard Myers, a prominent practicing lawyer in Calgary. Subsequently, I became acquainted with the background.

To assert that C.V. Myers was one of the world's most colourful characters is an understatement. The account of my professional encounter with Mr. Myers is the stuff to which Richard Wagner could have devoted another twenty years of feverish composition, with its overtones of Nibelungen gold. We know from both history and literature that when the precious metal gold is prominent in human interaction, there is dirty work afoot.

The dirty work that provides the context for this saga is the perfervid pursuit of Citizen Myers by the catchpolls of the Canada Revenue Agency, at that time a.k.a. the Income Tax Department. The one thing that none of us wants is a red flag on our government tax file. Mr. Myers, having been branded with his scarlet letter, wore it like a medal. In 1976-1977, Myers had been vigorously prosecuted for alleged tax evasion. He was acquitted after a Provincial Court trial; the Crown appealed to the Court of Queen's Bench, which reversed his acquittal and found both Mr. Myers and his corporation Inter Publishing Company Ltd. guilty of two counts. The Appeal Court also sentenced Myers, at the age of sixty-five and in bad health, to two years in a federal penitentiary.

Charles Vernon Myers, resident in or about Calgary, was a well-known and highly regarded investment counsellor. His own shrewd forays into the mysteries of making money netted him considerable wealth, and he was pleased to pass on the mechanics of his good fortune to others, in particular in his monthly publication *Myers Finance and Energy*, which circulated for twenty-three years and gained three thousand subscribers worldwide. Many of these financial clients were prominent community leaders and remained loyally supportive of Mr. Myers throughout his imbroglio with the infernal revenue. Back in 1952, Myers founded *Oilweek Magazine* in Alberta, a trade magazine for the oil and gas industry that prevails to this day. In 1966, he began his finance newsletter in Calgary, advising investors to buy gold. If they started doing so in the early 70s, their investments would have increased fifty fold.

Myers was reputedly a somewhat eccentric character, one widely circulated story in particular illustrating this. In anticipation of selling his Midnapore, Alberta property, Myers and his brother were cleaning out the horse barn when they came across an old barrel. It appeared to have fluid in it and smelled strongly of horse manure, suggesting that it should be jettisoned. Between the two of them, they managed to hoist this inordinately heavy barrel into the back of their half-ton, and discarded it with the rest of their load at the local landfill. It was heavy, it turns out, because it was full of gold Krugerrands. A connoisseur of garbage came across the broken barrel in the waste and noticed a glint of golden treasure. Showing an admirably honest *presence d'esprit,* the garbage picker alerted the local RCMP. They did not have to engage their full investigative powers before concluding that the only person thereabouts who could have inadvertently thrown out a treasure trove of gold was one C.V. Myers. Accordingly, the police dispatched themselves to the Myers home with the question: "to whom do the Krugerrands belong?" Mrs. Muriel Myers, showing her own *presence d'esprit*, laid claim to the lot. A suitable reward was made to the honest finder.

The Backstory, Part Two

Myers was a tenacious litigant; witness his successful lawsuit against the Government of the United States of America in its attempt to revoke his U.S. passport. In 1985, having fled from Canada after being convicted of tax evasion, Vern applied to the State Department for a U.S. passport based on his documented claim that he was a U.S. citizen. An official concluded that Myers had proved he was indeed a U.S. citizen and issued him a passport. In 1986, the Immigration and Naturalization Service, disapproving of the issuance of the passport and stating it was attempting to deport Myers, demanded the return of his passport and threatened him with fines and imprisonment if he did not do so. Myers sued the U.S. Secretary of State, arguing that once the State Department issued a passport it had no authority to revoke it. In 1988, judgment was granted in his favour. The Secretary of State appealed, and in 1990 the U.S. Court of Appeals, Ninth Circuit, dismissed the appeal. Myers kept his U.S. passport, and delivered a good punch to the eye of the bureaucrats.

In or about 1975, the Canadian authorities handed Myers a massive reassessment followed by a prosecution for alleged tax evasion. Both Myers and his corporation Interpublishing Company Ltd. ("Inter") were jointly charged with tax evasion for stated years in a stated amount "from the operation of publications known as *Myers Finance Review, Myers Finance and Energy, Myers Finance and Petroleum* and other publications, and from dealings in gold and silver bullion and coin, and for financial counselling." Myers was charged personally with a second count of tax evasion for stated years and a stated amount for essentially the same alleged delicts. Following a trial in the Provincial Court of Alberta, the Provincial Judge dismissed those charges against Myers and found the corporate defendant alone guilty and assessed a $250,000 fine. The Crown appealed the dismissal of the charges against Mr. Myers, and the corporate defendant appealed its conviction and sentence.

These appeals came on before an Alberta Court of Queen's Bench Justice by way of what was called a "*trial de novo*," a now-discarded process by which an accused, instead of arguing on the record before the lower court, was retried all over again in the higher court. In the result, Myers' acquittals were set aside and both he and his company were convicted. Moreover, Myers was sentenced to the maximum penalty, being two years in a federal penitentiary.

The findings of the appeal judge on the *trial de novo,* dated February 3,1977, are neither dissected nor disputed in this account. That is a judgment of a court of competent criminal jurisdiction that stands. That die was cast long before I came into the picture.

Mr. Myers' tax transgressions, as found by the Court on a review of the evidence, were substantial, but sending a sixty-five-year-old man with no previous criminal convictions to a federal penitentiary for two years for an income tax offence is a bit much. The Crown proceeded throughout by the less punitive prosecutorial option of summary conviction, although it had the option to proceed by indictment and did not. This Draconian punishment in my experience was practically unheard of, most transgressions of that nature being subject to a fine and the payment of an exorbitant penalty to the taxman. In the result, Myers ended up the oldest serving prisoner in the Canadian federal penitentiary system, and if that is not "cruel and unusual punishment" contrary to Section 12 of the much-vaunted *Charter of Rights*, nothing is. The *trial de novo* was held in Mr. Myers' absence, although he was represented throughout by counsel Jack MacPherson. Myers, residing at the time in Spokane, Washington, was therefore tried and sentenced in absentia. The sentence being imposed, he was a fugitive from Canadian justice.

Whether this procedure — which amounted to double jeopardy — was the last such *trial de novo* in Canada, they were certainly done away with not long after his second piggyback trial, and this after his acquittal in Provincial Court, where he had been represented by two leading counsel at considerable expense. In effect, he was forced to fund his defence all over again. This being a Crown appeal, Mr. Myers was not required to be in court, a right he chose to exercise. Thus he was in the United States when the Queen's Bench verdict was delivered and sentencing was imposed. He had not escaped legal custody, but by remaining in the U.S. one could say he was then "on the lam."

The saga that follows could transfix and mesmerize even the most jaded audience. Subsequent to the successful Crown appeal of his acquittal and the dismissal of his Corporation's appeal by the Court of Queen's Bench in February 1977, Mr. Myers "took it on the Arthur Duffy" not once, but twice. To put it in the argot of the average citizen, Mr. Myers escaped from prison twice, to the more salubrious climes of Spokane, Washington. Income tax evasion was then not an extraditable offence from the United States, and he could sojourn there in relative tranquility: Myers, who had a rare sense of humour, would say that he was there for his health; it was not healthy for him to be in Canada. This socially uplifting loophole, somewhat akin to seeking sanctuary in a church, was purged some time ago, to the chagrin of upright tax evaders everywhere. There were, however, compelling reasons for him to return to Canada, the first of which, in 1979, was to endeavour to appeal his sentence.

Although by that time the window for an appeal from what could be argued was an unreasonably harsh sentence had expired, an approach was made to the Canadian authorities by Myers' Calgary lawyers offering for him to voluntarily return to Canada and enter custody if they would not oppose an application for leave to appeal the sentence. That did not mean they had to concede the actual appeal, but at least allow Mr. Myers to have his sentence reviewed by an appeal court. The exact circumstances have been obscured by the passage of time. Suffice it to say that Myers returned to Canada — and to jail — voluntarily, on his understanding that he could have his sentence reviewed. Accordingly, he returned to Canada and turned himself over to the RCMP in Calgary, January 1979. Too late, it was determined that the Canadian authorities took the position that they had not made any commitment to bind Crown counsel not to oppose the leave application.

Having returned voluntarily, Mr. Myers was thrown into the *Château d'If* to serve his two-year sentence. Thus he found himself first in the Maximum-Security Remand Center for twenty-one days and then incarcerated with serious criminals in the penitentiary eighty miles north of Calgary. On his transit to the pen, he was chained to a gunrunner who opined that he would not have been loath to shoot it out with the cops. No doubt chafing in *durance vile* in his eight by twelve cell, he identified with Edmond Dantes *a.k.a* the Count of Monte Cristo, according to no less an authority than Wikipedia,

> ... an adventure story primarily concerned with themes, of hope, justice, vengeance, mercy and forgiveness, it focuses on a man who is wrongfully imprisoned, escapes from jail, acquires a fortune and sets about getting revenge on those responsible for his imprisonment.

History repeats, with the blast of a Wagner tuba.

Worst-Case Scenario

There is always a worst-case scenario accompanying any sentence appeal, that is, the sentence could be increased. Sentence having been put in issue, the matter might end up before a judge who had the jurisdiction to vary the original sentence upward to a fine of one quarter to double the taxes owing — in this case, what Dr. Hunter S. Thompson would call "serious money" — *plus* maximum imprisonment, with extra prison time tacked on in the event of non-payment of the fine. On consideration of that sobering possibility, there was therefore no sentence appeal. Mr. Myers settled in to serve his penitentiary sentence of two years, which was a chilling prospect at the age of sixty-seven years. While we are dealing with Notes to Foreign Students, it should be observed that the original sentence imposed could have been "two years less one day," which would have meant that Mr. Myers would serve his term of imprisonment in a provincial minimum-security correctional institution, with a better prospect of day passes, halfway house privileges, and perhaps earlier parole.

There remained the prospect of parole. This wasn't much of a prospect. Ten U.S. Congressmen wrote on his behalf, which references were forwarded to the National Parole Board pending a parole hearing on July 18, 1979. Those and many other letters of support apparently were of no avail. At that time, it appeared to Mr. Myers that success of his parole application was influenced negatively by the fact that his re-assessed tax liability remained outstanding. Things looked grim. Mr. Myers felt that he was being held in a debtors' prison, which was difficult to accept, considering that such oppressive incarceration regimes had been discontinued a century before.

Mr. Myers escaped from prison on the second occasion in 1979 by failing to return after a forty-eight-hour weekend leave. On the determination that a prisoner was not likely to commit mayhem, after a certain amount of time in jail, a temporary absence could be given, and a forty-eight-hour unescorted temporary absence came Myers' way in July 1979. He had from five *p.m.* Friday to dinnertime Sunday, at which latter time he had to report back to the pen. At nine o'clock Monday morning, Myers was no longer in Canada. Certain imaginative planning went into this elopement: a two-car convoy was standing by to facilitate his escape. Mr. Myers was dining with his oblivious extended family at a downtown hotel, got up to go innocently to the men's room, and just kept going to the first car. He was driven to the second car, and they passed safely through to the American side. Myers recounts all this detail in his published autobiography *"Fifty Years in the Furnace: Autobiography of a Non-Conformist."*

Other than from such a master as Alexander Dumas, one would be hard-put to produce from mere imagination a more compelling narrative than this one: in his mind wrongfully imprisoned, an elderly prisoner escapes twice to another jurisdiction from which he not only evades re-incarceration but deliberately thumbs his nose at his former country's justice system. This goading raspberry was accomplished by Myers writing a monthly column "The Exile" — to use his term "hurling invectives from the safety of my U.S. haven" — that was gleefully published by the redoubtable Byfield clan in their *Alberta Report*, of its day a popular right-of-centre periodical in Western Canada. It did not invite the sympathy of his tormentors that he appeared on the *Merv Griffin Show* as an escaped convict. Myers also went to Louisiana and addressed a huge audience, after which a Congressman on the CBC television program *The Fifth Estate* gave the Canadian authorities a gratuitous piece of his mind as "pointy-headed bureaucrats," praised Mr. Myers' "brilliant analytical mind," and likened his persecution to having been burned at the stake.

He remained in the United States, publishing his newsletter — which always came out on time and never a day late, in accordance with Myers' intention that there was never an issue missed, even throughout his incarceration — the while thumbing his nose at the Canadian *custos morum*, until December, 1987.

Undertaking the Defence

By now I had determined enough of the background that I knew this would be an intriguing case. Particularly engaging was the unsporting manner in which he had been nabbed.

In December 1987, Mr. Myers had returned to Canada surreptitiously to be with his dying wife Muriel who was in palliative care at a Calgary hospital. He was able to spend her last lucid hour with her. One of the medical personnel, being on the alert not so much for Charles Vernon Myers as for one of his relatives who was expected by the cops to appear at the hospital in an agitated state in a non-related matter, recognized the fugitive and called the cops. Mr. Myers was forced to attend his wife's funeral two days later handcuffed and in prison garb and marched in and out by Constable Boot. This humiliation was visited upon him in his time of ultimate sorrow in the presence of his family and friends. He was then re-incarcerated in Bowden Federal Penitentiary, a "medium security" joint, that is, surrounded by barbed wire with the RCMP police dog training school across the road. He was mandated by law to serve the remanent of his unserved sentence, some fifteen months remaining, and was further charged with "being unlawfully at large" contrary to the *Criminal Code*, the procedure against him by indictment. Any sentence received on a conviction for that delict would no doubt be made consecutive to the rest of the time that he still had to serve. That's pretty tough on a seventy-five-year-old man suffering from numerous medical challenges including the cancer that eventually killed him.

Thus it was that on a blustery winter day I found myself motoring to the Bowden Penitentiary north of Calgary in the company of Jack Marshall QC, a partner in the prominent Calgary legal mill Macleod Dixon, and one of Mr. Myers' Calgary solicitors. Mr. Myers presented as impatient, irascible, and put upon. And likeable. He had been through both a physical and an emotional mill; he was suffering bad health and was in depleted physical shape. It was a bitterly cold winter, and in order to walk the three blocks to the visiting area his face had to be totally covered against the cold. I could readily see that he was afflicted with arthritis and shortness of breath, and that the closely guarded federal penitentiary was hardly a place to stick a sick old man. That said, I also gathered that he was treated with respect by his fellow inmates, some of whom watched out for "the old man," which is a godsend in a place like that.

My job was to defend Charles Vernon Myers on the new charge of being unlawfully at large. Presumably an example was to be made of this unrepentant felon, and of course the case attracted a great deal of media attention. The prosecutor who was assigned was a sanctimonious and humourless sort of fellow and no doubt this was the pinnacle of his career. He prosecuted with the right hand of a vengeful Old Testament God. As luck would have it, however, the trial — the process accelerated as my client was elderly, ill and in custody — came on before Mr. Justice Arthur Lutz at Red Deer, Alberta. My take on Art Lutz as a judge was that, if the Crown was laying it on and the circumstances were sufficiently mitigating, he was just the judge to sort things out.

I seldom ever listened to my clients' advice on how they should be defended. My usual practice was to tell the client to cower in the prisoners' box and look repentant and apologetic and to keep his/her mouth shut; if I needed help I would ask for it. Meanwhile, hope that the courthouse burns down or the Crown witnesses die, preferably of natural causes. In Myers' case, I had a very intelligent, canny, and erudite client.

Following Myers' 1979 return, Jack Marshall QC had unsuccessfully applied to the Federal Court of Canada on his behalf for a writ of *habeas corpus* — literally, "deliver the body" — the argument being that Mr. Myers was imprisoned under a sentence "unknown to law." There was as much success with that innovative argument in the Federal Court at that time as Edmond Dantes had to his gaolers and as I had at Myer's Red Deer trial.

I advanced the defence theory that his original conviction was unlawful, because his sentence was unlawful, and if it was unlawful, then so was his incarceration, and he could not be "unlawfully at large." The argument went this way: I submitted that it was trite law that there are two parts to a conviction, the finding of guilt and the sentence. The Income Tax Act of the day stated that a fine, or imprisonment and a fine, could be imposed upon violators; it did not, for some obscure reason, allow for a prison sentence alone. Thus, I argued, the two-year sentence imposed on him by the appeal court was illegal because it imposed a prison sentence without a fine. If the sentence was illegal, the conviction was unlawful. *Quod erat demonstrandum.*

That was the essence of the defence argument that was urged upon the learned trial judge. We didn't get the cigar or the ashtray in the final analysis, but there was sufficient information put before the Court that activated the judge's empathy, which was exacerbated by the unrelenting demands of the Crown that Myers be publicly burned at the stake. In the course of the trial, I called forensic psychologist Dr. Thomas Dalby, who examined and tested my client. Dr. Dalby advised the Court that Mr. Myers' first wife had been institutionalized in a psychiatric facility and he was afraid the same thing would happen to him. Dr. Dalby testified: "At the time of his departure he was clinically depressed, anxious and was terrified of two things: the possibility he might die in prison and the possibility he would go mad."

I had emphasized to the Court Mr. Myers' poor health, which was aggravated by his detention at the Red Deer Remand Centre where he was held during the trial, to be returned to the penitentiary thirty miles south for the evenings. The strain, Myers noted, "had taken a visible toll on my health and I guess on my appearance." During the course of a long day's hearing I had asked the Court for a recess in order to see whether my client could continue.

I added: "But my client is a tough old bird and he may want to go on." Mr. Myers wanted to go on, and the judge considerately ordered a more comfortable chair for him to sit in instead of the hard wooden prisoner's box. After the first day's court appearance, Justice Lutz ordered Myers returned to Bowden Penitentiary. However, the correctional escort employees detained him at the Remand Centre because he had missed the last van scheduled to return to the penitentiary. His medication, which was requested at nine in the morning, did not arrive until three-thirty in the afternoon. Justice Lutz told the Crown Prosecutor to contact the Solicitor General and "convey the displeasure of this Court with regard to the conduct of these people in doing this to this man." At that moment, I had that warm feeling that sometimes flows over the Bench to the defence table.

Beating Up on Bambi

Based upon the mitigating medical evidence and the deteriorating physical health of my client, his great age, and the rather sad circumstances of his being re-incarcerated after visiting his dying wife, I pulled out the stops on the mitigation argument, describing my client as "one of the world's last angry men" who felt that he had been treated unjustly, having been convicted after being acquitted earlier. I said: "He had in his mind being kept in something that hasn't been around for a couple hundred years, a debtor's prison." In *Fifty Years in the Furnace*, Mr. Myers recalls:

> Evans spoke most emphatically, dwelling on my tribulations and the life-threatening conditions, in my opinion, from which I had felt I must escape for the sake of my survival. When he was through, Evans was ready to deliver the final K.O. 'To harshly treat this man,' Evans said, 'would be like beating up on Bambi.' I think it was a good defence. I think it was a good line. And I think it was an extra lenient sentence.

Mr. Justice Lutz sorted all of this out. He was empathetic to my client who was in failing physical and psychological health, but the law must take its course. He found Charles Vernon Myers guilty of the offence of being unlawfully at large, but took careful note of the medical and other mitigating evidence placed before him in the matter of penalty, and — notwithstanding the Crown's pounding the table for life and lashes — sentenced my client to thirty days imprisonment, the sentence to be served consecutively to the fifteen-month balance of the original 1977 sentence Myers was now serving.

I had kept my learned colleague Leslie R. Weatherhead, Attorney at Law, Spokane, Washington, one of Mr. Myers' U.S. lawyers, abreast of the developments in the Canadian jurisdiction. Les Weatherhead was a capital fellow, and a very able counsel. He had argued Mr. Myers' passport case. As soon as Myers was returned to the precincts of Bowden Pen, the National Parole Board convened a hearing for him, and I appeared with him before the three-person panel. The Board chairman ran a fair hearing, at the end of which the prisoner was granted parole. He could be paroled in Canada but could not leave the country; or he could be paroled to the United States if they would take him, but would not be able to return to Canada.

Mr. Myers decided that he would return to the United States. His wife was deceased; his newsletter business was centered in Spokane, Washington; the Canadian tax department had an outstanding claim against him for some $2.3 million. The question was, would the United States Immigration Department let him back in? Les Weatherhead obtained a temporary court injunction requiring the Immigration Department to admit Myers into the U.S., but there was a tight time limit. Weatherhead succeeded in having the Parole Board in Saskatchewan issue an Order for Parole to the United States, which was electronically sent to Bowden Pen. The pen would not release Myers until the following Friday, which would be too late to get back into the U.S. through the injunction window. Weatherhead then prevailed upon the Board to reverse their local Red Deer order of release date, and Myers was released on the Thursday and departed with Weatherhead and his son Richard. They flew to Castlegar, B.C., were picked up in a two-car convoy by his Spokane lawyers, and crossed into the U.S. With Myers returned lawfully to Spokane, they all no doubt had jam for tea that day.

Throughout his ordeal, C.V. Myers never lost his sense of humour. After his flight in 1979, he advised *The Calgary Herald* in a rather unique way that he was coming back to serve his time. He told them that on his death, he would arrange to have his ashes sent to Revenue Canada and his ashes could finish out his prison term, on the understanding that Revenue Canada would return his ashes to his estate. In his autobiography, Myers wrote: "Apparently a lot of people thought this was funny but Revenue Canada was not among them. "

Is Tax Evasion a Victimless Crime?

Crime in the context of alleged tax evasion is a relative concept: some people would say it was a crime without a victim. Professor Kate Moss, writing in "Hart-Devlin Revisited: law, morality and consent in parenthood" makes the point that there is an ongoing debate within society with respect to certain alleged wrongdoing, "reconciling issues of law and morality." One looks at the investigation and prosecution of an alleged delict "within a historically specific social and political context." She adds: "What is defined as a crime is arguably more to do with the reflection of the interests of the powerful of the time and not necessarily to do with what is moral / immoral....Most people (whether justifiably or not) might view tax fraud or speeding as not particularly serious (or perhaps victimless) crimes."

At the least, Mr. Myers would be branded immoral by the majority of "right-thinking citizens," the persons the federal government placates by legislating minimal sentences for crimes without victims in return for votes. "No wonder they hated me," said Myers in his autobiography, "I relished it. I'd paid a high price for their hate."

His pontification that he "relished" the animosity of Revenue Canada might elicit the response from some members of the public that it was appropriate that he pay "a high price." Had Myers been a younger, vigorously healthy man, would he still attract the same judicial empathy? I kept, as a rule, arms length of all my clients, and seldom if ever evinced sympathy for any of them. Empathy is more objective than the more emotional sympathy. The Learned Trial Judge in the case I argued had empathy for Charles Vernon Myers, as did I.

This case therefore qualifies as an exceptionally "tough crime." Given that Mr. Myers, according to a Court of competent criminal jurisdiction, was a convicted tax evader, this remains a situation where his original sentence to imprisonment in a federal penitentiary was arguably too harsh in his unique circumstances. On the matter I defended, had he been sentenced to more than the compassionate thirty days and granted no early parole, I believe he would have died locked up in a medium security penitentiary, old and sick and alone. Myers did not deserve that end; and I consider my part in his avoidance of that cruel fate a moral victory, as well as a legal one. Moreover, I have always considered that there remained an element of sportsmanship in Canadian criminal jurisprudence that his cruel nabbing at the hospital nullified. I think he was piled on.

For those of us in the business of crime and punishment, it is certainly well understood that prisoners have their own scale of culpability for various crimes. Sex offenders are notoriously ill-treated and often have to be placed in protective custody. Murderers are generally well regarded, dependant upon the victim. If one is philosophizing about the relative morality of modern penal strictures, particularly in the area of "crimes without victims," it is noteworthy that a prisoner in Mr. Myers' unique circumstances would be shown a consideration by his rough fellows not forthcoming from greater society.

Juries are a lot better at refusing to find guilt for a victimless crime than are trial judges sitting alone. As my colleague Mark Brayford QC has pointed out in these pages, exhorting twelve good and true women and men to cut loose one's client if they don't like the law and didn't think he should have been charged in the first place is anathema to the Supreme Court of Canada; nevertheless, that is exactly what juries do of their own motion in the back rooms. One would not be surprised if a jury had acquitted Charles Vernon Myers on the tax charges.

And, exceptionally for me, I liked him. I liked him because — despite his antisocial bent — he was tough and cantankerous and an unapologetic contrarian. He disliked mindless authoritarianism and he detested bureaucrats. Mr. Myers was a breath of fresh air in a stale jurisprudential milieu. I add the fact that he was highly intelligent, a nice change; most criminal clients are what one might call, charitably, not unusually gifted. Mr. Charles Vernon Myers died in the U.S. in 1990.

Other than that, I have no strong views upon the morality of the matter.

As for me, I was well remunerated and graciously thanked for my efforts, and all in all, it was a hell of a case and C.V. Myers was a hell of a client. Mr. Justice Lutz's disposition of the case was a classic example of meting out justice tempered with mercy, of reconciling law with morality. And it is not every day that a client writes a book in which he compliments you on his defence.

C.D. Evans acknowledges the generous assistance of Richard Myers QC in the preparation of this chapter.

PART FIVE

Community

William Trudell

THE WALKERTON TRAGEDY

William Trudell is the Chair of the Canadian Council of Criminal Defence Lawyers, and an active supporter of the International Criminal Bar. He has served as a director of the John Howard Society, the Ontario Criminal Lawyers' Association, and The Advocates' Society. He is a Fellow of the American College of Trial Lawyers, and recipient of the Law Times first Lawyer of the Year award.

"Hi Stan, nice to see you."

Those six simple words, an unexpected neighbourly greeting, unlocked a door to a journey that would consume the next four years. In retrospect, as defence counsel of course, those years seemed to have sped by, but in the moments, they were electric with apprehension and almost overwhelming responsibility. Little did I know that that greeting would be the first of many simple lessons that I would experience. The memories will always be with me, a case like no other.

Walkerton is a small town in Southern Ontario, population in the Year 2000 was approximately five thousand souls. Not unlike thousands of small Canadian towns, it was nestled just far enough away from the big city to avoid urban pressures and pace. It was surrounded by beautiful rolling farm land, clothed in mountains of snow in the winter, but close to great bodies of water for the short drive to the peacefulness of a too-often short summer retreat.

On the long weekend in May 2000, situational events would change this sleepy Canadian town forever with ripple effects not only throughout Canada, but around the world.

Between May 8 and May 12, 2000, more rain than Walkerton would normally experience over sixty years thundered from the sky. On May 12 alone, over seventy millimetres fell. Rivers swelled, puddles gave way to flooded basements. The cracks of thunder and streams of rain were unending. Lying in wait were events that, together with the punishing rainfall, brought death and excruciating illness to this unsuspecting close-knit community. A staple of life became an agent of death. The water was poisoned.

In the weeks prior to this weekend, over seventy tonnes of manure was spread over a farmer's grain crop field which sat adjacent to one of three wells that provided drinking water to the town. Cattle from this farm were found to have had the same strain of the deadly E-coli 0157: H7 and Campylobacter jejuni as was found in those infected. Contamination by sewage or excrement presents the greatest danger to public health associated with drinking water, therefore requiring frequency of sampling and testing to insure maintenance of residual chlorination levels to combat water-borne diseases.

Well "5" had been constructed in 1978 and almost immediately had been identified as one potentially vulnerable to surface contamination given its location in proximity to agricultural areas and its relative shallow depth over the aquifer, an underground layer of water bearing rock; a reservoir for ground water. Early environmental assessments recognized its vulnerability to contamination and called for continuous chlorine residual monitors. It never happened.

Unfortunately, this was the main well servicing its citizens during the storms. Moreover, the chlorinator at the main Well "7" had been turned off for repairs.

As the unsuspecting residents of Walkerton opened their taps to quench their thirst, they filled their glasses with contamination. A shocking sense of denial set in as inquiries about the safety of the water were met with misinformation and wishful thinking. Ignorance, deceit, and lax environmental regulations were about to make Walkerton a household word and usher in a disaster — the first documented outbreak in Canada of Escherichia coli 0157.H7 infection associated with a municipal water supply.

At its centre was (soon to be my client) Stan Koebel, the respected, friendly Manager of the Public Utilities Commission (PUC). Stan had joined the Walkerton PUC in 1972 at nineteen years of age, following his father. He began as a general labourer and in 1976, became a hydro lineman. In 1981, he was promoted to foreman and in 1988, he took over as manager. Shortly thereafter Stan obtained a Level 2 certificate for the operation of a water distribution system through a voluntary grand-parenting process. Stan Koebel had extensive experience in running the Walkerton PUC but little knowledge about the importance of treating and monitoring the drinking water supply and no knowledge about the health risks at stake if proper chlorination did not occur. He was certified as an operator in a grand-parenting system based on experience rather than training and examination. In 1996, he upgraded to Level 3 to reflect the upgrade of the water distribution system itself. There was no need for a course, no need for examinations or testing.

Stan's brother Frank Koebel became the foreman of the PUC. Frank's certification process mirrored his brother's. In essence, their training and knowledge of municipal water operation was derived from long-standing practices, on the job experience, without the benefit of any 'sophisticated' education. Stan and his brother Frank were salt of the earth family men, long-time residents of Walkerton, and community pillars in their own humble ways. But on that weekend in May 2000, Stan Koebel's life changed forever. In short order, he became a pariah as 'human error' replaced an Act of God as the cause of contamination and the failure to report bad water samples was discovered.

The devastation was horrible. In short order, seven people died and more than 2,300 became ill. Someone was going to pay.

There was no doubt in many minds during those early swirling days of accusations and anger that Stan Koebel was responsible. It would not be long before this humble man would be banished, told he'd better get away for his own safety and in the interests of the people of Walkerton. He soon fled his community in shock, shame and confusion as the responders and media invaded the town.

The First Contact

During the days after the tragic weekend, pieces began to form a puzzle and a scenario was taking shape. There had been warnings of contamination, samples had failed. The Public Utilities manager was responsible. He'd stood mute and had not disclosed that the drinking water was impure as hospitals filled up and air ambulances screamed across the skies. Consequently, too late for many, a boil-water advisory was put into effect. The horror and suffering became the only news, the clamour for answers only surpassed by allegations of blame. It all centred on Stan Koebel.

Along with his brother Frank, on Saturday, May 26, 2000, Stan secretly entered my office in Toronto, his fear tangible and his body language that of a defeated man.

His obviously fragile emotional state frightened me so much that I contacted a psychiatrist who I hoped would be able to help. Not surprisingly, he was soon diagnosed as mentally and emotionally in a state of crisis with ongoing symptoms of major depression with impairment of sleep, appetite, and memory concentration. He exhibited sadness and anxiety, and later an indication of post-traumatic stress disorder.

Because of the suspected psychiatric and certain legal reasons, I advised Stan to remain silent as criminal charges, I suspected, would be imminent. I also explained to him that he and Frank needed separate counsel and that I would assist in recommending someone for his brother.

He seemed to understand but was silent in too many ways. I asked him to stay in contact until I could get my own bearings.

I felt like I had just entered a dark tunnel and the entrance had closed. It was obvious that he felt like an outcast and was worried for his family, his children, and his community. I sensed that the storm just passed, would soon be replaced by a different storm. Suicide was silently screaming in my head but he agreed to see a doctor. He left to retreat to his sheltered location away from his home to await hearing from me soon. The Public Utilities lawyers started to work with us to find out what happened and what lay ahead.

I had no concept of what was coming and no idea what to do, but I sensed that the longer he stayed away, the more dangerous the situation would be for him. The media were on the hunt, the accusations intense and the rumours unceasing. Moreover, Stan Koebel's absence from his community was seen by many as tangible evidence of a consciousness of guilt. I suspected that the anger directed at him would never dissipate, especially if he remained "in hiding."

Going Home

My first exposure to basic decency in the face of tragedy came unexpectedly and in surprising fashion. On my way to work the following Monday morning, listening nonchalantly to a local radio program, I heard words that almost drove me off the road. I stopped and listened to an interview of the various religious leaders in the Walkerton community discussing a joint denominational prayer meeting that had occurred the evening before in one of the local churches. Pastor Beth Conway of the Trinity Lutheran church spoke compassionately about the community's attempt to come together and pray for all affected, as well as for Stan Koebel, the beleaguered PUC Manager whom they were sure was in great distress.

Oh my God. Instinctively, I dialled my client. "Stan," I said, "it is time to go home."

The cavalcade to Walkerton was surreal. My client and I in one car, the psychiatrist I had referred him to in another, my co-counsel, the amazing Joe Di Luca, in a third. With great trepidation, we made our way to a pre-organized meeting and press conference in the church parking lot. We stopped midway and met up with the exceptional Pastor Beth who comforted and prayed with Stan and his wife, Carol, as they continued on the last portion of the drive.

It was surreal. The Walkerton Police knew we were coming. I had reached out to them for professional guidance and to address security issues. Here were the local police taking an incredibly decent approach to a man many were accusing of terrible crimes. But he was, in a way, one of their own. We parked the car a block from the church, now a media circus, and took a couple of timid steps towards our press conference.

It was Tuesday, May 30th, 2000. I was perhaps making the worst decision of my life in exposing a client facing eventual criminal charges, and then that greeting — "Hi Stan, nice to see you." The greeting gave me a sense that we could get through this, as breathing room was being supplied by a generous, forgiving, and an oh-so-wise small town resident.

I suppose defence counsel often do not take time to worry about the life-changing decisions they advise for their clients; whether to testify, whether to plead guilty, whether to give a statement, whether to surrender, whether to inform their family, friends, employer. But something in our makeup, fuelled by experience, guides us to look beyond the immediate with an eye to the future. Tough crimes demand tough decisions. I think we all must have a secret compass that points the way.

We met the assembled masses, I read a statement, expressed my client's concern for whatever had occurred, and asked for understanding and privacy in the days ahead. Stan then merged with and rejoined his community into the church hall. Some of the big city media who had gathered, I suspect, were disappointed that they did not hear cries of 'crucify him'. It was the opposite. I think choosing the parking lot adjacent to the church to make his appearance created an air of forgiveness. Moreover, a small town reception with home-made cookies and cakes in the church hall sent the message that Stan remained a member of the community, not an outcast.

The Inquiry

I then returned relieved to the big city having been taught one of many lessons about the depth of goodness surrounding this case and the benefits of loving community involvement. In the weeks that followed, the likelihood of criminal charges began to take a back seat to the urgent need for a Public Inquiry into the unprecedented tragedy that occurred in an era of Government cutbacks, including to the environment. The Provincial Conservative Government of the day acceded to the public and political calls for a full-scale inquiry and thus began an amazing journey of discovery. Indeed, the government, I suspect perhaps to its later chagrin, named then Associate Chief Justice Dennis O'Connor as the Commissioner to find out what happened, why, and most importantly, to make recommendations to ensure the safety of the water supply in Ontario. Consequently because of his outstanding work, O'Connor's report had repercussions throughout the world. Indeed, he did not let the government off the hook.

The Provincial Ministry of the Environment (MOE) had primary responsibility for regulating and enforcing regulations and policies that applied to the construction and operation of municipal water systems including inspections, qualifications and training of operators. The MOE was responsible for the oversight of testing results and monitoring adverse water quality reports. Unfortunately, the tragic events of May 2000 were accompanied by budget reductions that resulted in inspection cutbacks, monitoring failures and privatization of laboratory testing. Resulting from that was that there was no longer an automatic notification linkage from the Provincial Ministry of the Environment lab to the MOE. The lack of communication delayed the previous notification alerts that might have significantly resulted in earlier responses in Walkerton.

It had seemed that there was irrefutable evidence of wrong-doing by my client and he was the cause. Needless to say, the examination of what occurred and all the surrounding circumstances including the effect of government policies, procedures, and practices was for me a 'preliminary hearing' of a sort beyond expectations and the wildest dreams of a defence counsel. Moreover, finger pointing would not suffice for Commissioner O'Connor and over the next number of months, a much larger perfect storm, with many components, was uncovered.

I sensed before it began, and as it unfolded, that the conduct of Stan Koebel and his role at the inquiry would likely determine his fate before any criminal court. To cooperate or remain effectively silent were dangerous alternatives, given the uncertainty of what lay ahead and the predictability of him being found to be the cause of death and terrible illness. As the Commission investigators began their labourious reconstruction of the events, it became clear to them that the recorded information of years of chlorination levels that perhaps could have at least controlled the contamination, made little scientific sense.

On a rainy June afternoon in my office, the answer became clear. A tearful Stan Koebel, asked by me to assist in unravelling the mystery, solved it. The daily operating sheets that were at each well to record periodic chlorination levels were inaccurate, estimates unreliable, perhaps, to my horror, simply false. For years, sampling of water had not been taken properly. Therefore even if the emerging evidence of lax government regulation and oversight was environmentally unacceptable, deception at the wells seemed shockingly negligent — in fact stark in apparent criminality. To disclose was akin to a guilty plea before charges were laid. To withhold, would be a frustrating disaster for the Commission, those who had suffered, and the community at large.

My client's cooperation was clear. We were to make disclosure to Commission Counsel. I will remember for the rest of my career the stunned reaction of the Commission staff when they were advised that the recorded chlorination results were unreliable. At some point, I hoped this cooperation and disclosure would be revisited and considered in Stan Koebel's favour.

The stakes were enormously high. I was gambling with my client's future and perhaps making all the wrong decisions, as he was protected by a presumption of innocence that could not be displaced by an Inquiry. But the world was watching. It was also clear that Stan Koebel's emotional health was straw-like and he would be unable to withstand the examination, cross examination and skilled scrutiny that awaited him as a witness, no matter how compassionate and professional the Commissioner and his Counsel were likely to be.

I turned my attention to whether he could testify, be skillfully led through exhaustive scrutiny, or whether he would simply collapse in depression, concede misconduct without explanation or indeed, freeze in unfamiliarity with what really happened. The doctors shared my concerns. Most Counsel at the Inquiry were eminent and successful litigators. I recall a number of townsfolk remarking that they had never seen so many BMWs at Tim Hortons in their lives. It was the drivers I was worried about as they were all skilled examiners and as the Inquiry moved, on time, within budget, and efficiently, decision day was fast approaching. I knew that there had to be a message of remorse from my client. It would be genuine, but I doubted his ability to voice it.

No one was apologizing as the Inquiry logged hours and days of testimony. Finger-pointing was the order of the day. The government response, despite the mounting evidence of failed support and infrastructure, inconsistent adherence to their own regulations, privatization of laboratory testing and cutbacks throughout, remained unconvincingly one of 'the system was based on trust'. Their refrain was to shift almost all responsibility to the careless operators of the Walkerton PUC, Stan and Frank Koebel.

Stan's apology and acceptance of responsibility, especially given the national media scrutiny, was going to be essential to the Inquiry, its findings. Criminal court I was still hoping to avoid. A psychiatric report was prepared. In effect, it showed that my client was likely, from a health point of view, incapable of testifying and surviving the scrutiny of labourious and almost certain attack. Commission Counsel and the Commissioner became very concerned.

A further independent report was commissioned and Mr. Koebel again cooperated. The concerns remained acute. He would be almost in shock, perhaps unintentionally unreliable, and it might be unfair to him to be called by Commission Counsel and led through exhaustive and surely exhausting procedures and cross examination.

Although he was terribly afraid, Stan knew as did I that not appearing would be a repetition of his earlier forced escape from his community. He needed to face up to the events and take responsibility for the mistakes he made and I suspected, demonstrate his lack of sophisticated understanding and appreciation of the necessity and intricacy of proper chlorination and testing.

I knew he believed that deep well water from the earth — safe, clean, and unadulterated — did not need the 'big city treatment'. I also knew that Stan Koebel would testify to the fact that on that fateful night of Friday, May 19, 2000, when he knew something had gone wrong with the water, he single-handedly, alone, for hours, flushed the entire system. He figured that would fix the problem. The night was muggy and hot. He was tired, exhausted, and thirsty. He filled his helmet with water gushing from the hydrant and drank it to quench his thirst. I was determined that that evidence would be heard.

A compromise was reached. Unlike all other witnesses whose evidence began with Commission Counsel, I would call Mr. Koebel and take him through his evidence to offer some comfort as he began the public journey of hopeful redemption. He had met for hours with Commission Counsel in preparation, signalling his continued cooperation.

On the evening before he testified, a horrific snowstorm, all too common in Walkerton, hit like a pathetic fallacy ushering in the day everyone had waited for. With a sea of cameras flashing, Stan Koebel slowly took the witness stand. The cameras stopped. An eerie silence took over the Inquiry room. I approached the lectern and Stan Koebel spoke for the first time in seven months.

> I'm not very good at words so I wrote down a few things. Words can't begin to express how sorry I am and how bad I feel. I accept responsibility for my actions. I am one piece of the puzzle that came together in May and I am grateful for the opportunity to speak.

After a couple of more questions, to the surprise of many, I sat down and turned matters over to Commission Counsel. We had our apology and remorse on the record before a national audience.

For the next two days, barrage after barrage of questions illustrated the incompetence, lack of training, corner cutting, and perhaps deceit of my client. The attacks in the media were relentless and even cruel, given the shocking revelations of mismanagement, inaccurate and misleading sampling, and almost total lack of familiarity and comprehension of government regulations. Nevertheless, it was expected and my client had taken the stand. It could not get worse. I was hoping that at some point, those days of painful admissions would play out in his favour. I probably deluded myself that criminal charges could be avoided.

Report of the Walkerton Inquiry

Within months, the now-world-renowned *Report of the Walkerton Inquiry* was released and the blame game had failed. The responsibility for the tragedy was thoroughly documented and the conclusions clearly opened the door to shared responsibility. Among the conclusions were the following:

- The contaminants entered the Walkerton system through Well 5 on or shortly after May 12, 2000. The primary, if not the only, source of the contamination was manure that had been spread on a farm near Well 5. The owner of this farm followed proper practices and should not be faulted. Seven people died, and more than 2,300 became ill. Some people, particularly children, may endure lasting effects.
- The failure to use continuous monitors at Well 5 resulted from shortcoming in the approvals and inspection programs of the Ministry of the Environment (MOE). The Walkerton Public Utilities Commission (PUC) operators lacked the training and expertise to identify either the vulnerability of Well 5 to surface contamination or the resulting need for continuous chlorine residual and turbidity monitors.
- The scope of the outbreak would very likely have been substantially reduced if the Walkerton PUC operators had measured chlorine residuals at Well 5 daily, as they should have, during the critical period when contamination was entering the system. The other improper practices included failing to use adequate doses of chlorine, making false entries about residuals in daily operating records, and misstating the locations at which microbiological samples were taken. The

operators knew that these practices were unacceptable and contrary to MOE guidelines and directives.

- The PUC commissioners were not aware of the improper treatment and monitoring practices of the PUC operators. However, those who were commissioners in 1998 failed to properly respond to an MOE inspection report that set out significant concerns about water quality and that identified several operating deficiencies at the PUC.
- Had the PUC's general manager disclosed rather than concealed the adverse test results from water samples taken on May 15 and the fact that Well 7 had operated without a chlorinator during that week and earlier that month, the Health Unit would have issued a boil water advisory on May 19 and three hundred to four hundred illnesses would have been avoided.
- The provincial government's budget reductions 1) made is less likely that the MOE would have identified both the need for continuous monitors at Well 5 and the improper operating practices of the Walkerton PUC which the MOE's inspection program should have detected and corrected; and 2) led to the discontinuation of government laboratory testing services for municipalities in 1996. In doing so, the government should have enacted a regulation mandating that testing laboratories immediately and directly notify both the MOE and the Medical Officer of Health of adverse results. Had the government done this, the boil water advisory would have been issued by May 19 at the latest, thereby preventing hundreds of illnesses.

Most significantly, this unique type of preliminary hearing as we used it, emphasized that it was not very common at all to have an E. Coli O151.H7 outbreak in municipal water and that a number of key factors contributed to the tragedy. Moreover, expert opinion was that upping the chlorine dramatically would not necessarily have helped.

A subsequent agreed statement of facts, in the criminal proceeding, contained in part the following:

> It therefore cannot be said that the criminal conduct of Stan Koebel and Frank Koebel, and more particularly, their failure to properly monitor, sample and test the well water supplying the Town of Walkerton, was, in law, a significant contributing cause of the deaths and injuries caused by the contamination of Walkerton's municipal water supply.

The Last Chapter — Criminal Charges

Following an intensive police investigation and almost three years after the tragedy, criminal charges were laid against Stan Koebel and his brother, represented by an amazing lawyer, now Justice Michael Epstein. We had attempted to convince the Ministry of the Attorney General and the police that the public interest would not be served by reliving the nightmare and indeed lobbied and submitted that the situation was unique, and the clients had suffered enough.

Many in the public and among the citizens of Walkerton wondered why only the brothers had been charged. Despite the seriousness of the tragedy and the publically admitted failures of my client he was, to my enlightenment, still welcomed in his community and forgiven by many, who felt that others especially in Government were equally if not more responsible.

The acceptance of the people of Walkerton to the invasion of 'big city' lawyers and relentless media attention to their tragedy created an atmosphere of understanding. Something terrible had happened but there was a concerted effort to work together to find out what. Even though they knew that one of their own had failed them, they in large measure refused to spurn him.

For me, it was so tangible. The defence team including my son, Blair, now a lawyer but a student at the time, lived in a small rented farmhouse throughout the months of the inquiry, often with seemingly relentless waves of snow piling up around us. Very early many mornings, we awoke to the sound of our neighbour's tractor as he magically plowed our driveway, not asked, not answered, not surprising.

The fact of the criminal charges was disappointing but the charges alleged no causation. They were, in effect, common nuisance allegations that sounded tantalizingly trivial but in their essence, captured the horror and reality of what had occurred.

Section 180 (1)(a) of the *Criminal Code* sets out the criminal offence of Common Nuisance, as,

> Every one who commits a common nuisance and thereby, a) endangers the lives, safety or health of the public, or b) causes physical injury to any person, is guilty of an indictable offence and liable to imprisonment for a term not exceeding two years.

The evidence could not establish causation but by operating a well without a chlorinator, failing to properly monitor samples and test the well water supplying the town of Walkerton, failing to accurately record the required information in the logs and most particularly, by inaccurately completing the daily operation sheet for one of the wells knowing it would be relied on as if genuine, captured the essence of his involvement and reflected the disclosure he had made and the evidence years earlier.

Even though the inquiry process could not be used as evidence, his admissions and apology had been public. There would be no trial. Causation was off the table. Surely, I thought, the Crown would not be seeking a jail sentence and no judge would fail to recognize that Stan, in effect, really had been in a form of prison for over four years. We felt certain that we could put together an impressive brief for resolution and obtain a non-custodial sentence. We were heartened to hear that the very experienced, former defence counsel, then Regional Senior Justice Bruce Durno would deal with the matter. Pre-trial discussions occurred, an agreed statement of facts assembled and an impressive collection of character letters was filed. We had no agreement on sentencing. The Crown sought jail for Stan Koebel. The Judge was non-committal in pre-trial meetings but seemed sympathetic.

I think I was not firm enough to request that the Judge advise us what he had in mind. In retrospect, I was so close to the file and had walked so many miles with my client that I could not see the proverbial trees. I felt increasingly alone in my view as the victim impact statements were filed and chilling testimony hushed the courtroom at the sentencing hearing. We were reminded in emotional fashion that seven people had died and many more were seriously injured.

The decision was put over to a few days before Christmas. On the way to court, I dropped by my client's home in Walkerton to prepare him. His extended family, children, grandchildren, incredible wife, and friends were there. I assured them that this judge would do the right thing. I suppose, in retrospect, he did. At the time it seemed it was a kick in my empty defence counsel stomach; twelve months.

I was stunned. How could he? Surely my client had been through enough. I rose as the Court emptied and robotically walked to the prisoner's dock where my client now stood. "I'm sorry Stan. We can get you out on bail for Christmas."

Stan Koebel, in another lesson of the wisdom of uncomplicated people, looked at me and said "It's okay Bill. We already had our Christmas last weekend."

"Are you all right?" I asked. "I'm okay," he said, "Are you?" He reached into his coat pocket and handed me a candy cane, saying, "Have a good Christmas and thank you. We expected this."

Four months later, the Koebels had no lawyer at the parole hearing. Stan's wife Carol called me for advice but thought they would be okay. Stan Koebel was granted parole.

I asked Carol whether he had a job to go to. She said yes. Carol reported that a man whose wife worked at a gas station with a small store came and told the Parole Board that he would hire Stan. The Board apparently inquired why. The owner of the small-town service station where his wife worked had, at one point, taken a day off. She, a waitress, was alone waiting on tables and pumping gas. A long line of cars appeared and she was having real difficulty handling everything. Suddenly a man got out of his car, approached her, and quietly asked if she needed help. The man said he would be happy to pump gas and look after the customers while she attended to other duties. Her husband reported that she described him as a regular guy who wanted to help. They later found out his name was Stan Koebel.

Today, Stan lives quietly with his wife Carol and enjoys his seven grandchildren. Walkerton, Ontario has probably the safest drinking water in Canada.

I continue to practice each and every day, learning something new from the people I defend.

John Vertes

THE CASE OF HENRY INNUKSUK

John Vertes arrived in Canada with his parents in 1957 as refugees from the Hungarian Revolution. A Judge of the Supreme Court of the Northwest Territories for 20 years, he retired as Chief Justice, and is past president of the Canadian Superior Courts Judges Association. He was Commissioner for the Alberta Public Inquiry into Health Services Preferential Access. He pursues judicial and legal education initiatives.

TODAY IT IS COMMON-PLACE to speak of restorative justice as an alternative to standard criminal law practice in Canada's aboriginal societies. In Nunavut, where Rankin Inlet is now located, it is a regular practice of the court to have community representatives sit with the presiding judge to advise on the appropriate sentence for an offender. This practice leads to greater community involvement in the sentencing of aboriginal offenders. But in the 1970s, this type of community involvement was unheard of. Introducing it was a gamble I thought worth taking.

Yellowknife, Northwest Territories

In 1978 I was a young lawyer working in Yellowknife. I had moved to the Northwest Territories capital in the fall of 1977 from Toronto with my wife Louise. I had recently been called to the Ontario Bar and we took an opportunity to go North for what we assumed would be a two-year adventure. Our plan was to return to Toronto after that, but our two-year adventure turned into a thirty-four-year career for both of us. We never did return to Toronto.

My legal experience in Toronto was with a civil litigation firm specializing in insurance defence work and that was why I was hired by the Yellowknife firm of Searle, Richard and Kingsmill, as it was then known. And that was the work I got to do. But once I came North, I quickly developed a desire to do criminal defence work. I was drawn to the excitement of the Northern circuit — the Court party flying out from Yellowknife to hear cases in all the far-flung Northern communities.

My inexperience in criminal law notwithstanding, I put my name on the legal aid list and started taking on cases. I went on my first circuit in October 1977, a two-week trek around the Eastern Arctic in a DC-3 airplane that was older than I was, piloted by a former member of the Polish air wing of the RAF in World War II. But that is another story.

In April 1978, I received a call from the legal aid director asking me to go see a young man who was in custody at the Yellowknife Correctional Centre. The director did not call me because of my expertise; he called me because he knew I was keen to take on cases, and this one seemed somewhat problematic. The young man was Henry Suviserk Innuksuk, then eighteen years old, from Rankin Inlet. He had been arrested in Rankin Inlet on charges of breaking into various buildings in his community and setting fire to them. Essentially these were charges of arson. The buildings were all public buildings of importance to the community: the elementary school, the curling rink, the Hudson Bay Company store, the local Inuit Association office, the local housing association office, and a government office and public works shop. None of the buildings were completely destroyed but they were all damaged and repairs were costly. All the offences occurred in a short time frame in February and March 1978.

I was told that Henry could not communicate in English and there was some concern over his mental health. So when I first went to see him at the jail, I took with me a local Inuit interpreter, Ms. Mikle Langenham, who was of great help in establishing an on-going communication with Henry. I made it a point to have Ms. Langenham with me whenever I met with Henry and at every court appearance.

It took several sessions with Henry to build up his confidence enough, and his trust in me sufficiently, so that he would communicate with me in anything more than the most simple utterances. These of course were in Inuktitut and would have to be translated for my benefit. But it quickly became apparent to me, as it did to Ms. Langenham, that Henry was illiterate. More significantly, it seemed that he was also suffering from some type of mental dysfunction. Henry did not evade the fact that he had committed these offences or that what he had done was wrong. Indeed, he confessed to the arresting police officer at the first opportunity. But I had reservations about his mental state and possibly his legal culpability.

As it turned out, I was not the first one to have such reservations. After my first meeting with Henry, I sat down with one of the Crown Attorneys who showed me the prosecution file. In the Northwest Territories, then and still today, all criminal prosecutions are handled by the federal Department of Justice. Their Crown Attorneys had, for many years, the admirable policy of routinely giving full disclosure to defence counsel, usually by simply handing over their complete file for review. This was years before the Supreme Court of Canada formalized the disclosure obligations of prosecutors.

In the file was an assessment report written by a psychiatrist at the forensic services unit of the Alberta Hospital in Edmonton just a few days before I had seen Henry. Henry had been remanded at Alberta Hospital after his arrest in Rankin Inlet, for observation and assessment. That report noted that Henry was not suffering from a mental illness but was mentally retarded. More significantly, the report concluded that Henry suffered from psychopathic disorders and should be considered dangerous.

In those days a court-ordered forensic psychiatric assessment was normally conducted at the Alberta Hospital. It is fair to say that in those days the doctors there had little, if any, familiarity with Inuit culture and certainly no knowledge of Henry's home community. The assessment seemed very superficial even to my relatively untrained eyes. I was very concerned that if this report became the authoritative statement on Henry's psychological make-up, then his prospects on sentencing would be very grim indeed. Considering the nature of the charges, one could normally expect a relatively severe sentence, ordinarily one of several years of incarceration, even for a first offender such as Henry. So, if there was no alternative to pleading guilty, and I was hard-pressed to find one, I had to apply my resources to obtaining the best, or at least a less worse, sentence possible.

A Second Psychiatric Assessment

I realized that I had to counter the Alberta Hospital report in some way. I therefore took steps to arrange a second psychiatric assessment, this time at the Clarke Institute of Psychiatry in Toronto. I knew that they had flying teams of mental health specialists who travelled periodically to communities in the Eastern Arctic. I hoped that at least they would have greater familiarity with Inuit communities and that they might have the resources to conduct a more in-depth investigation into Henry's circumstances. In May 1978, I obtained an order for such a further assessment. The subsequent report from the Clarke

Institute confirmed much of what I had been thinking. Henry was found to be fit to stand trial and was not suffering from a mental illness. He was mentally retarded, likely due to several severe early childhood illnesses. But he was not considered to pose a danger to himself or to others. He did not exhibit signs of any significant psychological disorder. More important, his personality was described as meek, docile and passive and not one exhibiting dangerousness or a propensity to setting fires. Finally, the report viewed long-term incarceration as definitely unhelpful considering Henry's condition and background.

With this report now part of my arsenal, I started discussions with the Crown Attorney handling Henry's case on what might be a suggested disposition should Henry plead guilty. And I concluded by then that there was no alternative if we were to have any chance at minimizing the severity of the potential sentence.

I never determined Henry's motives for setting these fires. The psychiatrists thought it was a form of attention-seeking. He may have been influenced or pushed into doing these things by others who supplied him with liquor — somebody's cruel way of having a laugh at Henry's expense. Henry was certainly impressionable and easily led and the fact that all the offences occurred within a short time span suggested to me that there may have been some sort of triggering event, perhaps a threat or some type of encouragement for him to act so out of character. But nothing definite ever came out of any of this, and all inquiries with respect to motive came to a dead-end. Hence my decision to concentrate on sentencing.

Two of the most significant factors in the eventual outcome of Henry's case were: firstly, the Crown Attorney who prosecuted the case and, secondly, the judge scheduled to preside at the sentencing hearing. The Crown Attorney was John Bayly. John had come to Yellowknife in 1974 to work initially for several aboriginal groups appearing before the Inquiry conducted by Justice Thomas Berger into a proposed Mackenzie Valley gas pipeline project. He went on to a varied and extremely successful career in the North, in both private practice and, from time to time, as a Crown Attorney. By the time of his untimely death in 2004, he was rightfully considered a Dean of the Northern Bar, known for his integrity and professionalism. Henry's case was the first time I'd worked with John but I am pleased to say it was only the first of many cases and projects over the years. I quickly developed great respect for both his abilities as a lawyer and his commitment to the interests of the people of the North.

John quickly recognized my concerns. Sentencing precedents called for a significant term of imprisonment for these offences, but Henry's personal characteristics were such that imprisonment would be devastating for him.

John sympathized with his situation but there had to be sound arguments for deviating from precedent, especially since John was answerable to Department of Justice masters in Ottawa who did not necessarily share his empathy with people in the Northern communities.

On July 11, 1978, I appeared with Henry (who was still in custody on pre-trial detention) in court and entered guilty pleas to all charges. Sentencing was set for August 4 in Rankin Inlet. John had agreed with me that the case was sufficiently important to the community that the hearing should be held in Rankin Inlet.

I had decided to keep the case in the Territorial Court, which is the Northern equivalent of Provincial Court. I thought there would be advantage in an early guilty plea without protracted proceedings. I was also betting on the presiding judge, Chief Judge Jim Slaven. The late Jim Slaven was originally from Nova Scotia and had worked as a counsel for the Northwest Territories government before his appointment as a judge in 1973. In my brief time before the Northern courts up to that time, I came to appreciate the many human and humane qualities Jim brought to the bench. No one would ever accuse Jim of intellectual arrogance but he brought to his work, throughout his career, a sensitivity and appreciation for the situation of many of the people appearing before him. I thought that if there was a chance of convincing a judge to do something out of the ordinary then Jim was my best opportunity.

Prior to the guilty pleas and in preparation for sentencing, I started contacting people in Rankin Inlet who might be able to provide information on Henry and his family. One of the people I spoke to was Ms. Jean Williamson, one of Henry's grade school teachers. She then put me in contact with her husband, Dr. Robert Williamson who was a professor of anthropology at the University of Saskatchewan and the director of that university's Northern Research Centre. Of far more relevance was the fact that he had lived in Rankin Inlet for many years; spoke fluent Inuktitut, was familiar with the Inuit of that region, and was acquainted with Henry's family.

Dr. Williamson told me about the great interest in Henry's case amongst the Rankin Inlet community. Henry came from a very traditional family, a well-respected one but with difficulties since the death of Henry's mother several years earlier. Many people in the community, I was told, expressed regret over not being more attentive to Henry's situation. Dr. Williamson said that the case might be an opportunity for the people of Rankin Inlet to take a greater role in the criminal justice system and to show its strength as a community. In his opinion they could draw upon Inuit tradition wherein the responsibility for sanctioning, correction and control of members of the community who commit deviant acts is placed in the hands of the community who would act as his surrogate family.

Rankin Inlet

Rankin Inlet, or as it is known by its Inuit name, *Kangirliniq*, meaning "deep bay," is located on the northwestern coast of Hudson Bay, north of the tree line. Archaeological surveys revealed evidence of Thule hunting activities in that area since the twelfth century; the Thule people being ancestors of all modern Inuit. The town itself was founded in 1957 by the owners of the Rankin Inlet Mine, an underground nickel and copper operation. Inuit from different regional groups came there to work in the mine until its closure in 1962. After the mine closed, the community stagnated until the mid-1970s when it was designated a government regional centre. This also drew Inuit from different regional groups to live there. Its population in 1978 was approximately a thousand people; today it is twenty-two hundred. The community is notable for its Inuit art and artisans as well as for its chilling winds and severe winter storms — the average high in January is minus twenty-seven-degrees Celsius.

The important fact to draw from Rankin Inlet's history is that its Inuit population was made up of people from many different groups; people who had not lived together previously in any particular settlement. So, the community coming together to demonstrate a collective will was a ground-breaking event.

A few days prior to the date for sentencing I was contacted by Dr. Williamson and told that the Rankin Inlet Hamlet Council wanted to meet with me prior to the hearing. Apparently the Council had decided to assume responsibility for Henry, together with his family. The Council members recognized that this was an opportunity to demonstrate their strength as a community and their collective responsibility for each other.

On August 4, the Court party assembled at the Yellowknife airport for the four-hour flight to Rankin Inlet. Besides myself, there was Chief Judge Jim Slaven, prosecutor John Bayly, my interpreter Ms. Langenham, a court clerk, a court reporter, and a court sheriff's officer. Henry had already been transported to Rankin Inlet by an RCMP aircraft. We arrived in Rankin Inlet at ten in the morning and to nobody's surprise, it was a cool day with blustery winds. Court was scheduled to start at eleven *a.m.* but I had already told the judge and John about the request from the Hamlet Council to meet with me, so he agreed to delay proceedings until one in the afternoon.

Upon arrival, I immediately went to the Hamlet offices where I was greeted by a large throng of people including the mayor and the Council members, all of whom were Inuit except for one. Also in attendance were Dr. and Mrs. Williamson; Henry's elderly father; two of his older brothers, as well as many community members. One by one, they spoke to me about Inuit traditional ways and about their concerns for Henry. The mayor said that he and every member of the Hamlet Council would be willing to act as surety and supervise Henry in the community if that would mean Henry's avoidance of a jail sentence. They felt sad that they had not paid more attention to Henry in the community, previously knowing his limitations. And now they wanted to take responsibility for his future conduct.

The meeting initially lasted well beyond eleven *a.m.*, so I went to see Judge Slaven to request more time. He said that I could take as long as I need. I also took John Bayly, the Crown Attorney, back with me to hear what these people were saying. John was far more familiar with Rankin Inlet than I was at that time so he listened with great interest and empathy.

Court Proceedings

We finally started the Court proceeding at four in the afternoon. Public interest was so intense that the hearing was held in the largest facility in Rankin Inlet — the community hall. It was packed with people. Prior to commencing, John and I agreed that we would put forward a proposal that Henry not be given any more jail time, but instead be placed on probation under the supervision of a probation officer but with the active involvement of the community. John agreed to submit that, while jail was the norm in cases of this type, it would not necessarily be required in this case due to the special circumstances of Henry's condition and the willingness of the community to assume responsibility. We knew, however, that the final decision was strictly up to the judge.

The hearing lasted over seven hours. I called nine witnesses to testify as to Henry's situation, the strength of the family, and the community response to the case. Dr. Williamson testified as to how the action of the community represented aspects of Inuit culture that should be fostered and strengthened. All of the testimony was translated in open court between Inuktitut and English. The psychiatric reports were entered into evidence. After the witnesses were heard, Jim adjourned court and asked to see John and me outside the courtroom. What he really wanted was a smoke break. We all wanted one because at that time all of us smoked. So there we were, standing outside the community hall, smoking in a bitterly cold wind, when Jim looked at us and asked, in effect, "how can we justify a non-incarceration sentence?" We said that would be the subject of our submissions. After we finished our smokes, we went back inside, convened court again, and made our respective submissions.

Judge Jim Slaven suspended sentence on all charges and placed Henry on probation for two years. The formal order placed Henry under the supervision of a probation officer but with the *proviso* that the officer be in a supportive role to Henry's family and the community. In passing sentence, he made the following remarks:

> It is so refreshing for me to come into a community and find a family and a community who are willing to take the responsibility to try and help one of their own instead of throwing up their hands and saying, 'Judge, you and the other fellows, you do it.' His only real chance to be rehabilitated and take a worthwhile role in society is the chance offered him here in Rankin Inlet in the hearts of his family and his community. I have heard the nine witnesses, all residents of this community, who gave evidence today. I have seen them here today. From the evidence given here there was a meeting of the Hamlet Council today. I have seen the interest of the hundreds of people who have come to court today, and I am completely satisfied that the community and the family here afford the best chance for the long-term protection of society. I am satisfied that the family and the community can control this boy by supervising, directing, and supporting him.
>
> I thank the family and the community for taking this course of action today. If you had not done so, if you had not offered to support this boy, I would have had to send him to jail for a lengthy period, and I am certain that would have ruined him forever. You will have to be supportive to him for as long as he lives here. You cannot let your enthusiasm of today die out in a couple of months' time, and my greatest wish for your success and Henry's success goes with you.

Henry was released and the court party flew out of Rankin Inlet at midnight. Judge Slaven's willingness to delay proceedings until counsel were ready was nothing new. He recognized the need for flexibility considering the conditions in which the circuit court worked. He also recognized, in Henry's case, the importance of his disposition not just to Henry, but to the entire community. Jim was quoted in Jack Batten's book *Lawyers (Penguin Canada, 1985)* as saying, in reference to this case:

> It was the first time such a thing had happened in Rankin, the first time the local people had ever sat down together. You see, coming from all various backgrounds the way they had, different strains of

> Eskimo, they'd never managed as a real community. There was a professor up there, fellow named Williamson from the University of Saskatchewan, who'd been going to Rankin every summer for eighteen years, and he said this was the old traditional Inuit way of doing things, meeting together and looking after their own. Well, hell, under those circumstances the court was pleased to stand aside for a few hours. That might sound ridiculous to a judge in the south, but northern justice is different.

Northern Justice

I wish I could say it was my advocacy that resulted in Henry being able to go back to his family that night. But that result had far more to do with the understanding displayed by the prosecutor and the willingness of the judge to take a chance. Most of all it was the result of a community coming together to care for one of their own.

John Bayly's work on the case was not done, however. As I understood it at the time, his superiors in Ottawa were not only surprised by the sentence, calling it a miscarriage of justice, but were insisting that he file an appeal. He kept up a steady argument against it and in the end he convinced his superiors to drop the idea of an appeal.

I kept receiving information about Henry for some time after the hearing. In a letter from his former grade-school teacher Jean Williamson, in October 1979, she wrote that "he was doing extremely well and appears to be happy and contented." The last word I received about Henry was in February 1988 when the local director of community programs wrote that Henry was working in the hamlet garage, living with and under the care of one of his older brothers, and that "he gets along well with people." The general sentiment in the community, ten years after the fact, was that the court's decision was a good one and things worked out very well.

Over the thirty-five-plus years that I spent as a lawyer and a judge I often thought back to Henry Suviserk Innuksuk's case. It was not only the first case that opened my eyes to a different way of doing things, it was also the first example in the North of a community becoming an active participant in the justice system. It made me realize that the community at large has a stake in how an individual offender is treated, how a particular case is disposed of, and, because of that, its collective views and wishes should be heard and respected. In this case it was the community that was the victim. And it was that victim that extended mercy to Henry and a helping hand for his future.

Thomas Dalby

THE TABER SCHOOL SHOOTING

Dr. Thomas Dalby, described by the American Bar Association as one of North America's leading forensic psychologists, has provided expert opinions to courts and has published extensively for three decades. In 2013 he received his profession's highest honour, the CPA Award for Distinguished Contributions to Psychology as a Profession. He has taught at the university level since 1978, and holds specialist recognition in neuropsychology.

THE TOWN OF Taber, Alberta lies two hundred kilometres southeast of Calgary. Taber is known for its corn, as the crop grows well with the abundant sunshine that blesses the area. There is a large sugar beet factory there and a preponderance of devout Mormons. Having a little over seven thousand inhabitants, Taber had no reason to garner headline news — until the overcast, snowy afternoon of April 28, 1999.

Just after the lunch hour, a fourteen-year-old boy, who had been a former student, entered the W.R. Myers High School in Taber with a sawed-off semi-automatic .22 calibre rifle and shot randomly at students in the hallway who were rushing to get to class. Two boys were struck by the assailant's bullets and a third barely missed being hit. The lucky boy raced to the Principal's office and shouted a warning. After first laughing, the staff realized the threat was real and teachers were told over the PA to close classroom doors and keep the children inside. One of the injured boys, seventeen-year-old Jason Lang, later died of his wounds while the second injured boy eventually recovered.

The following day, details of this tragedy were carried on the world's newswires. Prime Minister Jean Chrétien rose in the House of Commons and voiced his shock at the shooting and commented, "The senselessness of this act of violence makes it even more painful and all the more difficult to accept and comprehend." A moment of silence followed in the House for the victims.

Several weeks later, I received a call from Balfour Q.H. Der QC, one of Canada's finest criminal defence lawyers who, along with colleague Lisa Burgis, would assist the accused boy in the court proceedings that would follow. As with many crimes that defy rational explanation, it would be from us, the mental health experts, that some form of enlightenment would be sought. But expectations for scientifically credible revelations of "why" are sometimes unrealistic and even after three decades of providing opinions in legal cases, I can occasionally only scratch my head and utter, "God only knows" as my best reply.

When a case is so obviously laden with questions of mental stability, the Courts will sometimes request an evaluation of the accused person, and public facilities are available for such purposes. With the case of the fourteen-year-old boy, whom I will refer to as Jeff (this is not his name as it was protected from public release under the then applicable Young Offenders Act), he was transferred from detention in Taber to the in-patient psychiatric assessment facilities for young persons in Edmonton. During a typical month-long assessment, a team of psychiatrists, psychologists, social workers, nurses, and other health professionals conduct evaluations and together craft a court report addressing the issues relevant to the case. After he was evaluated in Edmonton, Jeff was returned to the Calgary Young Offenders Centre (CYOC) in northwest Calgary where I was to meet with him on several occasions. He was held in custody under a charge of First-Degree Murder and Attempted Murder.

My first visit with Jeff was on September 23, 1999 at CYOC. I don't do very many evaluations of adolescents and the CYOC felt more like visiting a high school than a jail. Jeff was a gangly young man with glasses, blemished skin, unkempt hair and crowded teeth. He was emotionally calm and cooperated fully with my questioning and testing. In my first contact with this boy, the purpose was to gain an impression of who he was and what had brought him to this point in his life. He gave his personal history as follows, adding that not everything that he told the mental health team in Edmonton was accurate but that he would tell me the truth, as Mr. Der had instructed.

A Depressed Teen

Jeff was born in Ontario and was the youngest child of nine from the same parents. His mother was a nurse and his stepfather was a trucker. His early development was unremarkable, as described to me later by his mother. Jeff portrayed a close supportive family with no abuse within the family. However, as soon as he began school, bullies targeted him. Even at age six, he was doused with lighter fluid by other students who threatened to torch him. The physical and mental abuse continued throughout the school years where others would hit him in the face without provocation and he had required stitches to repair the lacerations. He was school avoidant and had average grades.

Psychological testing with him in his early school years clearly showed, however, that he was intellectually gifted. His handwriting was primitive and he never learned to write in script. The family had moved out to Alberta after his mother re-married and when Jeff was in grade six. The peer-assaults continued, despite this opportunity for a fresh start. On Jeff's first day attending high school in Taber, a female student approached him, called him ugly and kicked him in the crotch. The witnessed assault resulted in a two-day suspension for the girl. After another particularly bad beating, his mother complained to police but no action was taken. The investigative file was apparently "lost."

Jeff never retaliated or fought back in any of these physical assaults and he could not explain why he was the chosen target of hate. He was called "geek" and "loser" by many of his peers of both genders, particularly by the more popular ones. At trial, no evidence showed that Jeff had ever spoken poorly of anyone else or harmed another person. Others noted that he just took the abuse as a silent human punching bag. Unable or unwilling to fend for himself, Jeff eventually withdrew from school and his mother attempted to home school him. He tried to go back to school in December 1998 but had difficulty adjusting socially. The school counsellor visited him at home several times but his conversations with her were brief. He spent most of his time alone and on the computer immersed in fantasy and role-playing games. He later emphasized to me that he never lost his sense of reality in carrying out the shooting and it was not like playing a video game. Jeff did not present his bullying history in a self-serving way and the many episodes of his abuse were widely confirmed through interviews with his peers, teachers and mother.

His mother told me that Jeff had been depressed for about a year prior to the shooting and she took him for psychiatric help in March of 1999. The psychiatrist diagnosed him as having Attention Deficit Hyperactivity Disorder (ADHD) and prescribed Dexedrine, a stimulant that can be effective for this behavioral condition. Jeff provided minimal symptoms of ADHD when I evaluated him, concurring with school assessments that had rated his attention span as excellent. He took the prescribed medication for only two weeks but had no substantial change in his behavior. As the drug kept him awake at night, he discontinued taking it. That was the end of mental health care in the community.

Jeff had never had a girlfriend and had only minimal exposure to marijuana and alcohol; certainly no more than his peers and he did not seem interested. He and a friend had been caught playing with lighters and had started a little fire in a trashcan. He had shoplifted some chips from 7-Eleven. He had never hurt anyone nor had he been arrested for any antisocial behavior. Some mental health experts would later point at these adolescent typical behaviors as evidence of abnormal conduct. I called such interpretations pathologizing; making ordinary adolescent behavior the hypothetical result of some mental defect.

Psychological tests are usually given by forensic psychologists to help measure certain aspects of a person prior to trial. These tests are not magic but can be thought of as structured samples of behaviour and abilities/traits can be reliably quantified with these tools. Jeff's IQ was in the Superior range; above ninety-five percent of his age peers. His Principal had noted that he was considered very bright but unmotivated. A test of mental health for adolescents called the Minnesota Multiphasic Personality Inventory — A (MMPI-A) showed that Jeff had no significant mental disorder and when I repeated this MMPI-A test closer to trial, the finding was the same. The test did show that he was a very introverted young man.

The Crime

At home by himself, Jeff watched television for many hours and played computer games such as *Diablo* and *World of Warcraft*. He often drew pictures with themes of automated violence from the computer games. His world changed on April 20, 1999 when Eric Harris and Dylan Klebold killed twelve of their fellow students and one teacher, and wounded twenty-three others, before taking their own lives at Columbine High School in Colorado. Although school shootings were not uncommon in the United States, the scale and methodical nature of the Columbine attack captured the attention of the world. Jeff's mother reported that he was fascinated with the case and watched it on television and read about it with interest. To me, he described being fascinated and obsessed with this "solution." He indicated that he hated Taber and the kids at school who tormented him.

The week before the shooting, he was noted to be markedly depressed and had trouble sleeping. The day prior to the Taber shooting, Jeff took the key to his stepfather's gun locker, took out all four guns (all had trigger locks and ammunition was locked in a shed away from the guns) and tried to match up ammunition to each weapon. He had some experience in shooting gophers and

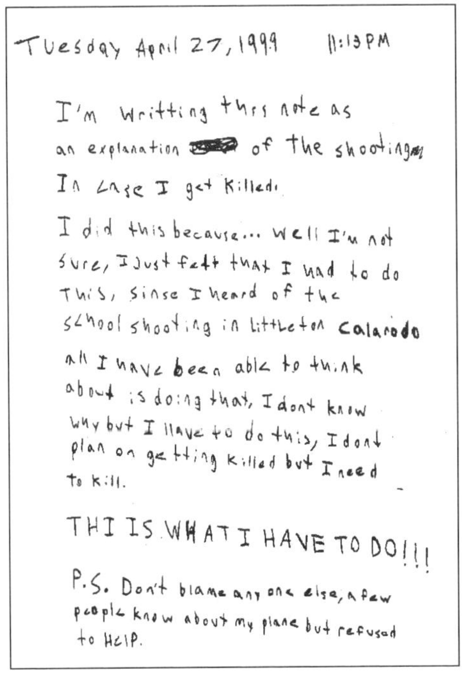

Tuesday April 27, 1999 11:13 PM

I'm writting this note as an explanation of the shooting In case I get Killed.

I did this because... well I'm not sure, I just felt that I had to do this, sinse I heard of the school shooting in littleton Calarodo all I have been able to think about is doing that, I dont know why but I have to do this, I dont plan on getting killed but I need to kill.

THI IS WHAT I HAVE TO DO!!!

P.S. Don't blame any one else, a few people know about my plane but refused to HELP.

Violent pictures drawn by the young man in the days preceding the Taber shooting.

clay pigeons supervised by his stepfather. He chose a semi-automatic rifle as it had a bigger ammunition clip. He wrote a note that night that he knew would be read after the event and had been drawing violent pictures in the days preceding the shooting.

The following morning, Jeff sawed off the barrel and the butt of the rifle with a hacksaw in his room. He skipped breakfast, watched television for a while and went to school at noon to have a smoke with several friends. He told his friends of his plan to shoot up the school but they laughed and did not believe him. He then showed them the gun he had under his green vest and the cartridges he had brought from home. At trial one of the boys smoking with him that day told Jeff that he "did not have the nuts" to shoot people. Jeff returned home as it had turned cold and he put on the only winter coat he had — a long dark coat, later misinterpreted to be like the trench coats worn by the perpetrators at Columbine. He then drank a glass of orange juice and went straight back to school with the gun under his coat — a pocket lining had been torn so he could reach the now-fifteen-inch-long gun. He recalls feeling no emotion as he prepared for the shooting. He had carried with him a quantity of 355 cartridges, some already packed into clips for reloading. He had left the makings of a bomb back in his room. When Jeff arrived at the school, he looked in one door and avoided being seen while he walked to the other door. Outside he checked that the gun was loaded and shot one round into the ground as a test. He then ran into the school and started to shoot randomly. He recalled someone yelling his name and that student told him to run. Jeff thought that he would be shot so he simply dropped the gun and allowed himself to be handcuffed by the town's popular school resource police officer, Dennis Reimer, who had heard the commotion (and who the local schools had just that day considered cutting for budgetary reasons). Jeff cried repeatedly that he was sorry as he was apprehended.

Jeff had never had any conflict with the victims of his violence. He added that he tried afterward not to think about his victims. He had met Jason Lang once but their interaction had been minimal and not unpleasant. When Jeff met with his mother several hours after the shooting he again expressed his remorse for his actions and told her not to blame herself.

My Involvement

The purpose of all forensic investigations is to answer legal questions; it is not a fishing expedition. Mr. Der had asked if there were any mental health issues sufficient for a legal defence. My answer was flatly no — although I could clearly talk about the effects of chronic bullying on his behaviour and that he was depressed prior to the shooting, although this information fell short of any formal defence. There would be other questions to come as we waited for trial.

During the routine physical examination of Jeff after he was arrested, physicians at CYOC noted that he had a serious heart defect that threatened his life. Surgical repair of his heart problem was arranged and was carried out at the University of Alberta in Edmonton in November 1999. A second surgery had to be conducted the following day and during that procedure Jeff suffered two cardiac arrests and a subsequent cerebral stroke that impacted both sides of his brain. He later told me that he "died" three times but saw no white lights.

Immediately after his stroke, Jeff was paralyzed on his right side and had great difficulty expressing himself. He became confused easily and overall was weak. He steadily improved over the next five months. He was sent to see my colleague, Dr. Robert van Mastrigt, a highly respected pediatric neuropsychologist, at Alberta Children's Hospital to understand how his brain damage had affected his major cognitive functions. He found that Jeff had significant expressive aphasia and Dr. van Mastrigt noted that Jeff was quite enthusiastic about the assessment. When conducting such assessments, we always incorporate tests measuring effort to ensure that the test results are valid and not manipulated for some reason by the patient. Jeff was found to give valid and sincere efforts on all tests. His overall IQ had dropped from the superior level into the average range and the speed of his information processing was especially slow. He now had poor attention skills. Even his mathematics ability had dropped by fifty-eight percent. His understanding of vocabulary was still superior but he had difficulty expressing himself and choosing the right words when he spoke. He also had motor impairment — poor strength and dexterity. Jeff began a programme of cognitive remediation to improve, as best as possible, some of the important skills that had been adversely impacted. The trial date was put off to help Jeff heal.

As the trial date began to loom, Mr. Der asked me to evaluate Jeff again to determine if he was fit to stand trial and if he could instruct counsel. A person must be able to understand why they are facing a trial, what the possible outcomes might be, and must be in a position to help their lawyer and express wishes about defence positions and decisions. When I met again with Jeff in September of 2000, he remembered me and the main thing I noticed was his slow speech and thinking ability. He recalled the events of the shooting with no difficulty. Although changed, he was still capable of assisting his defence and I found no evidence that he would be unfit to proceed.

What was the trial about if Jeff acknowledged that he had planned and carried out a violent act? The only real issue was in which court the young man, who was now sixteen-years-old, would be tried, given his age at the time of the crime — youth court, or adult (ordinary) court. The Crown, capably represented by Gordon Falconer, felt that given the gravity of the crime, Jeff should be tried and sentenced in adult court and he made that application. Mr. Der felt otherwise and opposed Jeff's transfer to adult court. The trial then became a transfer hearing to decide this key issue.

To decide a legal issue, experts don't just put in their two cents worth and see what the average is. The law guides experts as to the issues to address in formulating an opinion. In the case of transfer hearings, the Young Offenders Act (YOA), then in force, laid out the factors to be considered — the age, maturity, character, background and prior offences of the accused, as well as the availability of treatment if this is required.

The transfer hearing at the Lethbridge Courthouse began in late August 2000 with the Crown calling witnesses and its mental health experts. Unfortunately, these psychiatrists and psychologists failed to turn their minds to the specific scope of the issues under the act. They diagnosed a conduct disorder in the accused, which projected a negative view of his treatability. Conduct Disorder is a mental disorder with a standard set of criteria that are published in a reference book used by mental health professionals called the Diagnostic and Statistical Manual of Mental Disorders (DSM).The multiple experts called by the Crown suggested that Jeff could be tried and sentenced using adult criteria and sentencing principles. I disagreed with their diagnostic opinion and with their equivocal approach to Jeff's treatment in youth or adult court. With DSM in hand on the witness stand, I reviewed each of the fifteen criteria listed for Conduct Disorder and Jeff had none of them! The idea that Jeff had some persistent pattern of antisocial behavior was easily refuted and cross-examination by a skilled Crown attorney did not change this. Next in my testimony, I turned to the issues in the YOA. Using standardized tools, Jeff was seen as low-risk for violence, despite his single ultimate violent act, and he had no diagnosable mental disorder. He was immature and now handicapped both socially and cognitively. Where was the treatment in the adult correctional system to assist him? Had any of these other experts even been in an adult prison? I have seen the inside of many prisons and none would have had anything remotely helpful for this young man. If Jeff had been relentlessly bullied in the school system, what was going to happen when he went to a maximum-security prison for men? In the youth detention system, he would continue his education and I listed the specific therapy that he certainly needed and would receive by competent professionals. If there was ever a chance for Jeff, it was not to be found by transferring him out of the youth justice system.

Now don't think for a minute that I am one of those mushy softhearted people that always see the best in people and simply side always for the person accused. Opinions in court are only valuable if they are based on evidence and they are tested under fire — a biased expert would not last long in this business. I have certainly seen some hardened psychopaths who were still in their teens and would have suggested a different course if it fit the bill. In this case it just didn't.

Judge Gerald DeBow, after hearing all the evidence, decided in Jeff's favour and retained the case in Youth Court; a decision that the Crown did not appeal. On November 17, 2000, Jeff, through his lawyer Mr. Der, pled guilty to a count of first-degree murder and two counts of attempted murder. He was sentenced to three years of incarceration, which also was not appealed by the Crown. The maximum that he would have faced under the YOA was six years in jail and four years of community supervision. In the adult or ordinary courts, a conviction of first-degree murder would have brought an automatic life sentence with parole possible after five to seven years.

Reflections

There had not been a high school shooting in Canada for over twenty years prior to the Taber tragedy. Had we drifted into the American gun culture? Were our youths being desensitized to violence, and what role did the media play in this case? Was justice served appropriately through the youth justice system and was our dealing with young offenders sufficiently tough for major crimes? What about the issue of bullying and its effects? All of these questions circulated during and even long after the Taber shooting and trial.

There was no doubt that the Taber shooting was influenced by the Columbine case which had come just eight days before. Indeed, when the media descended upon Taber immediately after the shooting, the good folk of the town withdrew their customary welcoming nature. At least in part, the general public had laid the responsibility for the violence on the media. The feeling was that if the media had not obsessively reported every detail of the Columbine shooting (including school video of the acts), it would not have been repeated in their town. They openly insisted that the media all go home.

The memorial for Jason Lang was held at his school and broadcast live across Canada. It was attended by many dignitaries. Jason's father, Anglican minister Reverend Dale Lang, conducted the service and drove to the school in Jason's 1983 black Camaro that Jason had purchased only three days before the shooting. Reverend Lang showed remarkable courage forgiving his son's killer and embarking on a speaking circuit that brought to the fore many of the issues related to the tragedy of his son's death including bullying. Ironically, Jason reportedly was a quiet boy and would befriend kids who were picked on by others. By shining light on bullying, much academic work has been done to understand the effects that bullying has on the mental life of a young person and it has become firmly established that bullying is a clear risk factor for the development of various mental disorders in adolescence. Some cities have since enacted anti-bullying bylaws and schools have developed policies to deal more directly with such events. Reverend Lang did not want the death of his son to be in vain and the awareness of the negative influences of bullying has certainly assured that. In Jason's memory, the Alberta Government established the Jason Lang scholarship programme which rewards high academic achievement at Alberta post-secondary schools. From 2012 to 2014, three-hundred- sixty-five cheques of a thousand dollars each were mailed to deserving students.

In 2002, the Young Offenders Act was replaced by the Youth Criminal Justice Act (YCJA), which eliminated transfer hearings and increased the incarceration term lengths for serious crimes such as murder that are committed by young people. Under the YCJA, an adult sentence can be imposed for certain crimes such as murder, that are committed by young persons. Youths aged fourteen or over are expected to receive adult sentences unless the Crown chooses not to proceed with this penalty range, or there is some other important factor preventing such a decision. The issue of sentencing under the new YCJA would occur after a finding of guilt, not before, like it did in Jeff's trial. It is just speculation what would have happened to Jeff under these new legal provisions. Was the penalty for Jeff tough enough? There is no way to balance the worth of a victim's life against any criminal sentence for the offender. The penalty attached to a criminal offence carries multiple purposes under Canadian law: general and specific deterrence, to contribute to respect for the law, and the maintenance of a just, peaceful, and safe society. Other purposes of criminal sentences include: to denounce unlawful conduct, to separate offenders from society, to assist in rehabilitating offenders, to provide reparations for harm done to victims or the community, and to promote a sense of responsibility in offenders. Weighing these factors is a tall order for any judge to undertake when imposing a sentence; different offences and different cases weigh each of these factors uniquely. There has been a persistent perception among the Canadian public that we are "soft" on criminals, and in particular, young offenders. I have never found any truth behind these suppositions. Indeed, those who hold these strong beliefs rarely have any knowledge about how our criminal justice system works. How could they? Most of their knowledge comes from mass media reports. How do you condense a complex trial and all the issues it had into a few inches of print in the newspaper? Yet, after a major trial has been concluded and reported in the media, everyone seems to have an opinion. To my way of thinking, those opinions stem more from each individual's belief system than any facts distilled from the specific case.

School shootings are far more common in the United States than any other western country. Our southern neighbour continues to have disproportionately high levels of gun violence. There has been no dramatic rise in gun violence in Canada over the past decade or so, despite the violence we see on American television. Although Alberta has about the same percentage of gun ownership as the United States, associated with a large rural population, we have no greater gun violence than Ontario, which has a gun ownership percentage that is only a third of Alberta's. When gun violence erupts in Canada it is often gang related. So gun culture is not a creeping epidemic in Canada. Our national outrage over mass killing of innocents in the United States, such as in Newtown, Connecticut in 2012, and our lack of understanding over the illegitimate and blatant historical misinterpretation of the "right to bear arms" in the United States signals that Canadians should never face the internal strife over the gun issue that Americans do.

Can forensic psychologists predict who will be a school shooter and intervene before such a tragedy occurs? Very low incidence behaviours are the most difficult to predict. Because the United States has had many more school shootings than the few in Canada, most research of this sort comes from there. In the years *before* the Columbine shooting in Colorado, the "profile" of the school avenger began to emerge. Writing in the journal *The Forensic Examiner* in May of 1999, psychologists James McGee and Caren DeBernardo sketched the hypothetical individual who had the potential to be violent toward peers in a school setting. The typical perpetrator was immature and socially inadequate and usually was not interested in typical teenage activities. (They were often fascinated by guns, bomb making, and media violence — real and fictional). Their IQs were average to above-average and they had no cognitive deficits or major mental disorders other than depression. Depression in teenage boys often manifests in a sullen and irritable way. Prior to the shootings there were temper outbursts and risk-taking behaviours by the shooters. They acknowledged fantasies of violent revenge and there was evidence of both mental and real rehearsal, dismissing any "impulsive" motive. Triggering events were common such as humiliation, losses, or bullying episodes. School shooters had an average age of fourteen-and-a-half years and the guns they used were nearly all taken from home. Most school shootings took place in rural areas or towns under a population of fifty thousand. In most cases the perpetrator had been rejected and explicitly described a revenge motive for the shooting. There was a strong geographic clustering of school shootings in the United States (mostly Southern states) and most shooters knew about a prior school shooting (recall this profile was created before the Columbine shooting). Journal or letter writing by the offenders often spelled out intent and details planned.

A "profile" is a group amalgam and there is a large variability in how close each case resembled these factors. The Taber shooting had many of these profile dimensions. However, this knowledge is rarely helpful in predicting when and who will commit the next school shooting. After this case, I was often sent drawings by police investigators — drawings of violence by young persons — and asked if I thought the individual was a risk of violence. One piece of evidence rarely has any ultimate predictive value — many "normal" teens draw pictures of violence that they are so often exposed to. I also suggested to investigators that matching a set of features to some prototypic "profile" wouldn't help much either. Rather the elements of a profile must just be considered risk variables to consider and to guide intervention in individual cases. It is obviously better to intervene with a troubled young person than wait to see if the explosive combination reaches an igniting point. Against the risk factors that forensic experts define, more appreciation is being given to "protective" factors and how to build them. Protective factors increase the resiliency of youth at risk who can persevere despite adversity. Protective factors can include exceptional social skills, confidence, pro-social values and attitudes. A child who has a positive and supportive connection with an adult figure is likely to display less-negative behavior. Peer influences are exceptionally strong in young persons and just as associating with deviant peers is a risk factor, associating with pro-social children is protective.

The lessons from the Taber shooting have been multiple, as I have tried to indicate. Jeff has now served his sentence — did this change him for the better or worse? We really don't know what will happen to anyone who is sent to jail — hopefully the purposes of the sentence as I outlined will have some impact on him as well as others.

Hersh Wolch

THE YOUNG CROWN PROSECUTOR'S TRIAL BY FIRE

Hersh Wolch QC is a Fellow of the American College of Trial Lawyers and the International Society of Barristers. He is also a board member of the Canadian Association of Criminal Defence Lawyers. He has successfully defended wrongfully convicted persons, negotiated the safe release of hostages, acted in Commissions of Inquiry, and appeared frequently in the Supreme Court of Canada.

THIS STORY IS ABOUT a criminal lawyer's life in progress; mine, that is, with the stand-out feature being the 1970 prosecution of Ruth Thelma Piché. *R. v. Piché* remains a landmark case in Canadian criminal law, settling the issue as to whether any statement made by an accused, be it inculpatory or exculpatory, had to be proven voluntary before it would be admitted into evidence. Factually, it predates and is a variation of the "Burning Bed" cases of spousal violence. In any event, it was my first exposure to, and is a vivid illustration of, the kind of legal defence that is wonderfully captured in song in the Broadway play and musical *Chicago*, where a number of young women in jail awaiting trial explain their conduct in the song "He Had it Coming."

A Magic Transformation

Given that my University of Manitoba Bachelor of Commerce degree was, for me, a ticket to nowhere, I entered University of Manitoba law school, attending classes in the morning and articling for a law firm in the afternoon. At the conclusion of the four years, I obtained employment as a Crown Prosecutor for the

Province of Manitoba. It was 1965 and I was twenty-five years old. Most young prosecutors are self-righteous and make up for their lack of life experience and compassion for the unfortunate with an air of moral superiority and an unwarranted degree of confidence. I was no exception.

Fulfilling the role of a Crown Attorney was extremely enjoyable. I was magically transformed from powerless student to a man who made incredibly important decisions, appeared on a daily basis in court and, best of all, worked with and directed police officers many years my senior. Unlike today's Crown prosecutors who are closely monitored by upward reporting and political pressure, my decisions were my own. I only spoke to senior prosecutors when I needed advice. There was no decision by committee. Politics and media had very little influence. Life was wonderful.

The only disappointment was my social life, most particularly in bars. I thought if word got out that I was a Crown Attorney, it would have a very positive social effect but much to my surprise, Crown Attorneys ranked slightly above used-car salesmen and far below drug dealers.

On one occasion the police informed me that some fellow I had successfully prosecuted for a dog-bylaw violation was a bit off. They intercepted some communications that he was planning to kill me. Accordingly, they suggested that I carry a gun with me at all times. I was absolutely ecstatic to walk around with a loaded gun under my suit jacket and having full-time access to the police firing range allowed me to target practice. I was an armed Crown Attorney. Quite a transformation from my modest beginnings as a poor kid from Winnipeg's tough north end.

Winnipeg in those days was divided into local municipalities. The City of Winnipeg had a few prosecutors located in the downtown police station/courthouse. A few of us were assigned to local municipalities and some to travelling out of town to places like Selkirk, Steinbach, and Fisher Branch. My first case was a prosecution of a fellow for having consensual sex with a barely underage girl. He was defended by Harry Walsh QC, who was considered if not one of the best criminal lawyers in the country, perhaps the best. I prepared incredibly hard and after securing a conviction, I wrote a letter to the Chief of St. James-Assiniboine Police Service commending his men on a highly professional job they did in preparing this prosecution. The Chief must have laughed when he got the letter. The main investigator was so excited, he quit the force and entered law school.

A Quarrel and a Shooting

Among the municipalities under my direction was St. Vital. On November 1,

1968 I received a phone call from a sergeant advising me of a possible murder. I said I'd get down to the police station as fast as I could make it. I hopped into my car, exceeded the speed limit (hoping I would be stopped so I could tell an officer what I was doing), and got to the police station where I thought I was going to direct the investigation. The cops had already done their work. I got the message; that was not my role.

The theory of the prosecution was that a twenty-one-year-old woman, Ruth Thelma Piché, had shot her common-law-husband, Leslie Pascoe, to death. Ruth Piché had been living with Pascoe since 1964. The two had had an evening of drinking on October 31, 1968, along with others. They returned home about midnight. There was evidence of quarreling during the evening and also on their return home, and of more and heavier drinking, particularly on the part of Pascoe. At 2:30 *a.m.* on November 1, 1968, Ms. Piché, called a taxi, which took her and her infant child to her mother's apartment. At 10:30 *a.m.* on November 1, Pascoe's body was found in their apartment. He had been shot by a gun that was found on the gun rack in the bathroom. The police interviewed Ms. Piché, on the morning of November 2.

Ms. Piché made an original statement, the essence of which was that she was in an abusive relationship with the deceased, and it was because of that abuse that she fled with her young child to go to her mother's place. She described the earlier drinking and the quarrelling, and the return home to more of the same. Her statement was, in part:

> I lay there about five or ten minutes and couldn't go to sleep so I got up and telephoned my mother. She was home so I told her I was coming over to her place. I then phoned for a taxi, Duffy's, then went and dressed Lisa. I put a coat, a sweater, shoes and socks on her and I too got dressed. Les was still asleep. I left the house at 1:50 in the morning I think. After I arrived at my mother's I slept on the chesterfield with Lisa. When I got there my mother was up and so was her boarder Maurice Laliberte. I told them we'd had a fight and that I wanted to stay with my mom.

She stated that she had no knowledge of who would have shot Mr. Pascoe. This first statement of Ms. Piché is an "exculpatory statement"; in lay terms, it offered an innocent explanation of the events and a defence.

Neither the investigators nor I had any doubt it was she who had shot him.

She subsequently made additional, but clearly conflicting and contradictory, "exculpatory statements" in which she confirmed the abuse, but added that she had taken one of the rifles, decided to commit suicide, but prior to doing so she went to kiss the sleeping Mr. Pascoe goodbye. She stated that as she walked towards him, the gun went off accidentally and killed him. She had been in a daze and her five-year-old child started to cry. Ms. Piché put the rifle back in its place, phoned her mother and went over there to spend the night.

Absent the shooting of the husband, seeking shelter with her mother is something she had done on a number of unfortunate previous occurrences in the relationship. Medical evidence as to time of death and evidence from the taxi driver who conveyed her to her mother's place all worked against her original exculpatory statement that she was not there when the gun went off.

I instructed that a charge be preferred against Ruth Thelma Piché, charging her with the murder of Leslie Pascoe.

Counsel for Ms. Piché's defence was Saul M. Froomkin. Saul eventually became a Federal Prosecutor in both Winnipeg and Ottawa, which was his springboard to becoming the Solicitor General, and later the Attorney General of Bermuda. Saul is a very good lawyer and he and I had numerous cases together over a fairly brief period of time. We were competitive in a friendly way. I do have a vivid memory of one trial where he did not like the outcome or perhaps how I had conducted the prosecution. He jumped onto the counsel table after the judge rendered her decision and left, pulled down his pants and underwear and mooned me. I expect I am the only lawyer who has ever been mooned in Court by the future Attorney General of Bermuda.

In any event, I had conduct of the preliminary hearing and had no difficulty securing a committal for trial. The trial commenced before Mr. Justice John Hunt. Justice Hunt was definitely a law and order judge, thoughtful and well-respected. I had devised what I considered to be a brilliant prosecutorial strategy. The only one of Ms. Piché's statements that I was going to put before the jury was the exculpatory one where she denied being involved in the shooting. The latter statements where she admitted she shot him, I was not going to tender in the Crown's case. If she wanted to put the accident explanation before the jury, she would have to testify. I would then use her statement that she had not been there to show that she had a consciousness of guilt. Surely if you accidently shot your common-law-spouse, the first thing you would do is say so. You would not say you were not there unless you were trying to avoid criminal responsibility. Departmental policy was to tender all statements of the accused in murder trials but I persuaded my superiors that an acquittal was very likely without my opportunity to cross-examine Ms. Piché on her first statement.

Tendering the first statement would be no problem at all since the law was clear that exculpatory statements did not have to be proven voluntary. There was no *Charter of Rights* in those days, but nevertheless, inculpatory statements, which are admissions of criminal wrongdoing, had to be proven to be clearly voluntary; that is, as articulated in the classic formulation in a case called *Ibrahim*: "not obtained from the suspect either by fear of prejudice or hope of advantage exercised or held out by a person in authority." We did not have video in those days. If a statement was exculpatory, the common wisdom was that you cannot truly be forced to say you did not do it, and accordingly it was admissible evidence.

Saul came up with a novel approach. He argued that the first statement was partially inculpatory and therefore had to be proven voluntary. He argued that she talked in her statement about the rocky relationship, which speaks to motive, and she admitted to having knowledge of the rifles in the home — that made the statement partially inculpatory. After some deliberation, Justice Hunt ruled after a *voir dire* that the statement had to be proven voluntary. The *voir dire* is a trial within a trial in the absence of the jury to determine a point in issue between the Crown and the defence. This ruling did not cause me any serious concern, although I thought he was wrong. The second *voir dire* as to voluntariness would not be a problem. I had never had a statement ruled "not voluntary." In my experience, police never fabricated or made up what the accused said, but they clearly strayed miles from the truth in the evidence as to how they got the accused to say what he/she did say. Accordingly, in the *voir dire*, I took the police officer through the usual standard questions about threats and promise of favour, and then watched in absolute disbelief when Froomkin cross-examined the experienced police officer. The police officer conceded that he might have threatened Ms. Piché, coerced her and done all sorts of things to get her to make the statement. Unfortunately, I did not recover fast enough, not that it would have mattered, but I was in a state of virtual shock.

I later spoke to the police officer and asked about those startling answers and he looked at me like I was the idiot and said, "Of course I could have done all of those things, but I didn't. When he asked me if I could have done them, I simply said yes I could have, but that does not mean I did." I did not know whether to laugh or cry. I had lost my best weapon. The "exculpatory statement" of Ms. Piché was excluded by the trial judge. I learned the hard way the importance of re-direct examination, where I could have put some questions to the police witness in what may have been an unsuccessful attempt to rehabilitate him. Therefore, I could not cross-examine her on it if she took the witness stand in her defence. She did take the stand. In her evidence, she related the essence of her subsequent statement, to the effect that the shooting was an accident. As Ms. Piché testified one could easily see the sympathy of the jury was really quite high and deservedly so. She had been the victim of a very abusive relationship. She was frail, weak and very credible as to the abuse she had endured and absent her initial denial of being there, her evidence was quite believable. The listener wanted to believe that it was an accident but was comforted by the fact that even if the act was deliberate, just as in the aforementioned Chicago song, the deceased Had It Coming. Accordingly, she was acquitted.

I recommended an appeal which proceeded before the Manitoba Court of Appeal. I wrote my factum and was quite confident that I was right in law. My appeal submission was that if the statement was inculpatory, the ruling by the trial judge was not, in the circumstances of this case, subject to review; if exculpatory, the *voir dire* was unnecessary and the statement should have been admitted when tendered by the Crown.

The Crown Appeal

The Court of Appeal was more imposing than I had anticipated. Chief Justice Charles Smith was a former, highly respected Attorney General and the Court itself had Sam Freedman who became the Chief Justice of Manitoba; Brian Dickson, who become the Chief Justice of Canada; Alfred Monnin, who also became Chief Justice of Manitoba; and the agreeable Robert DuVal Guy.

At that time, I attended numerous bar functions. Judges from all the courts would attend. Also, in those days before security, you could run into the judges in the Law Courts and say hello. I learned a lot from talking to the judges. Other than one instance when a judge asked for the phone number of my client's mother, the conversations were always appropriate. I felt very fortunate that I got to know Sam Freedman well as he was a brilliant jurist with a great sense of humour. He was the perfect role model for any judge. I don't recall when it was, but a few years later I was asked by *Macleans Magazine* who my greatest heroes were and for some reason I stated Justice Freedman and Muhammed Ali. From then on when I would appear before the court, Justice Freedman would make a sly reference to boxing or Muhammed Ali and would never fail to stop me in the hall and say in his great voice "Muhammed Ali?", smile and walk on.

Justice Monnin was also an exceptional jurist and what would always amaze me was I hardly ever agreed with him on any issue. I learned from him that in spite of great differences, arguments can be made. He is a man who was exceptionally liked and deserved a great deal of respect. "Doc" Guy was an affable judge who always concurred with Justice Monnin. Brian Dickson was an exceptional judge who went to the Supreme Court, taking with him the best qualities of his fellow judges on the Manitoba Court of Appeal.

Following the argument of the appeal, Justice Sam Freedman dissented from the majority. His dissent was based on saying that I did not have a right to appeal because the finding that it was a partially inculpatory statement was a finding of fact and the Crown could not appeal. He also expressed his unhappiness that a statement so obviously not voluntary could be used. The majority of the Court found opposite. They were quite clear. The statement was exculpatory and therefore admissible. The law was fixed on that issue. No *voir dire* had been required. The matter was to go back for a new trial.

Supreme Court

With the dissent in her favour, and her original acquittal at trial, Ms. Piché appealed to the Supreme Court of Canada. I knew something was happening when I was advised that the Supreme Court had set down two cases to be heard back-to-back in the full court. The other case was *R. v. Wray*, which dealt with inculpatory information drawn out through use of forceful interrogation. The Court was going to hear both cases with nine justices sitting.

I truly believe that I was too young to really appreciate my experience at the Court of Appeal and marched onto Ottawa not really knowing what awaited and not heeding Justice Freedman's warning as we passed in the hall, "Don't be over-confident…you never know." He smiled as he said it.

It was really busy times before going to Ottawa. The week before I left there was a bridge tournament in Winnipeg in which I participated on the Canadian team. The fact that the tournament was being televised where everybody could see all the hands was probably more nerve racking than appearing in the Supreme Court. As soon as it was over I raced off to Ottawa. When I got there I felt I had a sore ankle. In those days I played a lot of floor hockey and soon found out my ankle was broken. So for my first appearance in Supreme Court, I was on crutches.

Luckily *R. v. Wray* was being argued first. *Wray* involved the fruits of involuntary questioning and whether real evidence obtained would be admitted. I was able to watch two exceptional lawyers, Clay Powell and Robert Carter, argue that case. I like to think I learned quite a bit from them. The Court reserved and then turned to the Piché case.

I was well prepared but it really wasn't that difficult of a concept to be arguing, even on crutches. Those were the days when we didn't have cell phones and faxes. Just before we were to begin, a courier came running in to the Court with a telegram, shouting 'telegram, telegram' and handed me a telegram. We had to use telegrams back in that day. The telegram was from my friend stating "We are with you all the way and we are cheering you on." I then looked over and the same courier handed an identical telegram to Saul Froomkin. He and I looked at each other and nodded our heads and started to laugh over the fact that one of our colleagues was playing a joke.

When it was my turn to argue, everything seemed to be going relatively well. Questions weren't very difficult until the judge sitting beside the Chief Justice had a question for me. I didn't even know his name, nor did I know most of the others. He told me that he thought I was right and that the statement was exculpatory and did not require a *voir dire*. Before I could feel too good he said to me "But who made the rule that exculpatory statements have to be admitted, voluntary or not?" Before I could answer he answered his own question, one that I didn't see coming. He said, "Don't we make the rules, are we bound by bad rules?" In spite of not seeing it coming, I did my best to answer the question, talking about precedent and the value of precedent as learned in law school and how you have to rely on precedent and he just sort of smiled at me, having the courtesy not to ask me how old I was.

The Court issued the decision on Piché on June 26, 1970. When the decision came out, the judge who asked me the questions, Justice Emmett Hall, stated:

> In my view the time is opportune for this Court to say that the admission in evidence of all statements made by an accused to persons in authority, whether inculpatory or exculpatory, is governed by the same rule and thus put to an end the continuing controversy and necessary evaluation by trial judges of every such statement which the Crown proposes to use in chief or on cross-examination as either being inculpatory or exculpatory. The rule respecting the admission of statements is a judge-made rule and does not depend upon any legislative foundation and I see no impediment to making the rule clear and beyond dispute.

Justices Douglas Abbott, Ronald Martland, William Ritchie, Wishart Spence and Louis-Philippe Pigeon agreed with Justice Hall. Chief Justice John Cartwright also agreed, but Justices Gérald Fauteux and Wilfred Judson dissented.

The Piché decision stands out as a landmark case in Canadian criminal law jurisprudence. The Supreme Court of Canada laid to rest the conflicting decisions surrounding the admission in evidence of all statements by an accused to a person in authority, be they exculpatory or inculpatory: the burden was on the Crown to prove voluntariness. Before leaving the Crown, I never acknowledged that I had lost the case. After all, I was always right. I could not help it if the highest Court in the land changed the rules. Maturity and years as a defence counsel have changed my view.

At least then I was comforted by the dissenting reasons of Justice Judson:

> The practical importance of the case under review is obvious. It is an essential part of the work of the police to ask questions of suspects. It is only when the stage of confession is reached that the confession rules apply. If a person chooses to give the police an innocent explanation of his conduct and then at the trial goes into the witness box and gives another innocent explanation inconsistent with the first, it is entirely appropriate for Crown counsel to cross-examine on this discrepancy and the reasons for it.

The year 2015 marks my fiftieth year of criminal law practice in Canada. I look upon the Piché case as it progressed through the courts as the curtain rising on my professional career. Appearing in the Supreme Court and benefitting from the maturing metamorphosis that accompanies litigating a major case was my real win, because it was a very eventful time. I did not know as we were arguing, innocent sixteen-year-old David Milgaard was being convicted of murdering Gail Miller in Saskatoon, Saskatchewan. Much later, after he had served twenty-three years in prison, I would represent him in proving his innocence. Also, years later, I would be sitting with my client Steven Truscott in his living room after his exoneration by the Ontario Court of Appeal and after having successfully applied for compensation for his numerous years in prison, many of them served on death row. Steven referred to his first unsuccessful review that occurred in the Supreme Court of Canada in 1966. He stated, "Emmett Hall was the only judge back then who got my case right." I smiled and replied "It was not the only time he got it right."

Index